AF412290

Christopher P.M. Waters (*editor*)
THE STATE OF LAW IN THE SOUTH CAUCASUS

Euro-Asian Studies
Series Standing Order ISBN 978–0–333–80114–7
(*outside North America only*)

You can receive future titles in this series as they are published by placing a standing order. Please contact your bookseller or, in case of difficulty, write to us at the address below with your name and address, the title of the series and the ISBN quoted above.

Customer Services Department, Macmillan Distribution Ltd, Houndmills, Basingstoke, Hampshire RG21 6XS, England

---

By the Same Authors

James A. Green, *The International Court of Justice and Self-Defence in International Law* (Oxford, Hart Publishing, 2009)

Christopher P.M. Waters, *British and Canadian Perspectives on International Law* (Leiden, Martinus Nijhoff, 2006)

Christopher P.M. Waters, *Counsel in the Caucasus: Professionalization and Law in Georgia* (Leiden, Martinus Nijhoff, 2004)

Christopher P.M. Waters, *Guide to International Law Careers* (London, British Institute of International and Comparative Law, 2010) [with Anneke Smit]

Christopher P.M. Waters (ed.), *The State of Law in the South Caucasus* (Basingstoke, Palgrave, 2005)

Conflict in the Caucasus

Implications for International Legal Order

Edited by

James A. Green

and

Christopher P.M. Waters

First published 2010 by
PALGRAVE MACMILLAN

Palgrave Macmillan in the UK is an imprint of Macmillan Publishers Limited, registered in England, company number 785998, of Houndmills, Basingstoke, Hampshire RG21 6XS.

Palgrave Macmillan in the US is a division of St Martin's Press LLC, 175 Fifth Avenue, New York, NY 10010.

Palgrave Macmillan is the global academic imprint of the above companies and has companies and representatives throughout the world.

Palgrave® and Macmillan® are registered trademarks in the United States, the United Kingdom, Europe and other countries.

ISBN: 978–0–230–24124–4 hardback

This book is printed on paper suitable for recycling and made from fully managed and sustained forest sources. Logging, pulping and manufacturing processes are expected to conform to the environmental regulations of the country of origin.

A catalogue record for this book is available from the British Library.

Library of Congress Cataloging-in-Publication Data

Conflict in the Caucasus : implications for international legal order / edited by James A. Green and Christopher P.M. Waters.
        p. cm.—(Euro-Asian studies)
      ISBN 978–0–230–24124–4 (hardback)
      1. Georgia (Republic)—International status. 2. Georgia (Republic)—Foreign relations—Russia. 3. Russia—Foreign relations—Georgia (Republic) 4. Humanitarian law—Caucasus. I. Green, James A., 1981– II. Waters, Christopher P. M. (Christopher Peter Michael), 1968–

KZ4316.C66 2010
341.26—dc22   2010027520

10 9 8 7 6 5 4 3 2 1
19 18 17 16 15 14 13 12 11 10

Printed and bound in Great Britain by
CPI Antony Rowe, Chippenham and Eastbourne

for Jane.
(a.k.a Mum).
   James A. Green

for Jennifer, Chris, Isabella and Greydon
   Christopher P.M. Waters

Contents

Map of the Caucasus

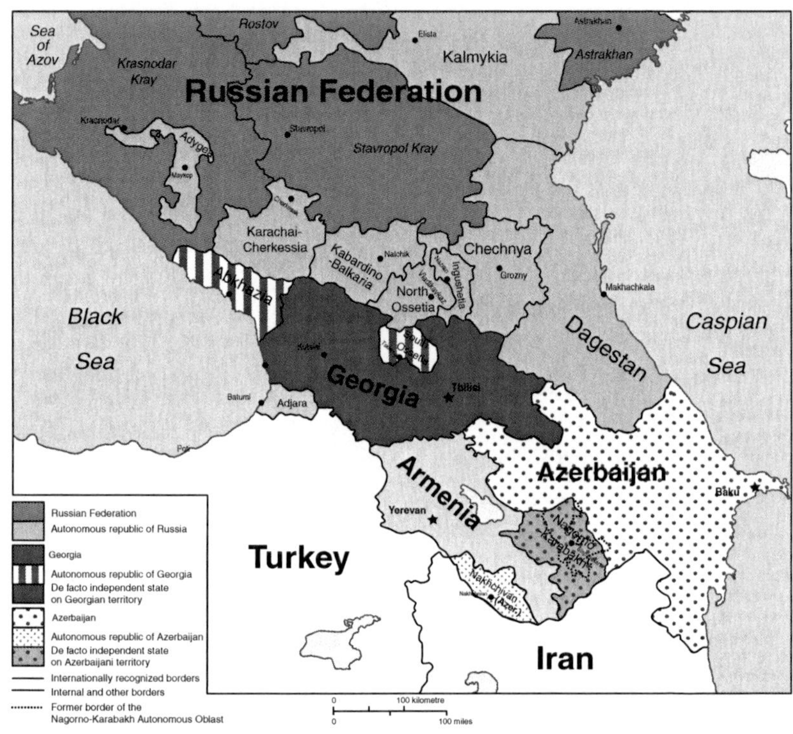

Acknowledgements

This volume was born out of an interdisciplinary conference on the subject of the 2008 Caucasus conflict, held on 15 April 2009 at the School of Law, University of Reading, UK and co-sponsored by the Centre for Transnational Law and Justice at the University of Windsor, Canada. The editors would like to gratefully acknowledge everyone who was involved in the organisation and administration of that conference (most notably David Leary, Valbona Barjami, David Hallam and Deborah Edwards), as well as all the contributors and attendees.

We would like to thank the contributors to this volume. This is very much a collaborative work, and we appreciate all the efforts of our contributors in producing such consistently excellent chapters.

Finally, we would in particular like to express our gratitude to Ashley Barnes – whose RA position was funded by the Law Foundation of Ontario – for her invaluable editorial assistance in preparing this work.

James A. Green
Christopher P.M. Waters
April, 2010

Foreword

The South Caucasus draws a lot of attention for such a distant and seemingly insignificant place. Since the three republics regained their independence in 1991, this attention has waxed and waned. In a first period, it reflected the eruption of a number of small but highly destructive conflicts, two in Georgia and one in Azerbaijan, that generated substantial population displacement and, when combined with the collapse of the Soviet economy, severe humanitarian challenges. As these crises faded, international interest was rekindled by the possibility that the region could serve as a transit corridor for the energy resources of the Caspian Basin. Later, after Georgia's Rose Revolution, it became a focus of American democracy promotion. And, as European and Euroatlantic economic and security institutions slowly crept eastwards, the region became a focus of interest for both the European Union (the Neighbourhood Policy), and for NATO (through Partnership for Peace and consideration of eventual membership for Georgia in particular).

Finally, in 2008, when Georgia attempted to regain control of its region of South Ossetia, Russia attacked the country, defeating Georgian forces, detaching the regions of South Ossetia and Abkhazia and recognising these as sovereign states in their own right. This conflict raised very serious questions for Europe and for the larger international order. Did the Russian action suggest a challenge to the post-Cold War settlement and the regional order that sprung from it? Was Europe a single security space, or was it being re-divided into two, each with different structures of power, rules and practices? What did the Russian use of force to seize and then to detach part of a neighbouring state suggest about the durability of United Nations Charter and European norms of territorial integrity and the peaceful settlement of disputes?

A considerable amount has been written about the war and its implications for the sub-regional, regional and international system. The bulk of that literature has concerned the causes, conduct and political and economic consequences of the conflict. Yet the military conflict was accompanied and followed by significant legal contestation. Each party sought to justify its position and to condemn that of the other with reference to legal doctrine and principle. As such, the conflict is an ideal case in which to examine the application of law in the contemporary international system on a central question (the use of force), to ask what that application suggests about the role of law in that system, and about the direction of development of law as an element of international order.

This volume addresses these questions in a tightly structured set of chapters examining numerous aspects of international law (e.g., human rights, self-determination, self-defence) as they relate to the conflict and then considering legal argumentation in international institutions (the International Court of Justice and the Council of Europe). The result is a comprehensive and extremely useful analysis of the legal dimension of the dispute and the implications of the dispute for the rule of law in the European and international systems. It is a distinctive and welcome addition to the literature not only on the Caucasus and Russia but also on the evolving role of law in international order.

S. Neil MacFarlane
Head of Department of Politics and International Relations,
University of Oxford

Contributors

Bill Bowring is Professor of Law in the School of Law, Birkbeck, University of London and joined the Law School in 2006. He is a practising barrister at Field Court Chambers, Gray's Inn. He has previously held posts at the University of East London, University of Essex, and London Metropolitan University, and was Director of the Pan-European Institute, University of Essex from 1997–2000, and Director of the Human Rights and Social Justice Research Institute, London Metropolitan University, from 2003–2006. He is currently a Fellow of the Human Rights Centre at the University of Essex. Professor Bowring has many publications on topics of international law, human rights and Russian law, in which he frequently acts as a court expert. Amongst numerous other professional memberships, Professor Bowring has been a Member of the Advisory Council of the European Union Russia Centre since 2005.

Dr Julie A. George is an Assistant Professor of Political Science at Queens College, the City University of New York. She specialises in comparative politics, focusing on ethnic politics, democratisation, and state building. Her current research examines how states undergoing significant transformation and reform address ethnic minorities. Dr George has conducted research in the former Soviet Union, particularly in the Russian Federation and in Georgia, where she was funded by the Fulbright Association. She is the author of *The Politics of Ethnic Separatism in Russia and Georgia* (Palgrave Macmillan, 2009), as well as articles in *Europe-Asia Studies*, *Post-Soviet Affairs*, *European Security* and *Central Asian Survey*. She received her PhD from the Department of Government at the University of Texas at Austin in 2005.

Prof. Sandy Ghandhi has been a member of the School of Law at the University of Reading since 1978. After studying for his first degree in Law at the University of Oxford, he graduated from the University of London, King's College with an LLM. Thereafter, he qualified as a Solicitor working for a niche practice in central London. He served on the Law Society's International Human Rights Committee for nine years (1998–2007) and was involved in a number of major projects with the Committee. He has also been consulted widely on issues of international human rights law and has advised in the preparation of *amicus curiae* briefs. In addition, he was a consultee of the Justice Department in the preparation of the recent periodic reports of the UK to the ICCPR and ICESCR. Professor Ghandhi is a member of the Leverhulme Trust Major Research Programme 'The Liberal Way of War'. He is currently engaged on research in the broad field of international human rights law with an emphasis on the work of the Human Rights Committee of the International Covenant on Civil and Political Rights.

Dr James A. Green has been a Lecturer in the School of Law at the University of Reading since 2006. He previously studied for his doctorate at the University of Nottingham, and, in 2005, was a visiting research scholar at the University of Michigan. Dr Green's primary research interests are international law on the use of force (particularly self-defence), the International Court of Justice and the formation of customary international law. He is the author of *The International Court of Justice and Self-Defence in International Law* (Hart Publishing, 2009) which was the winner of the Francis Lieber Prize, awarded by the American Society of International Law's Lieber Society for an exceptional work in the field of law and armed conflict. He has also published various articles in leading journals in both Europe and North America and has given papers on a variety of international law topics around the world.

Kristin Hausler is a Research Fellow in Public International Law at the British Institute of International and Comparative Law, which she joined in August 2007 to assist on a study relating to international courts and tribunals. Subsequently, she has worked on two projects commissioned by the Ministry of Justice, as a researcher on a project relating to human rights and as a director for a comparative study on access to justice. She has also written numerous articles and case notes on major court rulings for the Institute's Bulletin of International Legal Developments. Previously, Kristin worked for several years in Vancouver, Canada, on a repatriation project involving Indigenous communities. She holds a 'licence en droit' (Bachelor and Master of Law) from the University of Fribourg, Switzerland as well as an LLM from the University of British Columbia, Canada.

Prof. Robert McCorquodale has been the Director of the British Institute of International and Comparative Law since January 2008. He is Professor of International Law and Human Rights, and former Head (Dean) of the School of Law, at the University of Nottingham. Previously, he was a Fellow and Lecturer in Law at St. John's College, University of Cambridge and then at the Australian National University in Canberra. Before embarking on an academic career he worked as a qualified lawyer with leading law firms in Sydney (Mallesons Stephen Jaques) and London (Herbert Smith). Professor McCorquodale's research and teaching interests are in the areas of public international law and human rights law. He has published widely on these areas, and has provided advice to governments, corporations, international organisations, non-governmental organisations and peoples concerning human rights issues.

Dr Anneke Smit is Assistant Professor in the Faculty of Law, University of Windsor. She previously held a Lectureship at the School of Law, University of Reading, where she also completed her PhD in 2008. She is a former Visiting Study Fellow of the University of Oxford's Refugee Studies Centre. Dr Smit has worked with the Canadian Department of Justice; the OSCE Mission in Kosovo; the Caucasus Institute for Peace, Democracy and Development (CIPDD) in Tbilisi and Citizenship and Immigration Canada. She is the author of *The Property Rights of Refugees and Internally Displaced Persons: Beyond Restitution* (Routledge, forthcoming 2010) and co-author of *A Guide to International Law Careers* (British Institute for International and Comparative Law, 2010).

Dr Christoph H. Stefes is Associate Professor for Comparative European & Post-Soviet Studies at the Department of Political Science, University of Colorado, and the director of the University's undergraduate program in International Studies. He studied in Tübingen, Germany and Groningen, The Netherlands and received his PhD from the University of Denver's Josef Korbel School of International Studies. In his teaching and research, he focuses on political and economic developments in the former Soviet with a specific focus on the South Caucasus and Central Asia. He is the author of *Understanding Post-Soviet Transitions: Corruption, Collusion and Clientelism* (Palgrave Macmillan, 2006) and contributing co-editor of *The Politics of Transition in Central Asia and the Caucasus* (with Amanda Wooden, Routledge, 2009) and *Einführung in die Comparative Politics* (with Harald Barrios, Oldenbourg Wissensch. Vlg, 2006). His research has also been published in several journals and edited volumes.

Dr Christopher P.M. Waters is the Associate Dean of the Faculty of Law, University of Windsor. His previous academic post, from 2002 to 2007, was at the University of Reading. In 2006–2007, he was also a Visiting Research Fellow in the Changing Character of War Programme at the University of Oxford. Dr Waters' research interests include international humanitarian law, post-conflict reconstruction and law and politics in

Eastern Europe and the former Soviet Union. He has extensive field experience in the Caucasus and Balkans, including with the UN/OSCE's Kosovo Mission in 1999–2000. Dr Waters has frequently addressed military audiences on international human rights and humanitarian law in both Canada and the United Kingdom. His publications include *Counsel in the Caucasus* (Brill, 2004, winner of the Hart/SLSA Book Prize for early career academics), *The State of Law in the South Caucasus* (Palgrave, 2005) and *British and Canadian Perspectives on International Law* (Brill, 2006).

Introduction

James A. Green and Christopher P.M. Waters

On 7 August 2008, long-standing tensions in the Caucasus region came to a head when President Mikheil Saakashvili of Georgia ordered troops into the *de facto* independent region of South Ossetia with a view to re-establishing Georgian sovereignty. This intervention, which included the shelling and occupation of the South Ossetian capital, Tskhinvali, was the culmination of a number of more minor military exchanges over the proceeding months. South Ossetia's sponsor, the Russian Federation, responded swiftly to the Georgian action, with a large-scale military intervention into the state of Georgia. This use of force ultimately went beyond the boundaries of the South Ossetia region, both into the comparable breakaway region of Abkhazia and further into 'Georgia proper'.

Under international pressure for a peaceful resolution to the conflict, a six-point peace plan, drawn up by French President Nicolas Sarkozy, was agreed and signed by both Russia and Georgia on 12 August 2008 (as well as by South Ossetian and Abkhaz leaders over subsequent days). Yet, the withdrawal of the main Russian force, following the signing of the Sarkozy peace plan, was initially only partial. There remained Russian troops stationed for nearly two months around the cities of Gori and Poti in Georgia proper, as well as in other so-called buffer-zones outside of both South Ossetia and Abkhazia. Troops were ultimately removed from these areas when control was handed to the European Union observer mission on 9 October 2008, though, at the date of writing, Russian forces remain in the two disputed regions themselves.

The conflict led to the publication, in September 2009, of an extensive report produced by the Independent International Fact-Finding Mission on the Conflict in Georgia (IIFFMCG),[1] which was set up by the Council of the European Union.[2] The Report ran to three volumes and over a thousand pages.[3] Part of the Mission's mandate was to assess the facts surrounding the conflict with regard to international law[4] and, as such, it reached a number of preliminary legal conclusions. However, IIFFMCG was ultimately a fact-finding mission and so was unsuited to producing detailed legal analysis; as a result its legal conclusions were somewhat cursory and, at times, notably flawed.[5]

Additionally, the 2008 conflict has given rise to a contentious case on the docket of the International Court of Justice (ICJ): a case that, at the time of writing, has already led to a provisional measures order.[6] However, the ICJ's jurisdictional competence is severely limited in that case, with it having to restrict its judgments to alleged violations of the International Convention on the Elimination of All Forms of Racial Discrimination.[7]

While both IIFFMCG and the ICJ can be seen as contributing to our legal understanding of the conflict, both have only been able to legally assess it in a limited manner. This volume aims to offer a critical contribution to the understanding of the 2008 conflict between Russia and Georgia from the less restrained position of scholarly analysis. It will address multiple dimensions of the conflict and its aftermath; from the use of force to human rights and from transnational litigation to the use of international law 'rhetoric'. Contributions draw on various international legal sub-disciplines, and relevant international relations scholarship is also canvassed, particularly in the last chapter of the book. The overall goal is to probe the key issues arising from the particulars of this conflict and to explore their wider implications through several lenses.

Given this goal, it is clear that the contributors to this volume have embarked on a difficult task. The Russia–Georgia conflict of 2008 is not one that lends itself to straightforward analysis; the complexity of the situation in the region stretches back to the Georgia–South Ossetia conflict of the early 1990s and, indeed, to Soviet and pre-Soviet history.

Moreover, the 2008 conflict was one that – in spite of the globalised nature of the modern media – was clouded in a great deal of factual disagreement, propaganda and media misdirection. Gleaning what the 'facts' of the situation were at the time of the conflict, at least with any kind of reliability, remains rather difficult even this long after the end of hostilities, as the somewhat flawed IIFFMCG Report demonstrates. Therefore, legal and political analysis must necessarily be applied to disputed factual circumstances. Of course, this is to an extent true with regard to all conflicts.[8] Yet this was a problem that was particularly pronounced in the context of the Russia–Georgia dispute. Further, it was a problem that was exacerbated by the technological disruption of so-called cyber-attacks, which affected all parties and led to the disruption and occasional collapse of servers in the region.[9]

In spite of such evidential difficulties, each chapter in this volume offers a valuable contribution towards understanding the conflict. Indeed, beyond this, the entries collectively highlight the conflict's wider implications for international legal order, with respect to the actions of the parties and the legal and political claims (and counter-claims) made. The 2008 Caucasus conflict has a number of unique aspects, which will come into focus in the following chapters. This work, therefore, examines not only the application of international law during the conflict in the Caucasus but also *what that application tells us about international law*, and the possible future of international legal order.

Within and across the disciplines and sub-disciplines employed in this work the contributors take a variety of theoretical and methodological approaches. As foreshadowed by the diverse approaches taken, and in the light of the number of well-established and competing theories, this volume does not attempt to suggest a single definition of 'international order'. Having said this, all of the following chapters engage the general concept of the rule of law in international affairs, and the contribution the rule of law can, and, we would argue, *should* make to an international order that is stable, predictable and just. This link between the rule of law and international order is not new and is suggested in the literature[10] as well as a variety of international instruments, including the United Nations (UN) Friendly Relations Declaration.[11] Furthermore, we do not attempt to suggest that the rule of law is synonymous with international order. As Andrew Hurrell has put it, highlighting the importance of capacity for effective action and legitimacy: 'International order is made up of far more than simply law.'[12] Nonetheless, the benefit of an international order informed by the rule of law is, in our view, self-evident.

Of course, defining 'the rule of law' remains an unresolved issue: it is an amorphous concept with multiple definitions. However, as a general starting point, contributions to this volume employ Simon Chesterman's recent 'functional' understanding of the rule of law.[13] This functional approach rejects formal definitions and instead provides a common crucible to explore the connection between the rule of law and international order along multiple lines. Chesterman asks what function the rule of law has in the international arena, or, perhaps more accurately, what role we might wish it to have. For each of the functions normally desired of the rule of law, Chesterman suggests three benchmarks that must be met: i) non-arbitrariness in the exercise of power, ii) distinguishing rule of law from rule by law and iii) consistency of application.[14]

For Chesterman, non-arbitrariness in the exercise of power is reflected in the 'foundational' concept of *pacta sunt servanda,* as well as international law codification efforts and the establishment of international regimes designed to protect human rights, manage conflict and address other matters of global concern. Chesterman's second principle, distinguishing the rule of law from rule *by* law, looks to efforts to ensure the supremacy of law through, for example, greater acceptance of the compulsory jurisdiction of the ICJ and the full application of international law to a broader range of international actors than just states. The third aspect of Chesterman's definition, equality before the law, encompasses steps towards making the formal equality of states match the law in action, by, for example, reforming the structural inequalities of the UN Security Council. This approach to the rule of law – the use of the rule of law as *means* to a more stable, predictable and just international order – will, no doubt, not appeal to realists who would reject the entire inquiry as flawed. However, this volume is unashamedly internationalist in orientation, and, as such, it is worth keeping Chesterman's approach to the rule of law in mind throughout: it acts as a common, if flexible, theoretical link between the chapters.

As has already been noted, the contributions to this volume examine multiple aspects of the 2008 conflict, and its implications for international legal order, from distinct but interlinking perspectives. In Chapter 1, Christopher Waters seeks to frame the conflict by sketching the multiple points of contact between, hard power, on the one hand, and, legalisation and internationalisation, on the other. He argues that international law and international institutions and norms served to contain the conflict in terms of duration and intensity, though brutality was sadly in evidence. The centrality of law in the management of this dispute, Waters suggests, is highlighted by contrasting the 2008 dispute over South Ossetia with the predecessor conflict of the early 1990s, where international organizations and norms appeared to play little role, and where international courts played no role at all.

The origins of the conflict are multiple, but one key part of the factual matrix of the conflict – and any potential resolution – is the question of self-determination. In Chapter 2, Robert McCorquodale and Kristin Hausler outline the content, nature and scope of the right of self-determination under international law, and then apply that right to the South Ossetian and Abkhaz people. They argue that the necessary 'exceptional circumstances' to warrant the exercise of the right of self-determination by external methods – such as secession – are not currently present. Instead, the appropriate method of exercising the right for these peoples remains through internal self-determination.

In Chapter 3, James Green tackles the lawfulness of the use of military force. In doing so, and in contrast to many Western observers, Green takes the Russian claim of lawful self-defence seriously. He suggests that Russia's self-defence justifications do not depart from established legal categories *per se* – notably the concept of the 'protection of nationals abroad' – albeit that the application of this concept is problematic in the present case due to the 'passportisation' of the South Ossetian population. Where the conflict's legacy does threaten traditional understandings of the *jus ad bellum* is in the loosening of the strict interpretation of the criterion of proportionality as a key aspect of assessing self-defence actions, a trend that is also worryingly reflected in other recent examples from state practice.

The next two chapters consider the 'legalisation' of the conflict through international and regional fora. In Chapter 4, Sandy Ghandhi considers the Russia–Georgia case before the ICJ. In particular, he examines the Court's provisional decision on the novel question of the applicability of the Racial Discrimination Convention when one state acts in the territory of another. The ICJ was deeply split on the issue and Ghandhi suggests that, while from a rights and humanitarian-oriented perspective the decision that the Racial Discrimination Convention does apply extraterritorially may be welcome, this bold decision may have misinterpreted the Convention itself.

In Chapter 5, Bill Bowring then looks to a regional response to the conflict. He suggests that the Council of Europe played – and will continue to play – an important (though underestimated) role in the management of the conflict. Furthermore, he suggests that the judicial branch of the Council, the European Court of Human Rights, is taken seriously by both Russia and Georgia, although litigation arising from the Caucasus conflict underscores the structural reforms required for the Court's continued success.

One result of the conflict has been the displacement of thousands of individuals, forced to flee from their homes. Anneke Smit, in Chapter 6, analyses how the Georgian and international authorities have responded to this large-scale displacement. She suggests that the response, which has focused on the implementation of durable solutions – most notably local integration in Georgia proper – represents a healthy (if undeniably problematic) new approach to the handling of the internally displaced when return to home of origin is not feasible immediately following conflict.

Finally, in Chapter 7, Christoph Stefes and Julie George ask the 'international order question' from an international relations perspective. Avoiding binary rules-oriented/interests-oriented interpretations of the conflict, they point out a fundamental paradox hinted at in other places in this volume: while 'international rules and norms barely constrained the behaviour of Russia, Georgia, and the leaders of the two separatist regions [,] ... the aftermath of the conflict has shown that international rules and norms have played important roles in giving meaning to what happened and determining the ways governments talked to each other, to the outside world, and with their citizens'. They conclude that 'states find it inconceivable to engage in actions that other states might consider illegal without trying to justify their behaviour by invoking international law'. This latter point is a key thread running throughout the chapters of this volume; despite the lawlessness inherent in the short and sharp war of 2008, and the continued displacement and suffering of individuals, the rule of law in international affairs represents a key principle for the management, containment and resolution of the conflict.

Notes

1. The Report of the Independent International Fact-Finding Mission on the Conflict in Georgia (IIFFMCG) (30 September 2009), online: http://www. ceiig.ch/Report.html.
2. European Union Council Decision 2008/901/CFSP of 2 December 2008 concerning an independent international fact-finding mission on the conflict in Georgia, Official Journal of the European Union 323/66.
3. The Report is significant because, as it noted, '[t]his is the first time in its history that the European Union has decided to intervene actively in a serious armed conflict. It is also the first time that after having reached a ceasefire agreement the European Union set up a Fact-Finding Mission as a political and diplomatic follow-up to the conflict.' See IIFFMCG Report, *supra* note 1, Volume I, 2. It is worth noting that the Mission made it clear that the comparatively short Volume I of the Report should be viewed as authoritative, see IIFFMCG Report, *supra* note 1, Volume I, 1. Although, of course, Volumes II and III still represent the published conclusions of the Mission and so should not be dismissed.
4. European Union Council Decision 2008/901/CFSP, *supra* note 2, Article 1(2).
5. See, for example, C. Henderson and J.A. Green (2010) 'The *Jus ad Bellum* and Entities Short of Statehood in the Report on the Conflict in Georgia', *International and Comparative Law Quarterly*, 59, 129–139.

6. *Case Concerning Application of the International Convention on the Elimination of All Forms of Racial Discrimination (Georgia v Russian Federation), Request for the Indication of Provisional Measures,* Order of 15 October 2008, International Court of Justice, online: http://www.icj-cij.org/docket/files/140/14801.pdf.

7. In Chapter 4 of this volume, Sandy Ghandhi provides a detailed examination of the provisional measures order.

8. For example, the ICJ explicitly acknowledged the inherent difficulties involved in the gathering of evidence during an ongoing conflict in the jurisdictional phase of the *Nicaragua* case, see *Military and Paramilitary Activities in and Against Nicaragua (Nicaragua v United States of America)* jurisdiction of the court and admissibility of the application [1984] I.C.J. Rep. 392, para. 101. Yet, it is additionally worth noting that the ICJ unequivocally dismissed the objection, raised by the United States, that such evidential difficulties precluded the Court from examining the dispute in question at all, see *Military and Paramilitary Activities in and Against Nicaragua (Nicaragua v United States of America)* counter-memorial of the United States [1984] I.C.J. Plead., Part IV, 166–169 for the specifics of the objection raised. On the more general point of 'factual uncertainty in conflict situations', see R.N. Gardner (1991) 'Commentary on the Law of Self-Defence' in L.F. Damrosch and D.J. Scheffer (eds) *Law and Force in the New International Order* (Oxford: Westview Press), pp. 52–53.

9. See IIFFMCG Report, *supra* note 1, Volume II, 217–219 for a summary of the various 'cyber-attacks' that occurred during the 2008 conflict. Interestingly, 'cyber-warfare' is something that is becoming a notable feature of international relations in former Soviet regions. For example, the technological disruptions of 2008 follow the attacks on the technological infrastructure of Estonia in May 2007, which were alleged to have come from an official Russian source. See I. Traynor, 'Russia Accused of Unleashing Cyberwar to Disable Estonia', *The Guardian* (17 May 2007), online: http://www.guardian.co.uk/world/2007/may/17/topstories3.russia.

10. See, for example, R. Teitel (2002) 'Humanity's Law: Rule of Law for the New Global Politics', *Cornell International Law Journal*, 35, 355.

11. Declaration on Principles of International Law Concerning Friendly Relations and Co-operation among States in Accordance with the Charter of the United Nations, Annex to GA Res. 2625(XXV), UNGAOR, 25th Sess., Supp. No. 18, UN Doc. A/8018, adopted without a vote on 24 October 1970, Preamble.

12. A. Hurrell (2000) 'International Law and the Changing Constitution of International Society' in M. Byers (ed.) *The Role of Law in International Politics* (Oxford: Oxford University Press), p.334.

13. S. Chesterman (2008) 'An International Rule of Law', *American Journal of Comparative Law*, 56, 342. It should be noted that Chesterman's 'functional' approach to the rule of law and its connection to world order is not unique. See, for example, the manner in which Richard Falk has applied these concepts in R.A. Falk (2008) *The Costs of War: International Law, The UN and World Order* (Abingdon: Routledge).

14. Chesterman, *ibid.*, 359–360.

1
The Caucasus Conflict and the Role of Law

Christopher P.M. Waters

Introduction

At the turn of this century, the editors of a special issue of the journal *International Organization* suggested that a greater 'move to law' was occurring and that a trend towards the 'legalization of world politics' was taking place.[1] While this view was contemporaneously criticised as presenting a simplistic conception of law, one which failed to adequately account for the dynamic interaction between norms and policies and between legal and political actors,[2] the basic insight that international law and politics intersected seemed undeniable. The 2003 Iraq invasion shook this view. Realists (and 'neo-cons' who thought of themselves as realists) were quick to point out that hard power was back – if indeed it had ever gone – and that any 'liberal moment' that had emerged in the 1990s (evidenced by robust collective action through the Security Council and the creation of the International Criminal Court, among other things) had ended.[3] Many legal scholars perceived a 'crisis in confidence' for international law. Some responded to this 'crisis' by suggesting that international law reorient itself to new threats and new realities, chipping away for example at the 1945 United Nations (UN) Charter framework that restricted the use of force to narrow exceptions.[4] 'Norm-oriented' scholars, however, pointed out that the Iraq invasion had not dealt a death blow to the centrality of law in world politics. Indeed, the official justification for the war – even if flawed – was based on law (the implied Security Council authorisation argument), showing that the language of international law retained currency and was in fact shaping states' options. Further, they argued, there was actually broad consensus on the law but 'political and practical' problems over factually determining what constituted a threat and how to respond to those threats.[5] At any rate, most legal observers were able to agree, the Iraq war had served to mobilise public engagement with international law in a way not seen before; the large protests in London and the legality of the war as an election issue in the United Kingdom showed that law mattered even where hawks seemed to have won a round.[6]

At first glance, the August 2008 violent clash between Georgia and Russia over the breakaway Georgian territory of South Ossetia seems capable of being interpreted as another Iraq, another empirically observable blow to the notion that a normative framework, most notably that established by the UN Charter, has 'bindingness' when it comes to hard politics.[7] To believe that a legal framework could serve to constrain a great power like Russia – especially given the perceived weakness of that state's internal lobby for the rule of law in international affairs – seemed naïve.[8] Even some international lawyers expressed scepticism as to the logic of international law being accepted by the parties, or indeed by concerned third parties, notably the United States and the European Union (EU), as germane to the dispute.[9] This is understandable given the parties' actions. It is also understandable given the parties' rhetoric. At one point, during the August 2008 conflict, the Russian leadership was settled on a course of regime change in Georgia, with Prime Minister Vladimir Putin colourfully declaring to the French President that he intended to 'hang Saakashvili by the balls'.[10] Georgia's president, Mikheil Saakashvili – pressed on the home front as a result of his post-Rose Revolution authoritarian streak – has very deliberately invoked Cold War rhetoric in order to unify his domestic and Western audiences against Russian aggression. As he put it during United States Vice-President Joe Biden's visit to Georgia nearly one year after the conflict, demanding security guarantees from the United States, Georgia was 'building democracy at gunpoint' and that Russian artillery was 'pointed at…this palace, this city, right now as we speak'.[11]

The relevance of hard/coercive power and the concomitant illegalities in the dispute over South Ossetia are apparent. However, that is not the end of the story. This chapter contends that international norms and organisations played an important role in limiting the scope and length of the conflict, limiting the humanitarian suffering (tragic as it was) and managing the ceasefire. International norms and institutions also have a possible role to play in ensuring justice for those wronged by the conflict and a possible supporting role in finding a durable solution to the dispute over South Ossetia. Before addressing this main contention, it will be useful to briefly sketch the factual context of the conflict and introduce some of the legal issues that arise, most of which will be addressed in greater detail in the following chapters.

Conflict in the Caucasus

It would be simplistic to suggest that the conflict between South Ossetia and Georgia is based solely on the manipulation of ethnicity over the span of two decades.[12] However, as most Georgians and Ossetians will say – especially in contrast to the Abkhazia conflict – they *have* historically 'gotten along'. Ethno-political entrepreneurs, drawing on claims of history and identity, did radicalise what had been a largely peaceful co-existence until the late Soviet period. All the same, while this historical account begins in the late twentieth century, it should not be forgotten that the conflicts that led to secession are at least partly rooted in competing cultural historiographies and myths of ethnogenesis (which people were there first) and civilisation (which people had the more advanced culture) forged over time.[13] The national 'histories' and myths created by the opposing sides are often mutually exclusive and evoke strong feelings among the people involved. The competing myths make it difficult to sketch even a basic chronology of the conflicts, but a bare-bones chronology of 'recent' events is attempted here. Further facts are added in the next chapter.

During the Soviet Union's *perestroika* years, resurgent nationalism, both among titular ethnicities in each republic (Russians in Russia, Georgians in Georgia and so forth) and among the ethnic minorities in each republic, began to colour the democratisation process.[14] In 1989, the Supreme Soviet of Georgia's semi-autonomous South Ossetian region voted for greater autonomy within Georgia (South Ossetians, together with their ethnic confreres in North Ossetia in the Russian Federation, form a distinct ethnic group and have their own language). Georgian authorities, however, purported to annul this vote and strip South Ossetia of the limited autonomy it had before the poll. Violence was triggered by a demonstration of Georgian nationalists in South Ossetia itself, which quickly intensified into a full-scale conflict. Roughly 60,000 Ossetians and Georgians were displaced from their homes and, at present, there are a similar number of people remaining in South Ossetia. A ceasefire was signed in 1992 leaving the authorities in Tskhinvali, the South Ossetian capital, with *de facto* control over a good portion of the territory within the original borders of the province. Pursuant to the ceasefire agreement signed in 1992, Russian, Georgian and South Ossetian peacekeeping forces were deployed and international mediation efforts were launched under the auspices of the Conference on Security and Co-operation in Europe (later the Organization for Security and Co-operation in Europe or OSCE). These mediation efforts were unsuccessful in solving the conflict but they were successful in terms of confidence building and there was roughly a decade of calm between the ceasefire and Georgia's 2003 'Rose Revolution', which saw the removal of Soviet-era leader Eduard Shevardnadze from power and the ascension of the reformer Saaskashvili.

Indeed, for anyone who travelled into South Ossetia from the mid-1990s to the early 2000s, the idea that this 'frozen conflict' could have erupted so furiously would have come as a surprise. The Georgian–South Ossetian 'border' was porous; black-market trading between Georgia and Russia via South Ossetia took place in the open, and it was not unusual to hear Georgian spoken in the streets of Tskhinvali, the South Ossetian capital. The joint peacekeeping patrols between Georgians, Ossetians and Russians were successfully coordinated for the most part and there were tentative, small-scale efforts at return for displaced persons forced to flee after the 1991/1992 conflict.[15] However, as suggested above, the issues stemming from the conflict of the early 1990s were only frozen and never resolved. Georgia had strenuously insisted on its territorial integrity since the break-up of the Soviet Union and this had been backed by the international community. Calls for Georgia's reunification – by force if necessary – grew steadily louder since the coming to power of Saakashvili during the Rose Revolution. Saakashvili promised a high degree of autonomy within Georgia for South Ossetia and sought to woo ordinary Ossetians back to the Georgian fold through a variety of enticements, from the distribution of farming aids such as fertiliser to the promise of integration into a renewed Georgian democracy and economy.

Yet, over a decade and a half of *de facto* independence, South Ossetians had built up the institutions of a microstate – with a legislature, courts and even at least one relatively (for the region) fair presidential election – and a determination not to return to the Georgian fold.[16] Before and during the conflict, President Saakashvili portrayed South Ossetia as simply a stooge for Moscow.[17] This is, like so much of the rhetoric surrounding the conflict, a half truth. While it is true that South Ossetians look to Russia for protection – and that in the year or two before the conflict the Russian state including its security apparatus absorbed elements of the South Ossetian government – this was for many the reality of living in an unrecognised and threatened mini-republic. Russian protection – and ultimately absorption into the Russian Federation – is seen as the best available option by the vast majority of ethnic Ossetians in the Tskhinvali region. This was crystallised after the Rose Revolution, when Saakashvili suggested that if the 'carrots' to reintegration did not work, more bellicose means of restoring Georgia's territory would be tried.[18]

Given the broad desire for independence followed by autonomous status within the Russian Federation, obvious questions of self-determination arise that clash with Georgia's claim to territorial integrity.[19] It should quickly be noted, however, that South Ossetians were not a people facing a colonial-like oppression under Georgian suzerainty before 1991/1992; as suggested earlier, Georgians and Ossetians lived quite peacefully together before the conflict, albeit with occasional ethno-political tension. Further, the roughly 10, 000 ethnic Georgian internally displaced persons from South Ossetia (whose ranks have now been joined by those people displaced in the latest fighting), many still residing in collective centres in Georgia proper, are adamant that they be given an effective right to return and that the region remain Georgian. The various issues that arise along the self-determination-territorial integrity axis have been judicially and theoretically explored elsewhere, including in Chapter 2 of this volume, and will not be addressed further here.[20] Suffice it to say that while international law probably does not give South Ossetians a right to external self-determination (i.e. secession), nor does it make the creation of new states from an existing one illegal *per se*.

Temporarily overshadowing the self-determination question was the use of force in the summer and early fall of 2008. One of the still debated facts is who 'started' the conflict. Both Russia and Georgia blame the other for breaching the decade and a half old ceasefire on 7 August 2008. Sifting through the evidence, it seems the most accurate view is that Georgia launched an attack on the capital of Tskhinvali on 7 August.[21] However, the 'who fired first' on 7 August question in some ways misses the point as the broader question of causation depends on what frame of time one is looking at. Skirmishes between Georgian and South Ossetian (with Russian support) forces had been occurring for months prior to 7 August, and the latter date simply represents the final breakdown of the ceasefire. In using force on 7 August, Georgia may have breached its international legal and political commitments. Even though it was primarily seeking to restore its own territorial integrity and was therefore not in obvious breach of the basic UN Charter prohibition on the use of force,[22] the reckless Georgian attack on Russian-protected Tskhinvali represents a failure to resolve through peaceful means what has been since 1991/1992 an internationalised dispute involving peacekeepers (even if those peacekeepers' neutrality and impartiality were suspect). That said, however, the Georgian and Russian actions are on altogether different scales, with Russia aggressively taking the conflict well out of its natural confines.

Russia's primary legal justification for its actions appears to rest on the defence of its nationals – with the vast majority of South Ossetians holding Russian passports – and its peacekeeping forces. While a state's citizenship policy is generally not a matter of public international law, it can become relevant where nationality grants are sham-like and affect the rights of other states. The wholesale and in many cases purely extraterritorial granting of Russian passports to the citizens of South Ossetia, a disputed breakaway region where Russia sought influence, was largely a self-serving sham (though one cannot blame individual South Ossetians for seeking the passports in order to pursue study, work and travel opportunities) and therefore the protection of nationals claim may fail on that basis in my view.[23] Furthermore, the extent to which protection of nationals abroad comes within the ambit of legitimate self-defence at all is controversial, though this topic is explored in greater depth in Chapter 3 of this volume. Undoubtedly a host of political factors – in addition to the legal justification given – account for Russia's aggression. Some of the factors are: Russia's desire to send a strong signal of its opposition to NATO expansionism eastwards (Georgia openly sought membership in NATO and American troops were arming and training Georgian forces), Russian resentment over the West's recognition of Kosovo's independence in the face of Serbian opposition, Russian desires to discourage additional oil and gas pipelines transiting through Georgia and bypassing Russia, and Russian desire to regain control over its traditional sphere of influence following a 'humiliating' period of weakness *vis à vis* the West.

However, even assuming that Russia has a legitimate self-defence claim on the basis of the protection of nationals abroad (and Russia might have had a stronger legal basis for its use of force if it simply cited defence of its peacekeepers and fidelity to their 1992 mandate, albeit a mandate in which genuine Georgian consent had become compromised, its actions have exceeded the well-known customary international law requirements for self-defence of necessity and proportionality.[24] In attacking far beyond the conflict zone, in both Western Georgia – with attacks launched from Georgia's other breakaway statelet – Abkhazia – and as far south as the capital Tbilisi, at least by air, Russia lost any plausible claim to acting in self-defence.[25] Indeed, the Russian President's claim that 'the aggressors have now been punished' is strong evidence, even given the usual caveat that political and legal claims must be considered separately, that Russia engaged in punitive reprisals rather than self-defence.[26] Not surprisingly, criticism of Russia's use of force in the West implicitly centred on the proportionality issue.[27]

Russia has also compounded its attack on the territorial integrity of Georgia by recognising the independence of South Ossetia, as well as of Abkhazia. Understandably, Russia's actions have sent a chill through other areas of the former Soviet Union that Russia has long considered its 'near abroad'.

Putting to one side the *jus ad bellum* question of whether the Georgian or Russian use of force was legal, there are also credible, independent reports of direct attacks on civilians as well as looting and pillaging of civilian property contrary to International Humanitarian Law.[28] Both sides have also accused each other of ethnic cleansing. South Ossetian militias in particular appear to have carried out brutal attacks on Georgian civilians and civilian property, with the apparent acquiescence of Russian authorities (and, given Russia's effective control of the region at the relevant time, Russia's legal responsibility).[29]

With the manifest illegalities noted above in mind, the next section will consider whether international norms and organisations can still be said to be central to politics in the context of this violent conflict.

The constraining roles of international norms and actors

Many at the time of the Iraq war, and in its immediate aftermath, suggested that international law and institutions had been rendered irrelevant in light of states' – particularly the United States' – preoccupation with national interests in light of threats from terrorists and rogue states. By contrast, Jutta Brunné and Stephen Toope argued, boldly for the time, that '[i]nternational institutions...provide an indispensable forum for the mutual engagement of States, a forum in which processes of deliberation and justification can take place' and that no fork in the road for international law had been reached.[30] Since then, even in the United States, reliance on unilateralism and hegemony as operating principles has declined. And, as suggested in the introduction to this chapter, rather than representing a body blow to the relevance of international norms and actors, the Caucasus conflict demonstrates the continued centrality of the law to international politics. The current section makes this point through an analysis of the roles played or being played by international organisations and courts applying international norms.

The European Union and other international organisations

There were tensions among EU member states during the crisis about how to respond to Russian actions in Georgia. To put it crudely, Western European states dependant on Russian oil were less militant than Eastern European states wary of Russian expansionism. These tensions underlined the continued constraints on the EU as an international actor with a common foreign and security policy. However, internal tension did not prevent the EU from playing a constructive role in limiting the scope of the conflict and brokering a ceasefire.[31] With the French holding the rotating EU-Council Presidency, Nicholas Sarkozy's shuttle diplomacy was ultimately effective in convincing the Russians to de-escalate and largely withdraw from Georgia proper back to the separatist enclaves where they had been present prior to the August clash. Indeed, Sarkozy's visits to Moscow and Tbilisi on 12 August – a mere five days after the conflict began – appears to have been the main catalyst for the start of Russia's pullback on 18 August. It is important to stress that Sarkozy's actions were not the product of EU consensus – Lithuania, for example, was critical of the Sarkozy brokered ceasefire because it made no reference to Georgia's territorial integrity – and also that the 1 September 2008 meeting of all 27 EU member states failed to agree on imposing sanctions on Russia despite the urging of Poland the Baltic states. Nonetheless, the EU-Council President's crisis management was timely and bold and the 1 September meeting did result in a coherent and fairly comprehensive diplomatic response.[32] Indeed, EU efforts have paid off. While there are breaches, the ceasefire has largely held and the main Russian pullout is complete. Furthermore, EU monitors also give the organisation an important ground presence to ensure the complete Russian pullout and adherence to the terms of the ceasefire, and there are ongoing talks between Russia, Georgia and South Ossetia in Geneva at the time of writing on 'incident prevention' mechanisms, among other things. To be clear, the talks are fragile and first attempts to launch them broke down on various points, including who was to be at the table. But that they are occurring at present is due in no small measure to the EU's engagement.

Another EU initiative that provided clarity into the war's causes – and raised the applicability of international law to the conflict – was the establishment of a fact-finding mission. The International Independent Fact-Finding Mission into the Conflict in Georgia (IIFFMCG), which was comprised primarily of experts rather than politicians, had as its mandate an investigation into 'the origins and the course of the conflict in Georgia, including with regard to international law, humanitarian law and human rights, and the accusations made in that context'.[33] The Mission reported in the autumn of 2009 and – despite subsequent attempts by both Russia and Georgia to hijack the Report's findings – has provided a fairly credible narrative of the war using international legal criteria – notably the UN Charter – as a guide.[34] It found, among other things, that Georgia wrongly attacked Tskhinvali, that Russia's response was disproportionate and that violations of international humanitarian law (IHL) occurred that require criminal sanction.

While the EU has been the international organisation most effectively engaged with conflict resolution over South Ossetia, other organisations have played a limited role as well. For example, the OSCE and the UN are co-sponsors with the EU of the Geneva talks. Unfortunately, Russia has used the consensus-based decision-making process of the OSCE to end the Organisation's mandate in Georgia when it expired at the end of 2008 (and again to end the OSCE's participation in the EU monitoring mission at the end of June 2009). The UN Security Council has been similarly dislodged by Russia from the role it had been playing in the related Abkhazia conflict. The Security Council created a peacekeeping mission in 1993 for Abkhazia (UNOMIG) and regularly extended its mandate, including in October 2008 and February 2009. In June 2009, however, Russia used its veto to prevent the continuation of the mission,[35] highlighting – as if further evidence were needed – the sometimes debilitating nature of the P-5 veto. In fairness, Russia has argued that the legal basis of UNOMIG and the OSCE presence in Georgia had been removed by Georgia itself, following the latter's repudiation of the accords that brought an end to the Ossetian and Abkhaz conflicts of the early 1990s.[36]

Other organisations including, surprisingly, the Commonwealth of Independent States (CIS) and the Shanghai Co-operation Organisation (SCO) quickly sought to play a calming role after the outbreak of hostilities by calling on the parties to adopt a diplomatic, international-law based approach to the conflict. The 'de-escalate' stances adopted by the CIS and SCO were taken despite Russia's attempts to secure endorsement of its military actions, and are surprising given the leading role Russia usually plays in these organisations, particularly the CIS (with China playing the role of counterweight in the SCO).[37]

Before moving to the next internationalised forum addressing the conflict, it is worth noting that the European Union (or the European Economic Community as it then was) was only a 'bit player' in resolving the secessionist conflicts in the Caucasus in the early 1990s. Indeed, the earlier secessionist conflict was 'resolved' directly by Russia, Georgia and the South Ossetian separatists, vaguely under the auspices of the CIS, but essentially without the direct and effective influence of a disinterested party like the EU in 2008.[38]

The European Court of Human Rights

The Council of Europe (CoE) was founded in 1949 by a handful of Western European states. Over the last 60 years, through gradual expansion and a 'big bang' at the fall of the Iron Curtain, it now has 57 members, including Russia (which joined in 1996) and Georgia (which joined in 1999). Like its European regional counterparts, the EU and the OSCE, the CoE was actively engaged at a political level in trying to broker a ceasefire and preserve human rights in the early days of the conflict. The CoE remains actively seised of the continuing humanitarian issues arising from the fragile ceasefire, which has shown cracks. In addition to its politico-diplomatic engagement, however, the CoE plays a role through its judicial branch, the European Court of Human Rights (ECtHR).

The ECtHR hears petitions brought by individuals against member states for breaches of the 1950 European Convention on Human Rights (ratified by both Georgia and Russia) and indeed the Court recently witnessed a flurry of cases filed by South Ossetians against Georgia and by Georgians against Russia for alleged human rights violations during the conflict.[39] These petitions claim, among other things, shelling and air attacks on undefended villages and deliberate burning and looting of civilian property, contrary to several Convention rights, including the right to life (Article 2) and the freedom from torture and inhuman treatment (Article 3). This is not the first time Russian Federation citizens have pressed claims against Georgia, and Georgian citizens against the Russian Federation. Georgia has even used the rarely resorted to inter-state complaint mechanism against Russia under the Convention in the past (dealing with mass expulsions of Georgians from Russia in 2006), and it launched a second inter-state complaint following the August 2008 outbreak of hostilities. While both the conflict-related individual petitions (numbering over 3000) and the most recent inter-state complaint will take some time to adjudicate – the Court is backlogged with thousands of cases – the President of the Court did provide for interim measures shortly after the invasion of Georgia proper by Russian forces, at the request of Georgia, calling on all parties to take measures to respect the Convention in the conflict and to report to the Court on these measures.[40] Russia and Georgia have complied with the Court's orders to compensate wronged individuals in the past (though Russian compliance with other more systemic remedies granted by the Court, particularly over Chechnya, have been less rigorous)[41] and both states appear to be actively and vigorously relying on the Court to press their claims now. Russia – which has been the defendant in roughly 25% of cases before the Court in recent years – has even established a special 'brigade' of jurists through its Procuracy to prepare cases on behalf of South Ossetians.[42] The interaction between the CoE, the ECtHR and 2008 conflict will be examined in more detail in Chapter 5.

For present purposes, what is important to note is that the mass channelling of human rights complaints from the conflict into a judicial forum seen here is in marked contrast to the 1991 secessionist conflict over South Ossetia, where there was no possible recourse to an internationalised human rights court. The next section moves away from regionalised justice and into an international judicial forum, the International Court of Justice (ICJ).

The International Court of Justice

Mere days after the conflict began, Georgia launched an action against Russia before the ICJ, contending that:

> [The] Russian Federation, through its State organs, State agents, and other persons and entities exercising governmental authority, and through the South Ossetian and Abkhaz separatist forces and other agents acting on the instructions of, and under the direction and control of the Russian Federation, is responsible for serious violations of its fundamental obligations under CERD [the International Convention on the Elimination of All Forms of Racial Discrimination], including Articles 2 [prohibition of racial discrimination], 3 [prohibition of racial segregation], 4 [prohibition of incitement to racism], 5 [equal treatment] and 6 [right to effective remedies].[43]

In other words, Georgia was using CERD to advance its claim of Russian and Russian-backed ethnic cleansing. The reason CERD was relied upon is partly a matter of practicality on Georgia's part. While all members of the UN are parties to the ICJ, the Court does not automatically have jurisdiction in a case. The parties can grant jurisdiction to the Court by special agreement between the parties, through the so-called optional clause automatically granting jurisdiction to the Court (which Georgia but not Russia accepts) or through a compromissory clause contained in a treaty. It is this latter 'hook' to the jurisdiction of the ICJ that

CERD provides, given that both Russian and Georgia are parties to the Convention. Article 22 of CERD states that '[a]ny dispute between two or more States Parties with respect to the interpretation or application of this Convention, which is not settled by negotiation or by the procedures expressly provided for in this Convention, shall, at the request of any of the parties to the dispute, be referred to the International Court of Justice for decision...'

While it will take until at least the end of 2010 for a decision on the merits of the case, the Court did grant provisional measures at Georgia's request on the basis of potential ongoing irreparable harm, in a decision that is analysed in depth in Chapter 4 of this volume. The provisional order required both parties to refrain from acts of racial discrimination and 'to do all in their power...to ensure, without distinction as to national or ethnic origin...security of persons...the right of persons to freedom of movement and residence within the border of the State and...the protection of the property of displaced persons and refugees'.[44] The parties were also ordered to facilitate the delivery of humanitarian assistance and 'refrain from any action which might prejudice the rights of the other Party in respect of whatever judgment the Court may render in the case, or which might aggravate or extend the dispute before the Court or make it more difficult to resolve'.[45] There are several interesting jurisprudential dimensions to this case, which in itself is an example of the increasing frequency with which human rights issues are being litigated before the Court. The extraterritorial application of CERD is particularly noteworthy. The Court found that Russia's obligations under CERD applied even when Russia was acting beyond its borders, as it was in South Ossetia, Abkhazia and other parts of Georgia.[46] This finding has potential implications for a consideration of what international human rights obligations apply to military forces acting abroad in a variety of contexts, including Western states' deployments in Afghanistan.

Professor Payam Akhavan of McGill University's Faculty of Law is representing Georgia before the ICJ. He argues, persuasively in my view, that the Court action matters:

> The fact is that one can be cynical and say that what difference does international law make in this situation ... but it's very clear that legitimacy is important, not least because Russia has constantly invoked international law as a justification for its policies. ... Already there has been a certain moderation of the situation since we got this case before the court because it puts Russia on notice that its action

is being scrutinized, and that there will be consequences attached to that.[47]

Before moving to the next section, it should be stressed that this case is the first between Russia and Georgia before the ICJ and that no resort to a judicial body was made in the early 1990s following the original secessionist conflicts in the region.

We now turn from inter-state accountability to the accountability of individuals.

The International Criminal Court (ICC)

The 1998 Rome Statute of the ICC provides for the prosecution of individuals accused of acts of genocide, crimes against humanity or war crimes. In order to come within the jurisdiction of the Court, the suspected perpetrator of one of these serious (and usually mass) crimes must have a territorial or national link to a state party.[48] While Georgia is a state party, Russia is not. Thus the Court has potential jurisdiction over Georgian nationals committing crimes in Georgian territory. However, the Court also has potential jurisdiction over the actions of Russian soldiers who may have committed crimes in Georgia, because of the territorial link. Both Georgia and Russia have contacted the ICC's Office of the Prosecutor and over 3000 communications regarding the conflict have been received at the Court.[49] The Office of the Prosecutor has indicated that it actively monitored the conflict,[50] though whether the Prosecutor will act on his own initiative to indict individuals, or whether Georgia will formally refer cases to the ICC, remains to be seen. The possibility of prosecution of individuals (including commanders under the doctrine of command responsibility) may well be one of the reasons why, despite serious breaches of IHL, the war at first blush appears to have been somewhat less savage (it was certainly shorter) than its predecessor. Needless to say, the ICC, which only became operational in 2002, did not exist as a possible venue for accountability in the context of the 1991–1992 South Ossetian conflict. Nor in 1991/1992 had the *ad hoc* tribunals for the former Yugoslavia and Rwanda begun operation. These international tribunals have played an important role in delineating the customary and conventional obligations of IHL and advancing the notion and reality of individual accountability. Thus, when in 2009 the IIFFMCG reported, it was able to rely on an IHL/International Criminal Law framework far advanced from 1991 to 1992 in matters such as mixed intra/inter-state conflict and gender-related crimes.[51]

Conclusion

Georgia's territorial integrity is ruptured and thousands remain displaced from their homes. Only a fragile ceasefire is in place in South Ossetia and Abkhazia and conflict in other separatist tinderboxes in the Caucasus region (most notably the Nagorno–Karabakh dispute between Armenia and Azerbaijan) is foreseeable. On top of all this, there is overblown rhetoric of a 'new cold war'. Clearly, this is no time for Pollyannaism about the role of international actors and norms in conflict prevention or resolution. However, the facts remain that both Georgia and Russia have framed their actions in the language of international law and the current mechanisms and norms of international order have limited the extent and duration of the conflict. International law also provides the possibility of state and individual accountability. The internationalisation and legalisation of the current conflict of this conflict through international organisations, courts and norms stand in stark contrast to the character of the earlier South Ossetian conflict and underline the continued – or indeed enhanced – centrality of law to international politics, even when violent clashes occur. Of course, legalisation is not synonymous with the rule of law under most definitions, including Chesterman's functional definition referred to in the Introduction to this volume. However, the manner in which the Caucasus conflict has been legalised and institutionalised has served to limit and dampen the arbitrary exercises of power exhibited during the short, sharp war of the summer of 2008 and contributed, haltingly, to the rule of law in international affairs.

Notes

1. J. Goldstein, M. Kahler, R.O. Keohane and A.-M. Slaughter (2000) 'Introduction: Legalization and World Politics', *International Organization*, 54, 385. More generally, see W.A. Bogart (2002) *Consequences: The Impact of Law and Its Complexity* (Toronto: University of Toronto Press), p.5: 'A survey of the last five decades of Western industrialised society would highlight, as a defining element, the insinuation of law into all manner of human endeavour.' The present chapter draws on an earlier work by the author; see C.P.M. Waters (2009) 'The Legalization of the Georgia-Russia Conflict of 2008', *Journal of Parliamentary and Political Law*, 3, 351.
2. See, for example, J. Brunnée and S. Toope (2000) 'International Law and Constructivism: Elements of an Interactional Theory of International Law', *Columbia Journal of Transnational Law*, 39, 72. Brunnée and Toope suggest that the 'legalisation' view unwittingly accepts law as a binding, external force, without explaining where it comes from. By contrast, they argue for a

focus on 'the mutual generative normative activity of agents and structures in international law and politics'.

3. On the dismissal of 'soft power' by the Bush Administration, see, for example, J.S. Nye, Jr. (2004) 'The Decline of America's Soft Power: Why Washington Should Worry', *Foreign Affairs*, 83, 16.
4. For a recent example, see N. Rostow (2009) 'International Law and the Use of Force: A Plea for Realism', *Yale Journal of International Law*, 34, 548.
5. C. Gray (2007) 'A Crisis of Legitimacy for the UN Collective Security System?', *International & Comparative Law Quarterly*, 56, 157.
6. D. McGoldrick (2004) *From '9–11' to the Iraq War 2003* (Oxford: Hart).
7. On empirically measuring the relevance of international law to politics, contrast J.L. Goldsmith and E.A. Posner (2005) *The Limits of International Law* (Oxford: Oxford University Press); with M. Scharf (2009) 'International Law in Crisis: A Qualitative Empirical Contribution to the Compliance Debate', *Cardozo Law Review*, 31, 46.
8. Indeed, the most vocal domestic opposition to the Russian government's handling of the conflict was to the effect that the response to Georgian 'aggression' was insufficiently aggressive. H.-H. Schroder (2008) ' "A Short, Victorious War?" Russian Perspectives on the Caucasus Crisis' in H.-H. Schroder (ed.) *The Caucasus Crisis* (Berlin: German Institute for International and Security Affairs), p. 8, online: http://www.swp-berlin.org/en/common/get_document.php?asset_id=5524. Though for a contrary view, one which argues that 'being part of the international system has become a fundamental ambition of Russian foreign policy', see N.N. Petro (2009) 'The Legal Case for Russian Intervention in Georgia', *Fordham International Law Journal*, 32, 1524.
9. H.-H. Schroder (2008) 'Editorial: Georgia', *European Journal of International Law*, 19, 896.
10. C. Bremner, 'Vladimir Putin "Wanted to Hang Georgian President Saakashvili by the Balls"', *The Times* (18 November 2008), online: http://www.timesonline.co.uk/tol/news/world/europe/article5147422.ece.
11. B. Whitmore, 'Reset-Phobia in Tbilisi', RFE/RL (22 July 2009), online: http://www.rferl.org/content/ResetPhobia_In_Tbilisi/1783230.html.
12. I am grateful to Brad Roth for a thought-provoking discussion on this point.
13. See G. Smith et al. (1998) *Nation Building in the Post-Soviet Borderlands: The Politics of National Identities* (Cambridge: Cambridge University Press).
14. See generally, R.G. Suny (1994) *The Making of the Georgian Nation* (Bloomington: Indiana University Press).
15. On the challenges facing the return of refugees/internally displaced persons to their homes of origin, see A. Smit (2006) 'Property Law Aspects of Refugee and IDP Returns: Case Studies of Georgia and Kosovo' in P. Shah (ed.) *Migration, Diasporas and Legal Systems in Europe* (London: Cavendish), as well as her chapter (Chapter 6) in this volume.
16. See C.P.M Waters (2005) 'Rule of Law in the Secessionist States' in C.P.M Waters (ed.) *The State of Law in the South Caucasus* (Basingstoke: Palgrave); and (2006) 'Law in Places That Don't Exist', *Denver Journal of International Law and Policy*, 34, 401.

17. M. Corso, 'Georgia Holds Steady as Moscow Inches Closer to Abkhazia, South Ossetia', *Eurasia Insight*, EurasiaNet (17 April 2008), online: http://www.eurasianet.org/departments/insight/articles/eav041708c.shtml.

18. See D. van der Schriek, 'Georgia Uses Carrot-and-Stick Approach with South Ossetia', *Eurasia Insight*, EurasiaNet (1 June 2004), online: www.eurasianet.org.

19. In this regard there are obvious parallels to Kosovo's experience despite claims by Western states that the Kosovo case is unique.

20. See *Reference re Secession of Quebec*, [1998] 2 S.C.R. 217; and, generally, J. Crawford (2006) *The Creation of States in International Law* (Oxford: Oxford University Press).

21. C. Chivers and E. Barry, 'Georgia Claims on Russia War Called into Question', *The New York Times* (7 November 2008), online: http://www.nytimes.com/2008/11/07/world/europe/07georgia.html?_r=1&hp=&oref=slogin&pagewanted=print.

22. The basic UN Charter provision on the use of force is set out in Article 2(4), which provides that: 'All Members shall refrain in their international relations from the threat or use of forces against the territorial integrity or political independence of any State or in any other manner inconsistent with the Purposes or Principles of the United Nations.' The only recognised Charter exceptions to the prohibition on the use of force are self-defence and action authorised by the UN Security Council. In addition, Article 2(3) states that 'All Members shall settle their international disputes by peaceful means in such a manner that international peace and security, and justice, are not endangered.'

23. The leading case on citizenship in international law is the *Nottebohm* case (*Liechtenstein v Guatemala*) merits [1955] I.C.J. Rep. 4, 23; a 'genuine connection' with the state purporting to confer nationality is required.

24. See C. Gray (2006) 'The Use of Force and the International Legal Order' in M.D. Evans (ed.) *International Law*, 2nd edn (Oxford: Oxford University Press).

25. By analogy, see *dicta* from the International Court of Justice in *Armed Activities on the Territory of the Congo* (*Democratic Republic of the Congo v Uganda*) merits [2005] I.C.J. Rep. 116, para. 147, to the effect that 'the taking of airports and towns many hundreds of kilometres from Uganda's borders would not seem proportionate ...' Georgia is of course much smaller than the Congo and Russian targets in Georgia proper were not hundreds of kilometres removed from South Ossetia, but Russian actions do appear to have gone far beyond what the logic of self-defence would have warranted.

26. J. Meikle, 'Attacks on Georgia Continue Despite Russian President's Calls to Halt', *The Guardian* (12 August 2008), online: http://www.guardian.co.uk/world/2008/aug/12/georgia.russia5.

27. For example, a joint statement of G7 foreign ministers decried 'Russia's Excessive Use of Military Force'. See 'Statement on Georgia by G7 Foreign Ministers', Department of Foreign Affairs and International Trade News Release No. 185 (27 August 2008), online: www.international.gc.ca.

28. Human Rights Watch, 'Up in Flames: Humanitarian Law Violations and Human Victims in the Conflict Over South Ossetia' (2009), online: http://www.hrw.org/en/reports/2009/01/22/flames-0.

29. S. Talmon (2008) 'The Responsibility of Outside Powers for Acts of Secessionist Entities', *International and Comparative Law Quarterly*, 58, 493.
30. J. Brunné and S. Toope (2004) 'The Use of Force: International Law After Iraq', *International and Comparative Law Quarterly*, 53, 797.
31. See generally, A. Bendiek and D. Schwarzer (2008) 'The EU's Southern Caucasus Policy under the French Council Presidency: Between Consultation, Co-operation and Confrontation' in Schroder, *supra* note 8.
32. U. Halbach (2008) 'The Regional Dimension: Georgia and the Southern Caucasus after the War' in Schroder, *ibid.*, 20. At least one of the reasons for EU success in responding to the crisis was the EU's long-standing engagement with both Russia and Georgia through a variety of mechanisms and policies, including the European Neighbourhood Policy.
33. European Union Council Decision 2008/901/CFSP of 2 December 2008 concerning an independent international fact-finding mission on the conflict in Georgia, Official Journal of the European Union 323/66, Article 1(2).
34. The Report of the Independent International Fact-Finding Mission on the Conflict in Georgia (IIFFMCG) (30 September 2009), online: http://www.ceiig.ch/Report.html.
35. 'Russia Vetoes Extension of UN Mission in Georgia', *UN News Centre* (15 June 2009), online: http://www.un.org/apps/news/story.asp?NewsID=31151&Cr=georgia&Cr1=.
36. See Petro, *supra* note 8, 1529.
37. A Schmitz (2008) 'The Caucasus Conflict and the Future of the CIS' in Schroder, *supra* note 8. It should be noted that following the conflict Georgia indicated that it would withdraw from the CIS (the withdrawal took place on 12 August 2009), sparking a debate within Georgia as to whether in doing so Georgia was 'cutting off its nose to spite its face'.
38. Though as noted earlier, the OSCE (and its forerunner, the Conference on Security and Co-operation in Europe) did have an important role in monitoring compliance with the ceasefire.
39. 'Seven Applications against Georgia Concerning Hostilities in South Ossetia', Press Release of the Registrar of the European Court of Human Rights (14 January 2009).
40. 'European Court of Human Rights Grants Request for Interim Measures', Press Release of the Registrar of the European Court of Human Rights (12 August 2008). Interim measures are available under Article 39 of the Rules of Court, which states, in part: 'The Chamber or, where appropriate, its President may, at the request of a party or of any other person concerned, or of its own motion, indicate to the parties any interim measure which it considers should be adopted in the interests of the parties or of the proper conduct of the proceedings before it.'
41. For an argument that the ECtHR faces a pattern of challenges to its authority from newer members of the CoE, see J.L. Cavallaro and S.E. Brewer (2008) 'Reevaluating Regional Human Rights Litigation in the Twenty-First Century: The Case of the Inter-American Court', *American Journal of International Law*, 102, 773.
42. V. Shishlin, 'Prosecutor General Chaika will Help the Victims of the War to Obtain Justice,' *Interfax* (August 12, 2008), online: http://www.interfax.ru/print.asp?sec=1484&id=26795.

43. International Court of Justice, 'Georgia Institutes Proceedings against Russia for Violations of the Convention on the Elimination of All Forms of Racial Discrimination', Press Release Number 2008/23 (12 August 2008), online: http://www.icj-cij.org/docket/files/140/14659.pdf.

44. *Case Concerning Application of the International Convention on the Elimination of All Forms of Racial Discrimination (Georgia v Russian Federation), Request for the Indication of Provisional Measures*, Order of 15 October 2008, International Court of Justice, online: http://www.icj-cij.org/docket/files/140/14801.pdf.

45. *Ibid.*

46. *Ibid.*, para. 109.

47. As quoted in J. Gilman, 'Georgia Files ICJ Case: McGill Prof. to Represent Republic', *The McGill Tribune* (3 September 2008), online: http://media. www.mcgilltribune.com/media/storage/paper234/news/2008/09/03/News/ Georgia.Files.Icj.Case-3413201.shtml.

48. Article 12 of the *Rome Statute of the International Criminal Court*, 17 July 1998, 2187 U.N.T.S. 3.

49. L. Moreno-Ocampo, 'Impunity No More', *New York Times* (1 July 2009), online: http://www.nytimes.com/2009/07/02/opinion/02iht-edocampo.html.

50. 'ICC Prosecutor Analyzing Alleged Crimes in Georgia', *International Herald Tribune* (20 August 2008), online: http://www.iht.com/articles/ ap/2008/08/20/europe/EU-War-Crimes-Georgia.php.

51. See, for example, IIFFMCG Report, *supra* note 34, Volume I, 36–37, para. 10.

2
Caucuses in the Caucasus: The Application of the Right of Self-Determination

Robert McCorquodale and Kristin Hausler

Introduction

> The peoples of South Ossetia and Abkhazia have several times spoken out at referendums in favour of independence for their republics. It is our understanding that after what has happened [with the bombardment by Georgia of] Tskhinval [in South Ossetia] and what has been planned for Abkhazia, they have the right to decide their destiny by themselves. ... Considering the freely expressed will of the Ossetian and Abkhaz peoples and being guided by the provisions of the United Nations Charter, the 1970 Declaration on Principles of International Law Governing Friendly Relations between States, the CSCE Helsinki Final Act of 1975 and other fundamental international instruments, I signed Decrees on the recognition by the Russian Federation of South Ossetia's and Abkhazia's independence.[1]

In August 2008, the Russian President, Dmitry Medvedev, after receiving the support of the Russian Parliament, decided to recognise the independence of South Ossetia and Abkhazia from the state of Georgia.[2] According to the official statement by the President, quoted above, this action was based on international law. Each of the documents directly referred to in the statement has provisions about self-determination of peoples as do 'other fundamental international instruments', which include the International Covenant on Economic, Social and Cultural Rights 1966 (ICESCR) and the International Covenant on Civil and Political Rights 1966 (ICCPR), to both of which Russia is a party.[3] During the conflict, the Georgian government and other governments similarly appealed for international law to be applied.[4]

This chapter will explore the extent to which there is a right of self-determination of the South Ossetian and Abkhaz people, and the application of that right under international law. In so doing, it will consider the actions by both the Georgian and Russian governments, and the extent to which they were consistent with this international law. This discussion will also raise issues about the requirements of a rule of law based international legal order.

The right of self-determination in international law

The use of self-determination in an international legal context[5] primarily developed during the immediate post-First World War period, with both United States President Wilson and Lenin supporting self-determination.[6] In 1945, the Charter of the United Nations proclaimed that one of the purposes of the United Nations (UN) was 'respect for the principle of equal rights and self-determination of peoples'.[7] As will be discussed below, since that time, self-determination of peoples has been restated, clarified and reinforced in the international law instruments referred to by President Medvedev – the Declaration on Principles of International Law 1970 and the Helsinki Final Act 1975 – as well as in the two major human rights treaties referred to above (the ICESCR and the ICCPR), in decisions and opinions of the International Court of Justice (ICJ), in resolutions of the Security Council and the General Assembly, and in state practice.

While the UN Charter upheld the 'principle' of self-determination of peoples, the two international human rights Covenants made clear that self-determination was a human right. Common Article 1 of the Covenants (being the only substantive human right protected in both Covenants) provides:

1. All peoples have the right of self-determination. By virtue of that right they freely determine their political status and freely pursue their economic, social and cultural development.

2. All peoples may, for their own ends, freely dispose of their natural wealth and resources without prejudice to any obligations arising out of international economic co-operation, based upon the principle of mutual benefit, and international law. In no case may a people be deprived of its means of subsistence.

3. The States Parties to the present Covenant, including those having responsibility for the administration of Non-Self-Governing and
Trust Territories, shall promote the realization of the right of self-
determination, and shall respect that right, in conformity with the
provisions of the Charter of the United Nations.

Further, the Declaration on Principles of International Law, which is
generally considered to be internationally agreed clarifications of the
principles in the UN Charter, states that:

By virtue of the principle of equal rights and self-determination of
peoples enshrined in the [UN] Charter, all peoples have the right
freely to determine, without external interference, their political status and to pursue their economic, social and cultural development,
and every State has the duty to respect this right in accordance with
the provisions of the Charter.[8]

This Declaration confirms that the principles of the UN Charter
must now be understood as providing for the self-determination of
peoples as a human right, which is binding under international law
on all states.

It is evident from these international instruments that the right of
self-determination is a right that is applicable in economic, social and
cultural contexts, as well as in political contexts. It is also clear that it is a
right of 'peoples' as distinct from individuals.[9] However, the Covenants
do not give much greater clarity on the definition of the right.[10]

The right of self-determination outside of the colonial context

Initially the right of self-determination was applied solely to colonial
territories. In 1960, self-determination was considered in the context
of 'the necessity of bringing to a speedy and unconditional end colo-
nialism in all its forms and manifestations'.[11] The ICJ has consistently
held that the right of self-determination applies to all peoples in all
colonial territories,[12] and state practice confirms this. The position is
evident not only from the vast number of colonial territories that have
exercised their right of self-determination to become members of the
UN but also because of the acceptance by the colonial powers that they
have a legal obligation to allow this exercise.[13] Some writers have concluded from this consistent state practice, *opinio juris*, and lack of any
denial by states, that the right of self-determination of colonial peoples
is now a matter of *jus cogens*.[14]

However, state practice shows that the right of self-determination has definitely been applied outside the colonial context. For example, when East and West Germany were united into one state in 1990, it was expressly stated in a treaty signed by four of the five permanent members of the UN that this was done as part of the exercise of the right of self-determination by the German people.[15] The right of self-determination is also referred to in the context of the dissolution of the Soviet Union and Yugoslavia,[16] and internally within states (see further below). Additionally, the ICJ confirmed that the right of self-determination applies to the Palestinian people in its *Wall* advisory opinion.[17] Indeed, the ICJ has gone further and has declared that the right of self-determination is 'one of the essential principles of contemporary international law' and has 'an *erga omnes* character'.[18] This means that there is an obligation on all states to protect the right of self-determination. As such it is clear that self-determination is not merely an obligation on colonial powers and so the right applies to peoples beyond the colonial context.

Since 1960, the right of self-determination has not been expressed in any international or regional instruments solely in the context of colonial territories. For example, the Declaration on Principles of International Law provides:

> [All States should bear] in mind that subjection of peoples to alien subjugation, domination and exploitation constitutes a violation of the principle [of equal rights and self-determination of peoples], as well as a denial of fundamental human rights, and is contrary to the Charter of the United Nations.[19]

Therefore, the right of self-determination applies to any peoples in any territory (including non-colonial territories) who are subjected to 'alien subjugation, domination and exploitation'. Indeed, it would be contrary to the concept of a human right if the right of self-determination could only be exercised once (such as by colonial peoples) and then not again. So, all peoples in all states have the right of self-determination.

Definitions of 'peoples'

There have been many attempts to establish a definition of 'peoples'.[20] However, they have all struggled to find an 'objective' definition that can be applied to all relevant groups around the world, or even be appropriate for those in colonial territories. This is because a key aspect is self-identification, where the group identifies themselves consciously as a 'people'. This is an essential part of the definition of a 'people', not least because 'nations and peoples, like genetic populations, are recent, contingent and have been formed and reformed constantly throughout history',[21] often due to the oppression that they have received or to attain certain ends.[22]

While external recognition by a state or group of states can be very useful for the group (such as the recognition by many states of the Palestinian people),[23] it is not conclusive of the group being a people for the purposes of the right of self-determination. Indeed, if such external state recognition was conclusive it would allow the possibility of the existence of a human right (as distinct from the ability of a human right to be exercised) being dependent on the whims of governments. Above all, dependence on the government itself for the existence of a right would undermine the concept of a human right as being, for example, inherent in human dignity.

In fact, in many situations, it is clear as to who are the 'peoples' with the right of self-determination. This can be because the relevant national constitution, legislation or practice indicates this. For example, the Scots in the United Kingdom, the Basques in Spain and the Aceh people in Indonesia are all accepted as peoples with the right of self-determination.[24] There is also, as will be shown below, universal acceptance that the right of self-determination applies to all peoples in colonial territories, and significant state practice that applies it beyond the colonial context. Consistent oppressive actions by those in power over another group may also indicate an acceptance of the group as a 'people', not least because it may be catalyst for the self-identification of the group as a people with the right of self-determination.

Exercises of the right of self-determination

The Declaration on Principles of International Law 1970 set out the principal methods to show how the right of self-determination can be exercised. It provided that:

> The establishment of a sovereign and independent State, the free association or integration with an independent State or the emergence into any other political status freely determined by a people constitute modes of implementing the right of self-determination by that people.[25]

While the vast majority of peoples in colonial territories exercised their right of self-determination by attaining independence, this was not the only method of exercise that was either available or was used.[26]

In non-colonial situations, a range of exercises of the right of self-determination have occurred. While many have been by attaining independence, such as Bangladesh from Pakistan and Montenegro from its union with Serbia, others have been by merger (e.g., the two Yemens), or by free association (e.g., Bougainville with Papua New Guinea). These are all exercises of external self-determination, as there has been a change in the international relationships between the peoples exercising their right of self-determination and the original state/colonial power, as well as with other states and international actors.

Self-determination can be exercised by internal means, where there is a change in the internal relationships and administrations within a state but no change in the external relationships. The Organisation of Security and Co-operation in Europe (OSCE – previously the CSCE), which comprises all the Western and Eastern European States, the then Soviet Union, the United States and Canada, accepted that self-determination could be exercised by external and internal methods. In its Helsinki Final Act in 1975 – specifically referred to by Russian President Medvedev in the statement quoted at the beginning of this chapter – it was declared:

> By virtue of the principle of equal rights and self-determination of peoples, all peoples have the right, in full freedom, to determine, when and as they wish, their *internal and external* political status, without external interference, and to pursue as they wish their political, economic, social and cultural development.[27]

The Declaration on Principles of International Law expressed internal self-determination as being where 'a government [is] representing the whole people belonging to the territory without distinction as to race, creed or colour'.[28] The Canadian Supreme Court considered that internal self-determination in relation to the peoples of the province of Québec enabled the 'residents of the province freely [to] make political choices and pursue economic, social and cultural development within Québec, across Canada, and throughout the world... [and be] equitably represented in legislative, executive and judicial institutions.'[29]

Accordingly, there is a range of internal exercises of the right of self-determination. After all, 'customary and treaty law on internal self-determination [do not] provide guidelines on the possible distribution of power among institutionalized units or regions'.[30] For example, outside the colonial context there has been devolution of some legislative powers to Scotland and Wales in the United Kingdom, control over cultural and linguistic matters within the Swiss cantons, and a form of federalism in Bosnia-Herzegovina, Iraq and Sudan. These methods are often called 'forms of autonomy' or 'internal governance'. In many instances, the method of exercise has been by agreement with the government for significant autonomy within a state, such as Crimea in Ukraine, Mindanao in the Philippines and the northern regions of Mali.[31]

All these examples show that there are many possible exercises by peoples of their right of self-determination. While independence – called 'secession' when it is from an existing independent state – is often seen as the only option in non-colonial contexts; it is but one option of very many forms of exercise, and not normally the first option lawfully able to be exercised under international law. The Supreme Court of Canada made this clear when it was considering the position of the province of Québec's potential request for independence:

> International law contains neither a right of unilateral secession nor the explicit denial of such a right, although such a denial is, to some extent, implicit in the exceptional circumstances required for secession to be permitted under the right of a people to self-determination, e.g., the right of secession that arises in the exceptional situation of an oppressed or colonial people.…The recognized sources of international law establish that the right to self-determination of a people is normally fulfilled through internal self-determination – a people's pursuit of its political, economic, social and cultural development within a framework of an existing state. A right to external self-determination (which in this case potentially takes the form of the assertion of a right to unilateral secession) arises in only the most extreme of cases and, even then, under carefully defined circumstances.[32]

What the Court is indicating – which is consistent with the generally accepted position – is that, in most instances outside the colonial context, independence will not be considered the legitimate first step in the exercise of the right of self-determination. However, there may be exceptional circumstances where the people could exercise their right of self-determination by external self-determination where it is a 'last resort', as all other means of exercise of the right have been tried and have failed.[33]

The exercise of the right of self-determination must be by the people themselves. The ICJ confirmed this when it emphasised 'that the application of the right of self-determination requires a free and genuine expression of the will of the peoples concerned'.[34] In most instances the will of the people can be determined by a popular consultation, such as by referendum or elections. For example, the European Union (EU) created Arbitration Committee of the International Conference on the Former Yugoslavia (the 'Badinter Committee') decided that the will of the peoples in Bosnia-Herzegovina had to be ascertained, possibly by a referendum carried out under international supervision.[35] However, there may be exceptional circumstances where there is no consultation, such as where the position is clear in all the circumstances and is not manipulated by a state, a government or international institutions. For example, during the dissolution of the Soviet Union few referenda were held.[36] In ensuring that the genuine will of the people is clear, it is important that the views of all within the group, including those of women and minorities, are heard and listened to equally.

Limitations on the right of self-determination

As with almost all human rights, the right of self-determination has limitations on its exercise. These limitations are to protect the rights of others (such as the rights of others to self-determination) or the general interests of the society (such as public order, public health, *et cetera*).[37]

The limitation on the exercise of the external right of self-determination to protect the general interests of the relevant society that is most often asserted by governments is 'territorial integrity'. This limitation on the right of self-determination was expressed in the Declaration on Principles of International Law:

> Nothing in the foregoing paragraph [recognising the right of self-determination] shall be construed as authorizing or encouraging any action which would dismember or impair, totally or in part, the territorial integrity or political unity of sovereign and independent States conducting themselves in compliance with the principle of equal rights and self-determination of peoples as described above and thus possessed of a government representing the whole people belonging to the territory without distinction as to race, creed or colour.[38]

This is an important potential limitation on the exercise of the right. However, it is only a justifiable limitation in certain situations, namely when an exercise of external self-determination (such as independence) is being sought and when a state is 'possessed of a government representing the whole people belonging to the territory without distinction as to race, creed or colour'. In other words, it can only be a legally justifiable limitation on the exercise of the right of external self-determination when a state is already enabling full internal self-determination for those people.

A particular aspect of this limitation on the exercise of the right of self-determination is the international legal principle of *uti possidetis juris*. This principle provides that states emerging from colonial administrative control must accept the pre-existing colonial boundaries. Its purpose was to achieve stability of territorial boundaries and to maintain international peace and security.[39] While this has been uniformly accepted as a principle applicable solely to colonial territories, it was surprisingly applied by the Badinter Committee to the former Yugoslavia.[40] This latter application was probably incorrect, as it confused historically established boundaries that had not resulted from colonial determinations with colonial determined boundaries. It should also be noted that many of the colonial boundaries were created to preserve the interests of the colonial states and were not related to natural or cultural boundaries understood by the peoples on the ground.[41] Therefore, the principle of *uti possidetis juris* is of questionable legitimacy as a limitation on the right of self-determination. It should only apply, if at all, in the (now very few) situations of decolonization.

Therefore, when the Russian President Medvedev claimed that Russia's actions were 'guided by the provisions of the United Nations Charter, the 1970 Declaration on Principles of International Law Governing Friendly Relations Between States, the CSCE Helsinki Final Act of 1975 and other fundamental international instruments', he was including all of the international law concerning the right of self-determination as set out above. It is necessary to determine if the actions by Russia and by Georgia were in compliance with this international law.

The context of the right of self-determination in the Caucasus

The statement by the Russian President quoted at the beginning of this chapter was made in a particular context. This context was historical and political, in terms of the break-up of the Soviet Union, developments within Georgia and, more recently, the declaration of independence by Kosovo, and arose after a period of armed conflict between Russia and Georgia. There has also been involvement of the international community in the region for some time.

Historical contexts

Before the new Bolshevik military forces (the Red Army) invaded Georgia in 1921, it had been a Democratic Republic since the end of World War I following the collapse of the Russian Empire.[42] Georgia was then integrated into the new Soviet Union, initially as part of the Transcaucasian Soviet Federative Socialist Republics with Armenia and Azerbaijan, and then as a separate Soviet Socialist Republic (Georgian SSR) from 1936. Abkhazia and Adjara[43] were made 'Autonomous Republics' within the Georgian SSR, with their own constitutions.[44] As Autonomous Republics, they had a level of autonomy, including being responsible for the economic and social development in their territories, and jurisdiction for all matters not falling within the scope of the Soviet Union or the Georgian SSR.[45] South Ossetia was considered an 'Autonomous Region', with a lesser degree of autonomy,[46] which meant, for example, that the Ossetian language could be used and taught in schools.

With the end of the Cold War and the crumbling of the communist party governments in Eastern Europe, nationalist sentiments developed, especially from 1988 onwards, within the central Georgian SSR's territory and also among the population of the Autonomous Region of South Ossetia. The South Ossetian regional council wanted to gain the same Autonomous Republic status as Abkhazia and Adjara, and a political party was formed with this aim. However, the central Georgian SSR's government resisted this, and in 1990 it adopted a law forbidding regional political parties and proclaimed that Georgian was to be the principal language across the entire territory. As a reaction to these new restrictions, South Ossetia declared its independence from Georgia (to become a Soviet Socialist Republic) on 20 September 1990 and adopted its own constitution. The Georgian SSR's elections later that year were boycotted by the South Ossetians, which eventually led to the central Georgian SSR's government ending the autonomous status of South Ossetia.[47]

In early 1991, South Ossetia sought to secede from Georgia and unite with the North Ossetian Autonomous Region within the Russian Soviet Socialist Republic. An armed conflict then occurred between Georgian SSR forces and South Ossetian forces. On 9 April 1991 Georgian SSR declared its independence from the Soviet Union and on 21 February 1992 it restored the constitution of the 1921 Democratic Republic of Georgia,[48] with nine regions but without providing any guidance with regard to the status of Abkhazia and Adjara (or South Ossetia).

On 23 July 1992, the Supreme Council of Abkhazia reinstated its 1925 Constitution, which stated that Abkhazia is 'united on the basis of [a] Union Treaty with the Georgian Soviet Socialist Republic'.[49] This triggered an armed conflict between the newly independent Georgia's forces and the Abkhaz forces, following which Abkhazia declared its independence, adopting a new constitution on 26 November 1994 in which it declared itself a 'sovereign democratic State'.[50] Adjara did not declare independence – though for some time it stayed *de facto* outside the control of the central Georgian government – and remained free of direct armed conflict; its autonomy is now defined by Georgia's law on Adjara and the region's new constitution.[51]

Russia mediated the ceasefire agreement (the 'Sochi' agreement) between Georgia and South Ossetia in 1992, after a UN fact-finding mission to the region.[52] The OSCE (the CSCE at the time) both facilitated these negotiations and monitored the ceasefire. This agreement created a Joint Control Commission (JCC) – of which the EU became an observer in 2001 – and a peacekeeping body, the Joint Peacekeeping Forces group (JPKF), which was under Russian command. While the armed conflict with South Ossetia had effectively ceased in 1992, the tension in the region remained and thus a settlement memorandum was signed in 1996. This memorandum indicated respect for both territorial integrity and self-determination rights, without qualifying precisely the level of autonomy granted to South Ossetia.[53]

Russia also mediated the ceasefire agreement between Georgia and Abkhazia in 1993, with the peacekeeping forces being provided by the Commonwealth of Independent States (CIS), though only Russia offered troops.[54] The UN sent an observer mission in 1993 (UNOMIG) that was mainly focused on supervising the implementation of the ceasefire agreement.[55] Further negotiations by the UN resulted in the 2002 Boden proposal, according to which Abkhazia would be a distinct sovereign entity under the Georgian Constitution, though this proposal was rejected by the Abkhazians.[56] The EU also attempted peace efforts, including through the Group of Friends of Georgia with regard to the conflict in Abkhazia.[57]

During this period, referenda on independence were held in Abkhazia and South Ossetia. The referenda took place on 3 October 1999 in Abkhazia[58] and on 12 November 2006 in South Ossetia, each with a very large majority in favour, though ethnic Georgians boycotted the vote.[59]

The ceasefires largely remained in place from 1992/1993 until early 2008. Tensions were still present, especially between the Georgian and Russian governments, with each maintaining military forces on their borders with South Ossetia, and Russia having bases in Georgia itself until 2007.[60] Russia also appears to have been providing considerable support to the South Ossetian and Abkhaz groups seeking independence, including military support (see further below).[61] They also issued Russian passports to inhabitants of both Abkhazia and South Ossetia.[62] The tensions were such that the UN Security Council unanimously passed Resolution 1808 in April 2008, which reaffirmed:

> [T]he commitment of all Member States to the sovereignty, independence and territorial integrity of Georgia within its internationally recognised borders and supports all efforts by the United Nations and the Group of Friends of the Secretary-General, which are guided by their determination to promote a settlement of the Georgian-Abkhaz conflict only by peaceful means and within the framework of the Security Council resolutions.[63]

On 8 August 2008, armed conflict occurred between Georgia, and South Ossetia, Abkhazia and Russia. The main conflict lasted 5 days. The ceasefire agreement was negotiated by the EU and an EU monitoring group was put in place in Georgia.[64] Subsequently, the EU established a fact-finding mission (the Independent International Fact-Finding Mission on the Conflict in Georgia (IIFFMCG)) to assess the responsibilities with regard to the events of August 2008.[65]

On 21 August 2008, meetings were held in South Ossetia and Abkhazia to ask Russia to support their independence. On 23 August 2008, Eduard Kokoity, the President of South Ossetia, travelled to Moscow to present his appeal to the Federation Council of Russia, and on 25 August 2008, Sergei Bagapsh, the President of Abkhazia, made a similar appeal. The latter added 'that Abkhazia and South Ossetia will never be part of Georgia'. The Russian Federation Council agreed with these appeals, and the Russian President issued decrees recognizing the independence of South Ossetia and Abkhazia as states.[66] To date the only other states that have recognised South Ossetia and Abkhazia as independent states are Nicaragua, Venezuela and Nauru.

Kosovo

Early in 2008 a situation elsewhere in Europe occurred that is of relevance to the situation in the Georgian region. On 17 February 2008, the Kosovo Assembly issued a unilateral declaration of independence.

Fifty-seven states, including the United Kingdom and the United States, have (to date) recognised Kosovo as being independent.[67] The Serbian and the Russian governments (and others) rejected this independence as being contrary to international law.[68] Interestingly, the independence of Kosovo is mentioned in the Russian President's statement of 26 August 2008 in which he recognised the independence of South Ossetia and Abkhazia.[69]

In October 2008, the General Assembly requested an advisory opinion of the ICJ on 'whether the unilateral declaration of independence of Kosovo is in accordance with international law'.[70] Hearings have been held and the opinion is expected in mid-2010. It is of note that the submission by the government of Kosovo (amongst others) is that the question as to whether the people of Kosovo have a right of self-determination is not relevant in terms of the question asked of the ICJ, as the question only asks if the declaration of independence was valid under international law.[71]

While the issue of the lawfulness under international law of the declaration of independence of Kosovo is outside the scope of this chapter, there are a few issues in that situation that are important to note. First, the Badinter Committee recognised that the Republics of the former Socialist Federal Republic of Yugoslavia (SFRY) had a right of self-determination, though this right had to be exercised in particular ways, such as to respect minority rights and requiring evidence of consent by the peoples concerned.[72] However, it did not include Kosovo within its considerations. This was because Kosovo was not a Republic of the SFRY but was an 'Autonomous Province' within the Republic of Serbia, though the Serbian government, prior to the dissolution of the SRFY, ended most of its autonomous powers. Second, the Badinter Committee considered that:

> [T]he demise of the Socialist Federal Republic of Yugoslavia, unlike that of other recently dissolved States (USSR, Czechoslovakia), resulted not from an agreement between the parties but from a process of disintegration that lasted some time, starting, in the Commission's view, on 29 November 1991, when the Commission issued opinion No. 1, and ending on 4 July 1992, when it issued opinion No. 8.[73]

This means that some of the former Yugoslav Republics that had declared independence before 29 November 1991 had done so by express acts of secession and those Republics, such as Montenegro, which had done so after this time had become independent due to dissolution. Third, the territorial integrity arguments of the Serbian government were recognised but, since Security Council Resolution 1244 (1999), Kosovo and Serbia had been governed separately, and the United Mission in Kosovo (UNMIK) had been exercising authority (legislative, executive and judicial) on the territory since then.[74] Thus, there had been international territorial administration of Kosovo, which arguably meant that there was no remaining territorial integrity of Serbia that Serbia could claim. Finally, after eight years of this separation of governance of Kosovo and after many negotiations, in March 2007 the Special Envoy of the UN Secretary-General recommended that Kosovo become independent under the supervision of the international community, due to the fact that after 'one year of direct talks, bilateral negotiations and expert consultations, it has become clear to me that the parties are not able to reach an agreement on Kosovo's future status'.[75]

There is one other issue concerning the unilateral declaration of independence of Kosovo that is relevant to this chapter. When many of the states recognised Kosovo as an independent state, they expressly stated that this was a *'sui generis'* situation.[76] They sought to indicate that this was a unique situation and could not be used as a precedent for either its application to other situations or for recognition in similar situations. Asserting that the situation is *sui generis* is neither definitive to prevent a precedent or effective in terms of decisions on recognition. Indeed, almost every situation of the exercise of the right of self-determination, especially outside the colonial context, is unique. The exercise of the right of self-determination by the people of Bangladesh, the peoples of the new states of the former Yugoslavia, the peoples in the new states from the dissolution of the Soviet Union, and by the German people in the merging of the two Germanys, were all unique. Whether a particular exercise by a peoples of their right of self-determination, such as by a unilateral declaration of independence, is lawful under international law would be decided in the particular context of that situation, as was made clear by the Canadian Supreme Court in the *Québec* opinion.[77] This context will include, as discussed above, the ability of the people concerned to exercise internal self-determination (autonomy) within the broader state, the negotiation/consultation possibilities within the broader state, and the extent to which there are other exceptional circumstances that may impact on the question of self-determination. Above all, the situation in Kosovo can never be *sui generis* as a matter of precedential impact on the development of international law.[78]

Application of the right of self-determination to Abkhazia and South Ossetia

Internal self-determination

It is evident from the historical context above that the central Georgian government has treated both Abkhazia and South Ossetia as having a large measure of autonomy, perhaps even *de facto* independence, since the early 1990s.[79] Thus, it could be considered that they now have a large degree of internal self-determination, albeit more through force and ceasefires than directly through negotiated constitutional arrangements. Indeed, the IIFFMCG Report considered that, due to the breadth of their autonomy, Abkhazia was a 'state-like entity' and South Ossetia was 'an entity short of statehood'.[80]

The external identification of Abkhazians as a distinct people for at least 60 years, with a clearly accepted and maintained autonomy by the Soviet Union and then the Georgian SSR, as well as their self-identification, makes it clear that they are a people. South Ossetians did not have the same acknowledged depth of autonomy as the Abkhazians but were nevertheless externally accepted by the Soviet Union and the Georgian SSR as having sufficient distinctive identity as a people. Nevertheless their self-identity appears to be as South Ossetians (though possibly as Ossetians, in that they have a link with North Ossetians).[81] It is clear that the external acceptance, the passing of legislation and practices in the area are all supportive of the position that both the Abkhazians and the South Ossetians are people with a right of self-determination.

External self-determination

Both Georgia and Russia are parties to all the major international treaties that protect the right of self-determination, and so accept the right to self-determination as an international legal obligation. International law generally requires, outside the colonial context, that internal self-determination is the first method of exercise of the right of self-determination. The reason for this is primarily because of the principle of the territorial integrity of the existing state. Security Council Resolution 1808 (2008) made this clear when it affirmed 'the sovereignty, independence and territorial integrity of Georgia within its internationally recognised borders'.

However, as noted above, this principle does not apply where a state is not allowing internal self-determination. There was some significant internal self-determination of Abkhazia and South Ossetia, at least until the early 1990s. Since that time, there have been actions by the central

Georgian government that can be seen to limit the exercise of internal self-determination, including by restricting South Ossetian language use. The issue is, therefore, whether there are exceptional circumstances sufficient to warrant overcoming the principle of territorial integrity.

It is only in exceptional circumstances that the people of part of an existing state who have had internal self-determination can exercise their rights by external self-determination. These exceptional circumstances may include the dissolution of a state, as happened in the former Yugoslavia, and possibly where the scale of the ongoing violations of the right of self-determination (and other rights) is such that external self-determination is a 'last resort' as all other means of exercise of the right have been tried and have failed.[82]

Even in those exceptional circumstances, the peoples must respect the rights of others. For example, in the *Québec* opinion, the Canadian Supreme Court noted that the rights of the indigenous ('aboriginal') peoples in the province were also affected by the right of self-determination of the Québécois:

> We…acknowledg[e] the importance of the submissions made to us respecting the rights and concerns of aboriginal peoples in the event of a unilateral secession, as well as the appropriate means of defining the boundaries of a seceding Québec with particular regard to the northern lands occupied largely by aboriginal peoples. However, the concern of aboriginal peoples is precipitated by the asserted right of Québec to unilateral secession.[83]

The Court not only acknowledged the rights of the indigenous people but also accepted the human rights and constitutional rights of other parts of Canada. It determined that, even if there had been a clear majority of the people of Québec who wished to secede, they could not do so without negotiations with the other parts of Canada. However, this does not necessarily give a permanent veto power to the other parts of Canada, as the internal right of self-determination of the people of Québec must not be oppressively restricted. Nevertheless, as noted above, it is essential that all minority rights (and the human rights of all) must be fully respected and guaranteed by all peoples exercising the right of external self-determination.

The August 2008 conflict, and the violations that occurred during it, must be considered in this perspective. The IIFFMCG Report determined that the state of Georgia was responsible for the escalation of the conflict and it must share the responsibilities for the serious human rights violations, including civilian casualties, which resulted from this conflict.[84] In relation to the use of force by Georgia, the general international legal position is set out in the Declaration on Principles of International Law:

> Every State has the duty to refrain from any forcible action which deprives peoples referred to above in the elaboration of the present principle of their right to self-determination and freedom and independence.[85]

So a state cannot use disproportionate force against a people seeking the right of self-determination. It is also the case that the Geneva Convention Protocols 1977 extend to wars of national liberation, being 'armed conflicts which peoples are fighting against colonial domination and alien occupation and against racist regimes in the exercise of their right of self-determination'.[86]

Although the 2008 Caucasus conflict has ceased, tension in the region remains high; another armed conflict is plausible, and a large number of internally displaced persons remain.[87] There has been attempts to put into place interim measures that would replace the Russian military forces and border guards in Abkhazia and South Ossetia by certain international presences, but the current negotiations indicate that there is 'no progress in working out solid security guarantees for Abkhazia and South Ossetia on the Geneva discussions'.[88]

Nevertheless, a situation of tension does not, by itself, provide an exceptional circumstance of a last resort to enable a people to exercise their right of self-determination by external self-determination methods. In this instance, there must be negotiations in good faith between the government of Georgia and representatives of the peoples of Abkhazia and South Ossetia. This would place a responsibility on Georgia to guarantee in law and practice that the peoples of Abkhazia and South Ossetia will have significant autonomy over their regions, perhaps by using a form of federalism, as an exercise of their right of internal self-determination. Where this guarantee is made and fully carried out (preferably with international monitoring) then the right of external self-determination does not arise. Further, external self-determination could not be exercised in this situation where the peoples who may be seeking such exercise refused to negotiate in good faith. If such a guarantee was given by Georgia, then the representatives of Abkhazia and South Ossetia would also need to guarantee in law and practice that they would protect the rights of minorities (including ethnic Georgians) in their regions and allow all internally displaced peoples (if they so wished) to return to the regions.[89]

If, and only if, all negotiations carried out in good faith break down, and all avenues of resolution were truly exhausted – which is not yet the situation here – then the peoples may be able to exercise their right of external self-determination. If this happens then external self-determination does not need to be by secession/independence. For example, there could be exercise of a free association with Georgia or with Russia in which Abkhazia and South Ossetia have sovereignty over all matters except over their defence and foreign affairs, or the possibility of the merging of South and North Ossetia into a single autonomous region within Russia. Should any of these forms of exercise of external self-determination occur, it is essential that there is a full and appropriate consultation of the peoples, including taking into account the wishes of ethnic Georgians in the regions (some of whom may have left the regions due to the conflict).[90]

Russia and the right of self-determination in Abkhazia and South Ossetia

Request to support peoples exercising the right of self-determination

The peoples of Abkhazia and South Ossetia are entitled to support from other states when forcible action occurs against them as a people seeking to exercise their right of self-determination. This is clear from the Declaration on Principles of International Law:

> Every State has the duty to refrain from any forcible action which deprives peoples referred to above in the elaboration of the present principle of their right to self-determination and freedom and independence. In their actions against and resistance to such forcible action in pursuit of the exercise of their right to self-determination, such peoples are entitled to seek and to receive support in accordance with the purposes and principles of the Charter of the United Nations.[91]

The support that these peoples can receive must be in accordance with the purpose and principles of the UN Charter. This would ensure that the general principles of the use of force, such as proportionality, necessity and consent are applied.[92] However, action by a state that was effectively an occupation of the territory of the entity or the use of force by that state that was disproportionate would fall outside the principles of the UN Charter.

In this situation, Russia assisted the peoples of Abkhazia and South Ossetia when force was used against them by Georgia in relation to their exercise of the right of self-determination. The initial actions by the Russian troops in protecting the Abkhazians and South Ossetians could be considered being consistent with international law as these actions were in response to the support requested by these peoples.[93]

However, this support must remain in accordance with the purposes of the United Nations and international law (as noted by the Russian President in the opening epigraph). What occurred was that Russian military forces fought over territory that was well outside the Abkhazia and South Ossetia regions, and remained in those regions once the immediate need for protection has ceased.[94] As James Green argues in the next chapter of this volume, this is contrary to the UN Charter principles and so amounted to a breach of international law.

Support for self-determination forces

Russia maintained a militarised presence in the relevant entities for many years, and also provided substantial military and financial support to the South Ossetians and the Abkhazians.[95] Such substantial military, financial and other support to peoples seeking the right of self-determination could mean that Russia is internationally legally responsible for breaches of human rights by those peoples during the conflict. This was held by the European Court of Human Rights in *Ilaşcu v Moldova and Russia*,[96] in relation to violations of human rights that occurred in Transdniestria, a region of Moldova under the control of a group calling itself the 'Moldavian Republic of Transdniestria' (MRT), which was seeking external self-determination. One of the claims before the Court was that Russia had been assisting and supporting the MRT through military and political means. When considering the responsibility of Russia, the Court took into account the history of the situation in which Russia had given long-term military and political support to the MRT, which included its participation in the fighting to help the MRT set up their regime. As a result, the Court held that:

> All of the above proves that the 'MRT', set up in 1991–1992 with the support of the Russian Federation, vested with organs of power and its own administration, remains under the effective authority, or at the very least under the decisive influence, of the Russian Federation, and in any event that it survives by virtue of the military,

economic, financial and political support given to it by the Russian Federation.[97]

Thus the Court held that the acts of the MRT were attributable to Russia, and Russia was in breach of its obligations under the European Convention on Human Rights (ECHR).[98] It would appear that Russia has provided very similar support to the peoples of Abkhazia and South Ossetia, and so it would be responsible for violations of the ECHR by those peoples.

There are a range of other issues that raise international legal concerns about the extent to which Russia may have interfered in the territorial sovereignty of Georgia while supporting the peoples of Abkhazia and South Ossetia. These include the recognition by Russia of Abkhazia and South Ossetia as separate states from Georgia, the granting of Russian passports to people in those regions, and actions in Russia against Georgians.[99] However, these are issues that are outside the scope of this chapter.

The Caucasus and International Legal Order

It is clear that the peoples of Abkhazia and of South Ossetia have a right of self-determination. They have exercised this right through internal self-determination for many decades, albeit with some interruption and, more recently, through ceasefires after armed conflict. An exceptional circumstance of a last resort to enable them to exercise their right of external self-determination has not yet arisen, as there must first be full negotiations in good faith with the central Georgian government, in case a guarantee of their full internal self-determination over their regions is achievable. Representatives of the peoples of Abkhazia and South Ossetia (and Adjara, if they wish) must be fully involved in any discussions (and caucuses) to resolve this situation, and the international community can assist in this. If a last resort situation does arise in the future, then there is a range of methods of exercise of external self-determination that are possible, and not only secession/independence.

The role of Russia is also important in any long-term solution. While the initial support by Russia to the Abkhazians and South Ossetians to resist the use of force by Georgia against them was in accordance with international law, the breadth, depth and extent of their subsequent actions meant that they did not remain within the parameters of international law. Russia may also be internationally responsible for violations of human rights (and probably also violations of international humanitarian law) by the Abkhazian and South Ossetian forces, both during the conflict and subsequently, for which they provide substantial military and financial support. There are also many other regions within Russia where peoples seek to exercise their right of self-determination for which this situation will be seen as a precedent and not as *sui generis*.

Indeed, the situation raises the broader question of how to apply the right of self-determination in the international system. David Milliband, the United Kingdom Foreign Secretary at the time of the armed conflict in August 2008, wrote:

> The Georgian crisis is about more than vital issues of humanitarian need and rule of law over rule of force. It raises a fundamental issue of whether, and if so how, Russia can play a full and legitimate part in a rules-based international political system, exercising its rights but respecting those of others.[100]

This is a good and appropriate question to ask. One reassurance here is that Russia used international law as its primary justification for its actions, as seen in the statement of its President at the start of this chapter. Russia did so carefully and accurately, even if its actions on the ground did not always match its international statements. This is important because, if a rules-based international order is to be a strong framework of the international system, then international law, including the right of self-determination, needs to be treated seriously as law and not just as a 'handmaiden' to international politics.[101]

There will be other pressures that may also be relevant to ensuring a rules-based international order. Economic pressures will ensure that most states recognise that a state that has a rule of law provides order and stability, transparency, good governance, justice and accountability, which will attract commercial investment, and other states' engagement.[102] This is especially the case in the Caucasus region with its oil and other energy resources. It is the same at the international level as:

> The protection of the interests of all states and the creation of international stability requires that state-to-state relations be subject to a long-term framework [of an international rule of law], which ensures that international law is applied in conformity with principles of justice ... [and enables states to have a] stable, safe and predictable world in which they can better pursue their political and economic goals.[103]

Therefore, it is essential that the situation in the Caucasus is resolved in accordance with the principles of the UN Charter and international law, with full respect for the right of self-determination.

Notes

1. Statement by Russian President, Dmitry Medvedev, to the Russian people, 26 August 2008, as translated in *The Financial Times* (United Kingdom) (26 August 2008).
2. The relevant Presidential Decrees are 1260 (recognising Abkhazia); and 1261 (recognising South Ossetia), online: http://kremlin.ru/doc.asp?ID=047559; and http://kremlin.ru/doc.asp?ID=047560.
3. Russia ratified both the ICESCR and the ICCPR on 16 October 1973 without relevant declarations or reservations for these purposes.
4. See the lengthy statement by the Georgian government to the Independent International Fact-Finding Mission on the Conflict in Georgia (IIFFMCG), IIFFMCG Report (30 September 2009), Volume III, 5–330, online: http://www.ceiig.ch/Report.html. See also the statement by David Milliband, United Kingdom Foreign Secretary, *The Times* (19 August 2008), in which he stated that '[i]nternational law must be obeyed'.
5. Much of the material in this section and the next section is based on R. McCorquodale (2010) 'Group Rights' in D. Moeckli, S. Shah and S. Sivakumaran (eds) *International Human Rights Law* (Oxford: Oxford University Press).
6. See W. Wilson (1918) *War Aims of Germany and Austria*, reproduced in R. Baker, W. Dodd and H. Leach (eds) (1927) *The Public Papers of Woodrow Wilson: War and Peace* (New York: Harper & Brothers), p. 177; and V. Lenin (1950) *The Right of Nations to Self-Determination* (Moscow: Foreign Languages Pub. House), whose views were supported by the new Bolshevik government in Russia in 1917 (see T. Musgrave (1997) *Self-Determination and National Minorities* (Oxford: Oxford University Press), p.17–22).
7. UN Charter, Article 1(2).
8. Declaration on Principles of International Law Concerning Friendly Relations and Co-operation Among States in Accordance with the Charter of the United Nations, Annex to GA Res. 2625(XXV), UNGAOR, 25th Sess., Supp. No. 18, UN Doc. A/8018, adopted without a vote on 24 October 1970 (Declaration on Principles of International Law), section on 'The principle of equal rights and self-determination of peoples', opening para.
9. See, for example, the UN Human Rights Committee (HRC) views in *Ominayak and Lake Lubicon Band v Canada*, Annual Report of the Human Rights Committee, UN Doc. A/45/40 Vol II, Annex IX (1990), p.1.
10. See also Article 20 of the African Charter of Human and Peoples' Rights 1981, 21 I.L.M. 58 (1982).
11. Declaration on Independence for Colonial Countries and Peoples 1960, GA Res. 1514 (XV) (14 December 1960), Preamble.
12. *Namibia* opinion [1971] I.C.J. Rep. 16, para. 52. See also *Western Sahara* case [1975] I.C.J. Rep. 12, paras. 54–55; and per Judge Dillard at p.121.

13. See, for example, the statement by the United Kingdom's representative in the Security Council on 25 May, 1982, (1983) *British Yearbook of International Law*, 54, 371–372.
14. See, for example, A. Cassese (1995) *Self-Determination of Peoples: A Legal Appraisal* (Cambridge: Cambridge Univeristy Press), p.140; and J. Crawford (2002) *The International Law Commission's Articles on State Responsibility: Introduction, Text and Commentaries* (Cambridge, Cambridge University Press) in relation to Article 41.
15. Treaty on the Final Settlement With Respect to Germany 1990, 29 I.L.M. 1186 (1990).
16. See, for example, the terms of the European Community's 'Declaration on Yugoslavia and its Declaration on the Guidelines on Recognition of New States in Eastern Europe and the Soviet Union', 16 December, 1991, 31 I.L.M. 1486 (1992).
17. *Advisory Opinion on the Legal Consequences of the Construction of a Wall in the Occupied Palestinian Territory* [2004] I.C.J. Rep., paras. 118 and 122.
18. *East Timor* case [1995] I.C.J. Rep. 90, para. 29. The HRC also requires all states party to the ICCPR to report on their protection of the right of self-determination: HRC General Comment 12 (1984), para. 3.
19. Declaration on Principles of International Law, *supra* note 8.
20. See, for example, the Final Report and Recommendations of an International Meeting of Experts on the Further Study of the Concept of the Right of People for UNESCO, 22 February, 1990, SNS–89/CONF. 602/7. See also R. Kiwanuka (1988) 'The Meaning of "People" in the African Charter of Human and Peoples' Rights', *American Journal of International Law*, 82, 80.
21. E. Kamenka (1988) 'Human Rights, Peoples' Rights' in J. Crawford (ed.) *The Rights of Peoples* (Oxford: Clarendon Press), p.133. See also P. Allott (1992) 'The Nation as Mind Politic', *New York University Journal of International Law and Politics*, 24, 1361.
22. C. Chinkin and S. Wright (1993) 'Hunger Trap: Women, Food and Self-Determination', *Michigan Journal of International Law*, 14, 262 propose, at p.306, that 'food, shelter, clean water, a healthy environment, peace and a stable existence must be the first priorities in how we define or "determine" the "self" of both individuals and groups, instead of the present definitions, which are based on masculinist goals of political and economic aggrandizement and aggressive territoriality'.
23. See J. Crawford (2006) *The Creation of States in International Law*, 2nd edn (Oxford: Oxford University Press), p. 434–448; and V. Kattan (ed.) (2008) *The Palestinian Question in International Law* (London: British Institute of International and Comparative Law).
24. See M. Weller (2009) 'Settling Self-Determination Conflicts: Recent Developments', *European Journal of International Law*, 20, 111.
25. Declaration on Principles of International Law, *supra* note 8.
26. For example, the British and the Italian Somaliland colonies joined into one state of Somalia, and one part of the British colony of Cameroon merged with the French colony of Cameroun to form the new state of Cameroon and the remaining part joined with the existing state of Nigeria.

27. Helsinki Final Act 1975, Principle VIII (emphasis added), Organization for Security and Co-operation in Europe, online: http://www.osce.org/documents/mcs/1975/08/4044_en.pdf.
28. Declaration on Principles of International Law, *supra* note 8.
29. *Reference Re Secession of Québec*, [1998] 2 S.C.R. 217, 37 I.L.M. 1342 (1998), Supreme Court of Canada, para. 136 (*Québec* opinion).
30. Cassese, *supra* note 14, 332.
31. For details of these and other exercises, see Weller, *supra* note 24, 111.
32. *Québec* opinion, *supra* note 29, paras. 112 and 126.
33. See *Aaland Islands* opinion, International Committee of Jurists, (1920) L.N.O.J. Spec. Supp. 3; and *Loizidou v Turkey* 23 E.C.H.R. 513 (1997) per Judges Wildhaber and Ryssdal.
34. *Western Sahara* case, *supra* note 12, para. 55.
35. Badinter Committee, opinion 4, 31 I.L.M. (1992) 1502, para. 4.
36. Referendum in the Soviet Union of 17 March 1991, Commission on Security and Co-operation in Europe, online: http://csce.gov/index.cfm?FuseAction=UserGroups.Home&ContentRecord_id=443&ContentType=G&ContentRecordType=G&UserGroup_id=101&Subaction=Reports&CFID=95720&CFTOKEN=1. See also, Centre for Russian Studies, online: http://www2.nupi.no/russland//elections/March91_ref_1.html. Note that Georgia did not participate in this referendum but held its own referendum on 31 March 1991. See the Decree issued by the Supreme Council of the Republic of Georgia on 'Organization and Holding the Referendum on Preservation of the USSR' issued by the Supreme Council of the USSR, online: http://www.parliament.ge/files/1_933_840995_13.pdf.
37. See, for example, common Article 5(1) of the ICCPR, 19 December 1966, 999 U.N.T.S. 171; and ICESCR, 19 December 1966, 993 U.N.T.S. 3.
38. Declaration on Principles of International Law, *supra* note 8.
39. *Frontier Dispute Case (Burkina Faso v. Mali)* [1986] I.C.J. Rep. 554 (Chamber of the ICJ), para. 25.
40. Badinter Committee, opinion 2, 31 I.L.M. (1992) 1497, para. 1.
41. Malcolm Shaw (1986) *Title to Territory in Africa* (Oxford: Clarendon Press), p. 51.
42. For histories of the regions, see, for example, K. Salia (1983) *History of the Georgian Nation* (Paris: N. Salia); and R. Suny (1994) *The Making of the Georgian Nation* (Bloomington: Indiana University Press).
43. Also written as Ajara or Ajaria.
44. See the USSR Constitution of 7 October 1977, Article 82, online: http://www.servat.unibe.ch/icl/r100000_.html.
45. See *ibid.*, Article 83 and Article 84.
46. See *ibid.*, Article 87(2) and Article 88. Note that 'South Ossetia' does not correspond directly to one of the specific regions within Georgia but covers parts of several regions. It is mostly situated within the northern part of the Shida-Kartli region (in particular the northern district of Java, Kareli and Gori) and smaller parts of neighbouring regions (Racha-Lochhumi and Kverno Svaneti, Imereti and Mtskheta-Mtianeti).
47. Law of the Republic of Georgia on Abolition of the Autonomous Region of South Ossetia of 11 December 1990, online: http://www.parliament.ge/files/426_5649_580559_10.pdf.

48. For more details see the Declaration of the Military Council of the Republic of Georgia, online: http://www.parliament.ge/files/1_5718_330138_27.pdf last accessed 12 July 2010.

49. The Constitution of the Soviet Socialist Republic of Abkhazia of 1 April 1925, Article 4, online: http://www.abkhaz.org/index2.php?option=com_content&do_pdf=1&id=147. Article 5 states that: 'The Abkhaz SSR is a sovereign state, which exercises state authority on its territory independently from any other powers.'

50. See Annual Report of the Secretary-General on the work of the UN 1995, United Nations, online: http://www.un.org/docs/SG/SG-Rpt/ch4d-10.htm.

51. The Law of the Autonomous Republic of Adjara on Structure, Authorities and Rules for Activities of Government of Autonomous Republic of Adjara, online: http://www.adjara.gov.ge/eng/index.php?page=law last accessed 12 July 2010. This provides that the head of the region's government, the Council of Ministers of Adjara, is nominated by the President of Georgia, who can dissolve the Adjaran assembly and government, and overrule local authorities when their measures are contrary to the constitution of Georgia. See also R. Giragosian, 'Crisis in Ajaria: The Military Dimension', Central Asia – Caucasus Institute and the Georgian Forum (May 2004), online: http://iicas.org/2004en/07_05_04_fr_en.htm.

52. Agreement of 24 June 1992, as noted, for example, in Annex 2 of the 17th CSO Meeting of 6 November 1992, Journal No. 2.

53. Update Report No. 2 on Georgia (12 August 2008), Security Council Report, online: http://www.securitycouncilreport.org/site/c.glKWLeMTIsG/b.4423477/k.DB51/Update_Report_No2brGeorgiabr12_August_2008.htm; and see Memorandum on Measures to Provide Security and Strengthen Mutual Trust Between Sides in the Georgian–Ossetian Conflict (17 April 1996), online: http://www.mtholyoke.edu/acad/intrel/georosse.htm.

54. There was also an Agreement between Georgia and Abkhazia: the 'Declaration on Measures for a Political Settlement of the Georgian-Abkhaz Conflict' (4 April 1994), which contained a formal ceasefire accord and a commitment not to use force against each other: see the Letter dated 17 May 1994 from the Permanent Representative of Georgia to the United Nations Addressed to the President of the Security Council, UN Doc. S/1994/583, United Nations Observer Mission in Georgia, online: http://www.unomig.org/data/moscow_agreement.pdf.

55. See Security Council Resolution 858, UN Doc. S/RES/858 (1993). See also Security Council Resolutions 934, UN Doc. S/RES/934 (1994); and 937, UN Doc. S/RES/937 (1994). UNOMIG ceased its activity in June 2009 following a veto exercised by Russia, United Nations, online: http://www.un.org/en/peacekeeping/missions/past/unomig/.

56. The Boden Document on the Principles for Division of Competences between Tbilisi and Sukhumi, Office of the State Minister for Reintegration, online: http://smr.gov.ge/en/abkhazia/documents/bodens_document.

57. This group included France, Germany, Russia, the United Kingdom and the United States, and were called 'Friends of the UN Secretary-General' after 1997.

58. See the 12 October 1999 Declaration of the Abkhazia representatives, Unrepresented Nations and Peoples Organization, online: http://www.unpo.org/content/view/705/236/.

59. S. Ostrovsky, 'Thumbs Up for Independence in Separatist Georgian Region', *Agence France-Presse* (13 November 2006).
60. See IIFFMCG Report, *supra* note 4, Volume II, 6.
61. See *ibid.* which also notes that this support was not always consistent.
62. The IIFFMCG Report states that this Russian policy took place 'on a massive scale', *ibid.*, Volume II, 8. By granting this nationality, it arguably provided a basis for Russia's intervention on Georgian territory, as Russia was then acting to protect its own citizens. For more on this issue, see the discussion by James Green in Chapter 3.
63. There were no Security Council resolutions directly on South Ossetia, primarily due to the threat of veto by Russia.
64. See European Union Monitoring Mission in Georgia, online: http://www.eumm.eu/en/about_eumm.
65. The IIFFMCG was established by European Union Council Decision 2008/901/CFSP of 2 December 2008 concerning an independent international fact-finding mission on the conflict in Georgia, Official Journal of the European Union 323/66.
66. See Presidential Decrees, *supra* note 2.
67. See the United Kingdom's Written Statement to the ICJ on its *Advisory Opinion on Kosovo*, (17 April 2009), para. 4.12.
68. See Russia's Written Statement to the ICJ on its *Advisory Opinion on Kosovo*, (16 April 2009).
69. See Statement by the Russian President, *supra* note 1: 'We repeatedly called for returning to the negotiating table and did not deviate from this position of ours even after the unilateral proclamation of Kosovo's independence.'
70. General Assembly Resolution 63/3, UN Doc. A/63/L.2 (8 October 2008).
71. Written Statement by government of Kosovo to the ICJ on its *Advisory Opinion on Kosovo*, (17 April 2009), 157–158.
72. See EC Declaration on Guidelines on the Recognition of New States, *supra* note 16, which provides that there must be 'guarantees for the rights of ethnic and national groups and minorities in accordance with the commitments subscribed to in the framework of the CSCE'. This was applied by the Badinter Committee in its various opinions.
73. Badinter Committee, opinion 11, 32 I.L.M. (1993) 1587, para. 2.
74. UN Security Council, Letter dated 26 March 2007 from the Secretary-General to the President of the Security Council, S/2007/168, 3.
75. *Ibid.*, 2. There are an array of views on the Kosovo declaration of independence, see, for example, B. Jia (2009) 'The Independence of Kosovo: A Unique Case of Secession' 8 *Chinese Journal of International Law*, 27; D. Fierstein (2008) 'Kosovo's Declaration of Independence', *Boston University International Law Journal*, 26, 417; and J. Vidmar (2009) 'The International Legal Responses to Kosovo's Declaration of Independence', *Vanderbilt Journal of Transnational Law*, 42, 779.
76. See, for example, the United Kingdom's Written Statement to the ICJ on its *Advisory Opinion on Kosovo*, *supra* note 67, paras. 0.17–0.27; and France's Written Statement to the ICJ on its *Advisory Opinion on Kosovo* (7 April 2009), paras. 2.16–2.39.
77. *Québec* opinion, *supra* note 29.

78. See R. Müllerson (2009) 'Precedents in the Mountains: On the Parallels and Uniqueness of the Cases of Kosovo, South Ossetia and Abkhazia', *Chinese Journal of International Law*, 8, 2; and O. Corten (2008) 'Déclarations unilatérales d'indépendence et reconnaissances prématurées: du Kosovo, à L'Ossétie du sud et à L'Abkazie', *Revue générale de droit international public*, 112, 721 (and response by P. Weckel (2009) *Revue générale de droit international public*, 113, 257).
79. See, for example, Minority Rights Group International, *World Directory of Minorities and Indigenous Peoples – South Ossetia: Overview*, 2007, online: http://www.unhcr.org/refworld/docid/4954ce12c.html.
80. IIFFMCG Report, *supra* note 4, Volume II, 35. The Report concluded that neither entity should yet be recognised as states as 'the preconditions for statehood are not met'.
81. See *ibid.*, Volume II, 129: 'South Ossetia itself had not unambiguously and consistently claimed to be a state: on the one hand the South Ossetian authorities have sought to be recognised as a sovereign and independent state, but on the other hand they have also advocated unification with North Ossetia through integration into Russia.'
82. See also R. Wilde, 'Kosovo: International Law and Recognition', Chatham House meeting, (22 April 2008), 10–11, who notes that such serious breaches of human rights need to be ongoing, as the right to self-determination may not be granted as a form of remedy for past violations, no matter how severe.
83. *Québec* opinion, *supra* note 29, para. 139.
84. IIFFMCG Report, *supra* note 4, Volume II, 231, 236.
85. Declaration on Principles of International Law, *supra* note 8.
86. *Protocol Additional to the Geneva Conventions of 12 August 1949, and Relating to the Protection of Victims of International Armed Conflicts* (Protocol I), 8 June 1977, 1125 U.N.T.S. 3, Article 1(4).
87. It is estimated that there are over 220,000 internally displaced persons who have fled the regions since the early 1990s due to the conflict: 'Protection of Internally Displaced Persons in Georgia: A Gap Analysis' (July 2009), UNHCR, online: http://www.unhcr.org/4ad827f59.html. See also the Institute for War and Peace Reporting, *Georgian Conflict Exploitation Concerns* (24 December 2009), CRS No. 525 and General Assembly Resolution 62/249, UN Doc. A/RES/62/249 (29 May 2008). For a detailed examination of the issue of forced displacement following the 2008 conflict, see the contribution by Anneke Smit in Chapter 6.
88. See the declaration of Russia's permanent representative to the OSCE, as reported online: http://www.abkhaziagov.org/en/news/detail.php?ID=28090. See also the IIFFMCG Report, *supra* note 4, Volume I at 38.
89. On the number of internally displaced persons resulting from the conflict, see *supra* note 87.
90. The practice during the dissolution of Yugoslavia varied considerably. In Bosnia-Herzegovina, it was assumed that 50% plus one was sufficient and a boycott by the Serbian population (who comprised over 30% of the population) did not affect the result with over 60% of all those eligible to vote in favour of independence. In Montenegro the EU stated that there had to be majority of 55% of votes cast and there had to be a participation of at least

50% plus one of those eligible to vote. This required majority was probably based on the opinion polls suggesting that approximately half of the population supported independence while a relatively large share of the population strongly opposed it. See 'Crnogorsko javno mnjenje uoči referenduma' (23 December 2000), online: http://www.aimpress.ch/dyn/pubs/archive/data/200012/01223–005-pubs-pod.htm. Our thanks to Jure Vidmar for this reference.

91. Declaration on Principles of International Law, *supra* note 8, section on 'the principle that States should refrain in their international relations from the threat or use of force'.

92. *Ibid.*

93. IIFFMCG Report, *supra* note 4, Volume II, 256: 'the Russian invasion itself did not occur prior to the Georgian operation and therefore did not constitute an armed attack in the sense of Art. 51 [of the UN Charter]'.

94. *Ibid.*, Volume II, 263: '[R]ussia was involved in the conflict in several ways. First, Russian peacekeepers who were stationed in South Ossetia on the basis of the Sochi Agreement were involved in the fighting in Tskhinvali. Second, Russian regular troops were fighting in South Ossetia, Abkhazia and deeper in Georgian territory. Third, North Caucasian irregulars took part in the fighting.'

95. *Ibid.*, Volume II, 263: 'Russia supported Abkhaz and South Ossetian forces in many ways, especially by training, arming, equipping, financing and supporting them.'

96. *Ilaşcu v Moldova and Russia*, no. 48787/99 (8 July 2004), European Court of Human Rights, online: http://www.echr.coe.int/echr/en/hudoc/.

97. *Ibid.*, para. 394.

98. *Ibid.*, paras. 392–394.

99. There is a current claim brought by Georgia against Russia to the European Court of Human Rights concerning the arrest, detention and collective expulsion of Georgian nationals from the Russian Federation, no. 13255/07 (26 March 2007). There is also a case brought by Georgia against Russia to the ICJ, being the *Case Concerning Application of the International Convention on the Elimination of All Forms of Racial Discrimination (Georgia v Russian Federation), Request for the Indication of Provisional Measures*, Order of 15 October 2008, para. 3, International Court of Justice, online: http://www.icj-cij.org/docket/files/140/14801.pdf. In Chapter 4, Sandy Ghandhi provides a detailed examination of the provisional measures order.

100. Milliband, *supra* note 4.

101. See P. Alston (1997) 'The Myopia of the Handmaidens: International Lawyers and Globalization', *European Journal of International Law*, 8, 435; and response by S. Scott (1998) 'International Lawyers: Handmaidens, Chefs, or Birth Attendants? A Response to Philip Alston', *European Journal of International Law*, 9, 750.

102. A. Gerson (2001) 'Peace Building: The Private Sector's Role', *American Journal of International Law*, 95, pp. 101, 111.

103. A. Watts (1993) 'The International Rule of Law', *German Yearbook of International Law*, 36, pp. 15, 25, 41.

3
Passportisation, Peacekeepers and Proportionality: The Russian Claim of the Protection of Nationals Abroad in Self-Defence

James A. Green

Introduction

The aim of this chapter is to apply the international law on the use of force – the *jus ad bellum* – to the events in the Caucasus in the summer of 2008. Specifically, it focuses on the claim of the Russian Federation that its intervention into South Ossetia and beyond into Abkhazia and 'Georgia proper' was justified in international law as an action of self-defence. It is notable that comparatively few western legal scholars have examined the lawfulness of the Russian intervention into Georgia.[1] It is therefore important that the Russian self-defence claim is properly assessed.

The Russian claim is here tested with regard to the existing conventional and customary international law governing the use of force. In doing so, this chapter has two main points of focus: the 'protection of nationals abroad' as a manifestation of self-defence and an application of the criterion of proportionality. With regard to the former, the basis for Russia's self-defence claim was that it was protecting its nationals within Georgian territory. While there is some state practice supporting the legal justification of protecting nationals abroad under the rubric of self-defence, this manifestation of the right remains a controversial justification for the use of force. Nonetheless, it is argued herein that the protection of nationals abroad concept may be a legally acceptable one in principle.

Having said this, the Russian claim, as applied with regard to the 2008 conflict in the Caucasus, is rather unique for a number of reasons, most notably Russia's policy of 'passportisation' in the region and thus the Russian 'manufacture of nationals' in South Ossetia. The specifics of the Russian justification mean that – even if one accepts the protection of nationals abroad argument in principle – the *application* of this manifestation of self-defence by Russia is questionable in this instance. Perhaps more importantly, the Russian use of force was notably disproportionate to the goal of protecting these nationals. It is this disproportionality that most fundamentally demonstrates the unlawful nature of the Russian intervention. This chapter concludes by looking at the wider implications of the Russian self-defence claim for international legal order.

The Russian legal justification

Following its military intervention on 8 August 2008 into Georgian territory,[2] Russia quickly made the explicit claim before the Security Council that it was acting in self-defence. Specifically, the Russian ambassador to the United Nations (UN), Vitaly Churkin, argued in a letter of 11 August 2008 that: 'the Russian side had no choice but to use its inherent right to self-defence enshrined in Article 51 of the Charter of the United Nations'.[3] As such, there is no question that Russia employed self-defence as a legal justification with regard to its actions in the breakaway regions and Georgia more generally.

That Russia claimed self-defence is unsurprising, given that this essentially constituted the only feasible legal justification that could be offered for its use of force. This is because the only universally accepted exceptions to the prohibition on the use of force as set out in Article 2(4) of the UN Charter are: a) military action authorised by the UN Security Council (a collective security action) and b) self-defence, as defined by Article 51 of the Charter and customary international law. As Russia had clearly received no mandate from the Security Council for its military intervention, it would appear that the only possible justification under international law for the use of force was that it constituted an action in self-defence. Having said this, before moving on to the substance of this chapter and an analysis of the Russian self-defence claim, it is necessary to question, as a preliminary matter, whether there existed an additional legal justification advanced by Russia to justify its intervention.

Some commentators have argued that Russia in part justified its intervention as an act of unilateral humanitarian intervention.[4] In simple terms, unilateral humanitarian intervention can be defined as the use of force to protect non-nationals from gross violations of human rights within the territory of another state, without Security Council authorisation.[5] This view is supported by the fact that Russia undoubtedly appealed to humanitarian concerns to legitimate its action in South Ossetia and other areas of Georgia. For example, both President Medvedev and, more notably, his foreign minister Sergei Lavrov, employed language that is evocative of a justification of unilateral humanitarian intervention. Russia accused Georgia of a massive onslaught on civilians amounting to 'genocide' and 'ethnic cleansing'.[6] Such statements have been taken by some to indicate that Russia was invoking humanitarian intervention as a legal justification, to be coupled with, or to be taken in the alternative to, its self-defence claim.

However, it seems evident that, in spite of its repeated use of humanitarian language, Russia did not in fact invoke the *legal* claim of unilateral humanitarian intervention. This is a justification for the use of force that is not provided for by the UN Charter and is, at best, extremely controversial in customary international law. Indeed, it is notable that any Russian invocation of a legal doctrine of unilateral humanitarian intervention would have been diametrically contrary to the long established Russian (and Soviet) rejection of the concept as an aspect of customary international law.[7]

This fact in itself does not, of course, establish that Russia did not make a legal claim of unilateral humanitarian intervention; dramatic reversals in international legal policy are far from uncommon. Interestingly, the Report of the Independent International Fact-Finding Mission on the Conflict in Georgia (IIFFMCG),[8] published in September 2009, took the view that Russia would be estopped from relying on the doctrine of unilateral humanitarian intervention anyway, given that it had so persistently objected to such a concept in the past.[9] This may go slightly too far, but Russia's previous practice would certainly undermine any such subsequent claim.

What is more important is that the appeals that Russia made to concerns of humanity were clearly advanced in a political or moral sense. They were aimed at justifying the military action, certainly, but they were not delivered in a 'legal' manner. When it came to the formalities of legal justification, Russia followed the example of the overwhelming majority of other states in the UN era – along with its own previous practice – and shied away from officially justifying its action as being based on a legal notion of unilateral humanitarian intervention. It is notable that in the 'official' legal justification for the intervention provided to the Security Council, Russia made an explicit and rather detailed claim of self-defence, while not referring to the dubious legal concept of unilateral humanitarian intervention at all.[10]

Moreover, although Russia used phrases such as 'genocide', and initially claimed mass casualties in the thousands, it later revised the death toll, at least on the Russian and Ossetian side, to around 150 dead.[11] This figure sits more comfortably with independent casualty estimates.[12] Such relatively small figures (even including the comparatively large number of displaced persons) would undermine any claim of unilateral humanitarian intervention had Russia made it, given that even those that advocate this right require a gross or large-scale violation of human rights before force can be employed.[13]

Given the above, it is apparent that the right of self-defence was the sole legal justification advanced by Russia. The remainder of this chapter will now go on to analyse that claim.

The key criteria for self-defence

There is near-universal acceptance that, under customary international law, all uses of force in self-defence must meet the dual criteria of necessity and proportionality.[14] The criterion of necessity requires that military action must be taken as a last resort; the responding state must show that non-forcible measures were either exhausted, or that it would have been unreasonable to expect the responding state to attempt non-forcible measures of resolution.[15] The requirement of proportionality refers not just to a numerical equivalence of scale between attack and response, but also to the need for the state to act in a manner that is proportional to the established defensive necessity. In other words, the response must not be excessive with regard to the goal of abating or repelling the attack being responded to.[16] We will return to these criteria, particularly that of proportionality, in later sections.

In addition to the two customary requirements of necessity and proportionality, a further key criterion for lawful self-defence, explicitly set out in Article 51 of the Charter, is the occurrence of an 'armed attack...against a Member of the United Nations'. As to the meaning of this phrase, the International Court of Justice (ICJ) has famously stated in more than one decision that an armed attack is to be considered 'the most grave form of the use of force'.[17] To put this another way, the attack being responded to must be of a particular level of 'gravity' beyond a use of force *simpliciter*.[18] Traditionally, such an attack – a grave use of force to which a state may respond with force in self-defence – has been viewed as necessarily being an attack against the territory of the state in question.[19]

Notwithstanding the difficulties concerning the reliability of the various factual accounts of the 7/8 August,[20] it seems relatively clear that Georgia fired the first shots in the South Ossetia region during these initial stages of the conflict, though of course this was in the context of a number of comparatively minor exchanges stretching back over the preceding months.[21] Somewhat obviously, a claim of self-defence cannot be valid if the state making that claim attacked first (other than arguably in the controversial context of anticipatory self-defence in response to an imminent threat).[22] In the context of the 2008 conflict in the Caucasus, then, it is important for the Russian claim that – as appears evident – Russia did not use force first.

Yet in spite of Georgia 'firing first' in the conflict, prior to the Russian military response, Russia had clearly not been the victim of an armed attack against its *territory*. The initial large-scale attack by Georgia was directed against a *de facto* autonomous region within its own borders. Indeed, it would have been difficult for Russia to argue that the Georgian action, notably 'Operation Clear Field' (initiated to capture the South Ossetian capital of Tskhinvali), constituted even an *imminent threat* to the territory of the Russian Federation itself.

Given the fact that Russia could not claim that it had suffered an armed attack against its territory from Georgia, it instead advanced the more controversial claim that it was responding to an armed attack against its nationals within Georgian territory, specifically within the breakaway region of South Ossetia. In its letter to the Security Council, Russia explicitly took the position that the actual and potential future harm to its nationals within South Ossetia was – in itself – enough to trigger the right of self-defence.[23]

An overview of the protection of nationals abroad

The Russian claim of self-defence therefore amounted to what is often referred to as the 'protection of nationals abroad' justification for the use of force. The core element to this particular version of the right of self-defence is relatively straightforward. The protection of nationals abroad concept can be defined as: the use of force by a state to protect its nationals that are under attack – actual or threatened – outside of its own territory, without the consent of the state against which the force is used or the authorisation of the UN Security Council.[24] It is a legal argument that has been made on a number of occasions by states.

However, equally, it can hardly be said to be a common claim in international law, and it is one that remains controversial. This chapter, with its specific focus on the Russian claim of self-defence of August 2008, is not the place to advance a detailed examination of the protection of nationals abroad concept in general terms.[25] Nonetheless, a brief overview of this disputed manifestation of self-defence is necessary to shed some light on Russia's legal arguments.

To the extent that a claim of protection of nationals abroad could be seen as being lawful, it can only be so as a manifestation of the right of self-defence. Despite some arguments to the contrary,[26] the use of force to protect nationals abroad would clearly amount to a breach of Article 2(4) of the UN Charter and therefore any such action must fall under one of the existing exceptions.[27] Neither the Charter nor customary international law provide for a separate exception to protect nationals abroad. Such an action, if taken unilaterally, cannot fall under the collective security exception. Therefore, the protection of nationals abroad justification for the use of military force *must* exist within the parameters of the right of self-defence if it is to be considered lawful.

Having said this, it has been argued that the protection of nationals abroad can be seen as a manifestation of unilateral humanitarian intervention.[28] Leaving aside the fact, noted above, that this justification for the use of force is in itself at best extremely controversial, a conceptual distinction should be made between such actions and those aimed at the protection of nationals abroad. One claim relates to the protection of a state's own nationals, the other to the protection of foreign nationals.[29] More importantly, it is apparent that when states do make a legal claim based on the protection of nationals abroad, they do so within the rubric of the right of self-defence.[30] This is presumably because arguing self-defence is in general terms far less controversial than arguing for either unilateral humanitarian intervention or a free standing right to protect nationals abroad.[31] Ultimately, then, the general framework for the protection of nations abroad, for those that advance it, is that the 'armed attack' required to trigger self-defence need not necessarily be directed against the territory of the state itself. Instead, it is enough that it is directed against the nationals of the state.

Many writers object to this avowed manifestation of self-defence. This rejection is based upon three interrelated arguments. First, objection has been raised on the basis that the language of Article 51 simply does not extend to the use of force to protect nationals abroad.[32] In other words, this argument holds that such actions cannot be seen as falling within the notion of an 'armed attack...against a Member of the

United Nations' because they do not constitute attacks against the territory of the responding state. Some writers take this view based simply on the traditional reading of Article 51 – that an 'armed attack' means an attack against the territory of a state.[33] Others better support the position by concluding that attacks outside of the territory of the state responding do not threaten its fundamental security or survival, and therefore necessarily fall outside of the scope of self-defence.[34]

Second, it has been argued that state practice does not support the concept of the protection of nationals abroad.[35] This is because, in a relatively large proportion of the limited number of instances where states have invoked the protection of nationals abroad, the majority of other states have held the action in question to be unlawful.

Third, there exists a policy-based objection. The protection of nationals abroad is viewed by many as constituting an extension of 'traditional' self-defence that would leave the right open to (further) abuse.[36] To put this another way, there is concern that the protection of nationals abroad claim can be used as a pretext for using force in support of other, less desirable, goals.

With respect to the first objection, following a close reading of Article 51, it is here argued that there is nothing in that article to preclude the extension of self-defence to attacks that occur outside of the territory of the responding state. As noted, Article 51 requires that an armed attack has occurred 'against a Member of the United Nations'. The article does not refer to the *territory* of a Member of the UN. It is also clear from state practice that self-defence is not restricted only to fundamental instances where the survival of the state is at stake.[37] Again, the text of Article 51 does restrict self-defence in this way and the ICJ has taken the view that an armed attack can occur outside of a state's territory, at least in principle.[38]

As such, the concept of an attack against a state could plausibly be seen as including the nationals of that state, as constituting a part of that state or an extension of that state. In the view of the present author, this is not an unreasonable stretch of the language of Article 51: 'People being a necessary condition for the existence of a state, the protection of nationals can be assimilated without great strain to the right of self-defence explicitly conceded in the text of the Charter.'[39]

Of course, the attack against nationals would have to be 'grave' as with all armed attacks. As such, it is worth noting that Russia was keen to stress when making this legal claim regarding its August 2008 intervention that the 'scale' of the attack against its nationals was large (large enough to constitute an armed attack, and therefore trigger self-defence).[40] This can be debated factually, in that it appears that the initial Russian claims as to scale here were somewhat inflated,[41] but after the ICJ's *Oil Platforms* decision it would seem that an attack on a single vessel may be considered to be 'grave' enough to constitute an armed attack.[42] By analogy then, it is possible to argue that the Russian assertion that an armed attack had occurred was correct in terms of the requirement of gravity, so long as the general concept that an armed attack can occur against nationals outside of the territory of the state responding is accepted.

If one adopts the position that there is nothing in Article 51 itself that precludes the extension of self-defence to allow for the protection of nationals abroad, it is necessary to respond to the second objection raised by critics of the concept. The question is whether this manifestation of self-defence has been accepted into state practice as a customary international law interpretation of the Charter right. In the UN era at least, the protection of nationals abroad version of self-defence has been a relatively rare claim.

Again, the current chapter is not the place to set out the existing state practice on the protection of nationals abroad in any detail.[43] Nonetheless, an examination of the state practice indicates that, for the most part, in instances where protection of nationals abroad has been claimed, states responding to the claim have seen the use of force to be unlawful. Taking this state practice at face value, the indication is that the notion of the protection of nationals abroad therefore does not form part of customary international law. However, when one looks more closely at the rejections by states of the claim in specific instances, an alternative conclusion may be reached. To highlight this, a handful of examples – being generally representative of the wider state practice – will be examined here.

A classic example – often used as an indication of the unlawfulness of the protection of nationals abroad – is 'Operation Urgent Fury', the large air and sea assault undertaken by forces of the United States against Grenada in 1983. Here, one of the legal grounds for the intervention by the United States was self-defence to protect its nationals on the island.[44] This was generally seen as an unlawful action by other states.[45] It is also fairly evident that the intervention was primarily taken in response to a socialist coup, with the protection of nationals abroad argument being merely used as a pretext.

However, condemnation by other states of the intervention by the United States into Grenada was for the most part based on its disproportional nature.[46] Over 7000 troops were deployed to protect fewer than a thousand nationals, and certain objectives of the initial operation, such as the securing of the Richmond Hill prison, clearly went beyond what was necessary to ensure the safety of American nationals.[47] Moreover, in the longer term, the United States overthrew the new socialist regime in Grenada, and remained afterwards to oversee the installation of pro-American government.

With regard to its intervention into Panama in 1989, the United States again argued that one legal basis for this was the protection of nationals abroad (indeed, it argued this even more forcibly than it did with regard to the intervention into Grenada).[48] As in 1983, states almost universally rejected this argument.[49] Again, though, the primary reason for these objections was the issue of proportionality. The large scale of the action – 10,000 troops being deployed to protect just a few hundred American nationals – coupled with the fact that forces of the United States remained to instate a democratically elected government, meant that the action was viewed by most states as being disproportional.[50] As with the Grenada intervention, the protection of nationals abroad claim can be seen as a pretext for other policy goals: in this instance the removal of military dictator Manuel Noriega from power.

Another famous example is the 1976 hijacking by forces representing Baader-Meinhof and the Popular Front for the Liberation of Palestine of a French plane flying from Israel. While discussions were being undertaken for the release of hostages being held at Entebbe airport in Uganda, Israeli Special Forces stormed the airport and rescued the hostages. International reaction to the Israeli action was mixed. Again, the majority of states that took a position on the action found it to be unlawful.[51] For some, this was admittedly an objection to the protection of nationals abroad concept in itself.[52] In contrast, many other states that felt that the action was unlawful because the criteria for self-defence had not been met in the particular case in question. This was either on the basis that there had been no 'armed attack' against Israeli territory (as the hostage crisis was not grave enough to constitute such an attack),[53] or that the Israeli action did not meet the requirement of necessity (because negotiations were being undertaken for the release of the hostages at the time of the intervention).[54] As such, the majority of states that took a position did not make a principled objection to the protection of nationals abroad concept.

Indeed, a number of states explicitly argued that self-defence did extend to the protection nationals abroad.[55] It is also worth noting that the Israeli response was relatively limited in this instance. Its special forces removed the hostages in a fairly 'surgical' manner. As a result, the intervention was seen by some states as being proportional and, therefore in some cases, lawful.[56] Importantly, most states took no position; there was a general acquiescence to the Israeli action.

Although the Entebbe incident does not confirm the lawfulness of the protection of nationals abroad by any measure – given that a group of states did object to the concept in principle – it is notable that some states supported the action, and many more chose not to condemn it. This response can be contrasted to the near-universal condemnation of interventions into Grenada and Panama in the 1980s. The factual distinction between these examples is that the Israeli response may be viewed as being a proportional one. Of the states that did view Israel's action as unlawful, this was again largely on the basis that the intervention did not meet the usual criteria for self-defence (in this instance, an armed attack or necessity).

Given these examples, it is here argued that the protection of nationals abroad aspect of the Russian claim is one that can be defended, at least in principle. This conclusion is admittedly controversial. Indeed, it may appear strange, given that the majority of states have rejected applications of the concept in the majority of instances where it has been claimed in practice. However, this view is taken on the basis that neither Article 51, nor customary international law (as evidenced by state responses to the claim in practice), rule out this extension of the right of self-defence *per se*.

Instead, the issue for the majority of states has been the *application* of the protection of nationals abroad justification, either on the basis that the response taken was disproportional, unnecessary, or that the attack or threat to nationals was not grave enough to constitute an armed attack. All that this practice indicates is that customary international law requires that any exercise of this manifestation of self-defence must meet the requirements of armed attack, necessity and proportionality: something that holds equally true for more traditional actions in self-defence. In cases where the factual basis for the legal claim made did not meet the criteria for self-defence, 'the international response cannot fairly be interpreted as an indictment of the exculpatory theory as distinguished from its particular application'.[57] If the protection of nationals abroad is not clearly 'ruled out' by the Charter or custom, it seems reasonable to rule it 'in', at least in principle.[58]

Finally, it should be noted that the third objection to the protection of nationals abroad concept – the policy based concern that this extension of self-defence is open to abuse and can be flexibly employed as a pretext for intervention – is one that appears to be borne out by the state practice. The examples of the interventions in Grenada and Panama, amongst others, support this conclusion. While such practice is undoubtedly concerning, it should not be viewed as a reason to reject the entire protection of nationals abroad justification.

Abuses of this version of self-defence simply underline the importance of a strict application of the existing criteria, most notably of necessity and proportionality.[59] Actions to protect nationals abroad must be restricted to situations where a state is faced with a *genuine* necessity to protect its nationals abroad through the use of force. Additionally, the force employed must be strictly proportional to that necessity: no more force may be employed than is required to abate the attack and protect the nationals in question. Such restrictions – particularly the proportionality requirement – would act as a good safeguard (albeit not a perfect one) against the claim being used as a pretext for more wide-ranging interventions and a shield for additional policy goals.[60] At the same time, the protection of nationals abroad, suitably restricted by the usual requirements for self-defence, allows for states to use force in circumstances where there is no option but to do so to protect the lives and safety of its nationals in the territory of another state.

Protecting peacekeepers and passport holders

It was argued in the previous section that it is possible to view the protection of nationals abroad as a valid manifestation of the right of self-defence, assuming that, in its application, it meets the usual requirements for 'traditional' self-defence. If this is accepted, then the core basis of the Russian claim is at least defensible in international law, in a general sense. In this section, the specifics of that particular claim will be examined in more detail.

The Russian claim of self-defence was based on the protection of two groups of Russian nationals in particular. The first of these groups were Russian peacekeepers stationed in the South Ossetia region. More crucially, the second group were individuals of Ossetian ethnicity that had been provided with Russian passports.

With regard to the first group, there were 500 or so Russian peacekeepers stationed in South Ossetia, as part of a joint peacekeeping force, along with ethnic Ossetians and Georgians. This multinational peacekeeping force was established under the 1992 Sochi peace agreement. This chapter is certainly not the place to discuss in detail the lawfulness of the Russian peacekeeping presence in Georgia. In simple terms, the legal basis for the initial presence of Russian peacekeepers in the South

Ossetia region under the 1992 agreement is uncontroversial. Less clear is whether the Georgian consent to the presence of such forces had been revoked prior to the 2008 crisis.[61] Whether such a withdrawal of consent in fact occurred, and, indeed, whether Georgia had the legal right to unilaterally require the removal of the Russian peacekeepers are issues that will not be explored here.

Irrespective of the lawfulness of the presence of peacekeepers of Russian nationality in the South Ossetia region in August 2008, there has been a widespread acceptance by commentators that the use of (necessary and proportional) force by Russia to protect its peacekeepers in Georgia could be viewed as being lawful.[62] Similarly, the IIFFMCG Report uncritically took the view that 'there seems to be little doubt that if the Russian peacekeepers were attacked, Russia had the right to defend them using military means proportionate to the attack'.[63] If one subscribes to the protection of nationals abroad concept in principle, it certainly may be said that the protection of Russian nationals present on Georgian territory in a peacekeeping capacity was the 'best' possible justification Russia could advance for its use of force. However, this does not mean that this argument is uncontroversial, even excluding the debate surrounding the protection of nationals abroad generally. This is not because of a substantive legal objection as such: if one is willing to accept the protection of nationals abroad in principle, then this would logically extend to Russia protecting its nationals in South Ossetia if attacked, be they peacekeepers or not. Rather, there may be a policy objection to this relatively rare extension of the protection of nationals abroad argument to peacekeepers. This is because it has possible implications for peacekeeping missions in the future.

States have intervened to protect peacekeepers in the past, the best example being the operation to protect peacekeepers in Rwanda in 1994, which met with essentially no international censure.[64] That operation was large in scale, but it was also multilateral, with seven states contributing to the rescue operation. In contrast, this aspect of the Russian claim in 2008 was unilateral. If states are entitled to forcibly protect their nationals on peacekeeping missions when they are under threat unilaterally, this could destabilise international peacekeeping mechanisms. This is because other states may be less likely to allow peacekeeping forces into their territories, for fear of this forming a later pretext for an intervention by a powerful state whose nationals form part of the peacekeeping force.

Again, in theory, the requirements of necessity and proportionality should guard against this concern to some extent, in that any action to protect peacekeepers should be genuine, a last resort and limited in scope. Nonetheless, peacekeepers are, by the very nature of their role, likely to face a degree of threat to their person, and the majority of peacekeeping operations include personnel from 'powerful' states (as they are best placed to provide the manpower). As such, there is scope for a 'protection of peacekeepers' claim to be made with a degree of regularity by powerful states, and the Russian claim of 2008 has the potential to act as a precedent in this respect. Many states – especially developing states – may therefore understandably fear the abuse of the protection of nationals abroad concept, where peacekeepers are (or are proposed to be) deployed on their territory. Such a fear of abuse could have wide-ranging implications, in terms of state consent to, and co-operation with, future peacekeeping missions.

While it is worth keeping in mind that the aspect of the protection of nationals abroad claim relating to Russian peacekeepers has such potentially problematic implications, this did not form the core element of the Russian legal justification in 2008, and as such shall not be discussed further here. The Russian peacekeeping forces in South Ossetia were few in number when compared with the second group of nationals that Russia was claiming to protect. As such, the crux of the Russian protection of nationals abroad claim rests on the protection of ethnic Ossetians who had been granted Russian passports.

The Russian Federation has had a policy of issuing passports to people in both South Ossetia and Abkhazia since the early 1990s, but this passportisation process accelerated considerably throughout 2008.[65] This widespread distribution of passports had led to what may be referred to as the 'manufacture of nationals' in the breakaway regions. By the time of the August 2008 conflict, around 90% of the population of South Ossetia held a Russian passport. That such a population of newly created 'nationals' formed the basis of a protection of nationals abroad claim involving the use of military force is unique in the state practice.

It must be said that in the vast majority of cases, South Ossetians have been eager to gain Russian nationality. A Russian passport represents a lifeline for South Ossetians, a way to get an education or a job in North Ossetia or Moscow. There are few jobs in the South Ossetian region; as such, many families have at least one member working in Russia and sending money back home.[66] However, there were additionally reports suggesting that a minority of individuals had actually been *coerced* into taking Russian passports.[67] It is difficult to confirm such reports with any degree of certainty,[68] but if this practice did in fact occur, this would amount to a concerning and seemingly unique situation of 'nationality at gunpoint'.

Leaving this possibility aside and assuming that the South Ossetians in question took Russian passports willingly (which was certainly true in at least the vast majority of instances), this practice nonetheless led to the accusation from some commentators that Russia had essentially 'manufactured' a population of Russian nationals within *de jure* – if not *de facto* – Georgian territory. Moreover, it has been argued that this practice of passportisation was a pretext for intervention, particularly given that a large number of these passports were issued in the period immediately prior to the conflict.[69] As Umland has stated, rather convincingly:

> Moscow's provision of Russian passports for the populations of these territories is designed to accelerate local conflicts, create a pretext for Russian involvement (including military). ... Moscow wants to use a grey area of international law – a state's right to protect, even by violent means, its citizens abroad – for revisionist aims.[70]

Of course, it cannot be known for sure whether the issuance of passports in this manner was intended to provide a subsequent justification for the use of force or, in other words, to establish the conditions for Russia to be able to viably make a claim of protection of nationals abroad in self-defence. Nonetheless, the widespread issuance of passports may be seen as indicative of a general premeditated tactic to annex the region. Further circumstantial evidence to support this is the fact that in July 2006, the Russian Duma passed a resolution explicitly authorising Russian troops to serve anywhere in the defence of Russian nationals.[71]

Admittedly, international law leaves it for a state to decide under its own domestic rules whether to confer nationality and upon whom. Therefore Russia was and is entitled to grant nationality to whomsoever it likes.[72] However, as the ICJ has indicated in the *Nottebohm* case, for an individual's nationality to be enforceable against *other states* at the international level there is a requirement of 'real and effective' nationality: a meaningful connection to the state in question must be shown.[73] Without going too deeply into the rules on nationality here, it is unclear whether the *Nottebohm* test would have been met in South Ossetia during 2008. It is arguable that there are many more *de facto* ties between the people in the region and Russians – ties of language, for example – than there are ties with Georgians. Irrespective of this, it may be difficult to hold that the ethnic Ossetians in question were 'really' and 'effectively' Russian enough to give rise to a right of self-defence against another sovereign state. The genuine nature of their Russian nationality, not just in fact but in international law, is debatable at best.

As such, even if one accepts the justification of the protection of nationals abroad in principle – as does the current author – the manner in which it was employed by Russia is open to question. This claim with regard to the protection of its peacekeeping forces is relatively defensible, if still one with concerning implications. In relation to the more important claim regarding South Ossetians with Russian passports, though, this 'manufacture of nationals' aspect raises questions of good faith in the application of the already controversial protection of nationals abroad justification, which seriously undermine the validity of the Russian self-defence claim. As the IIFFMCG Report put it, in the context of this 'group of "new" Russians, it seems abusive to rely on their need for protection as a reason for intervention, because Russia itself created this reason for intervention through its own policy'.[74] Furthermore, it is clear that the Russian claim is even more significantly undermined if the allegations of 'nationality at gunpoint' are true, even if only in a small minority of cases.

Applying the criterion of proportionality

In the last section, the validity of the Russian protection of nationals abroad claim was examined. The manner in which Russia applied the protection of nationals abroad manifestation of self-defence in the context of the conflict in the Caucasus is questionable, given the 'manufacture of nationals' within Georgian territory. Having said this, in fact, the issue of the protection of nationals abroad, and whether the claimed protection of those holding Russian passports could be viewed as legitimate, is ultimately something of a 'red herring' in the context of the final analysis of whether the Russian action was a lawful exercise of the right of self-defence. This is because the most fundamental issue with regard to the lawfulness of the Russian use of force is the application of the criterion of proportionality.

It has already been noted that all exercises of self-defence must be proportional under customary international law, and that 'proportionality' is calculated by reference both to the scale of the response, and, fundamentally, to the necessity of defence.[75] Let us accept for a moment, then, the general concept of the protection of nationals abroad *and* the Russian application of this to peacekeepers and ethnic Ossetians in the region holding Russian passports. If the response by Russia to any attack against such Russian nationals in Georgia was a disproportionate one, then that action would be unlawful, irrespective of the protection of nationals abroad issue.

The Russian intervention into Georgia in August 2008 was not limited to the South Ossetia region, but went well beyond into Abkhazia and Georgia proper. It included such acts as the bombing and occupation of Gori, the occupation of Poti and moves towards the capital of Tbilisi. It is here argued that such actions were 'manifestly excessive' in terms of scale when compared to the attacks on Russian nationals (be they 'true' nationals or not) present in South Ossetia, to which Russia was ostensibly responding.[76] Perhaps more importantly, such actions were also disproportional when assessed against Russia's defensive goal of protecting its nationals within the South Ossetia region.

The Russian response appears even more starkly disproportional if one takes the view that the only legitimate 'nationals' that Russia was entitled to protect were the small number of its peacekeepers in the region. However, the action should still be viewed as disproportional even if the Russian claim of forcible protection could be extended not only to its peacekeepers but also to the comparatively large number of ethnic Ossetians holding Russian passports. The scale and nature of the Russian intervention, into Abkhazia and in the context of attacks on certain cities in Georgia proper, appears disproportional irrespective of whether one accepts that the protection of nationals abroad claim can be stretched to cover Ossetians holding Russian passports or not. Indeed, the Russian action seems particularly disproportional when it is considered that the withdrawal of the main Russian force in late August 2008 was in fact only partial. There remained troops stationed for an additional two months around Gori and Poti, as well as in 'buffer-zones' outside of the South Ossetian and Abkhaz regions. Even after the removal of these troops following the appearance of the European Union observer mission in October 2008, Russian forces remain in the two disputed regions at the time of writing.

Of course, Russia itself was careful to argue that it was acting in a proportional manner, explicitly stating that 'the use of force by the Russian side is strictly proportionate to the scale of the attack and pursues no other goal but to protect the Russian peacekeeping contingent and citizens of the Russian Federation...'[77] However, in the view of the present writer, this was simply not borne out in reality. Similarly, the majority of commentators have taken this position,[78] though as one would expect, a minority of writers have attempted to argue that the Russian intervention can be viewed as being proportional.[79] Far more important than academic and media opinion is the fact that other states have also viewed the action as being unlawful for this reason: of the few states that gave an official response to the Russian claim of self-defence, it is notable that many explicitly condemned the action on the basis that it was *disproportional*. This issue of proportionality formed the crucial aspect of the legal criticism from the United States,[80] Germany,[81] France,[82] the United Kingdom[83] and Panama,[84] as well as from the Secretary-General of NATO.[85] It similarly formed a key objection to the Russian action coming from Georgia itself.[86] Finally, the IIFFMCG Report of September 2009 also found that the Russian use of force was disproportional, when measured either in relation to the protection of peacekeepers alone, or with regard to the protection of all Russian passport holders in South Ossetia.[87]

As such, it is difficult to argue that the Russian claim to be acting in self-defence was a valid one; the intervention into Georgia must be viewed as being unlawful. This is most fundamentally because of the disproportional nature of the Russian intervention.

Of course, it is worth keeping in mind that this conclusion in no way legitimates the prior military action taken by Georgia – most notably 'Operation Clear Field' – against the region of South Ossetia. It would be admittedly difficult to view the Georgian attacks of 7 August 2008 against that region as a breach of Article 2(4) of the UN Charter, as that provision is confined to the use of force between 'states' in the technical sense. It is therefore not applicable to an entity within a state – such as South Ossetia – however factually autonomous it may be.[88] In contrast, these actions were arguably contrary to Article 3(d) of the 1974 Definition of Aggression, which holds that an 'attack by the armed forces of a state on the land, sea or air forces, or marine or air fleets of another state' constitutes an unlawful act of aggression.[89] This is on the basis that Article 1 of that instrument indicates that the term 'state' is used therein without prejudice to issues of recognition or membership of the UN.[90] In addition, it is relatively clear that in the course of its attacks against South Ossetia in 2008, Georgia breached various provisions of international humanitarian law (as did Russia in the context of its response).[91]

Nonetheless, such breaches of international law by Georgia in the South Ossetia region do not in themselves mean that the Russian response was a lawful self-defence action. Having tested the Russian claim of self-defence from 2008 in this chapter, it must be concluded that Russia breached international law – specifically Article 2(4) of the UN Charter – by using military force against Georgian territory.

Implications for International Legal Order

It has been argued in this chapter that the core protection of nationals abroad argument advanced by Russia may in fact be a valid one in principle, despite the misgivings of many writers and its apparent rejection by the majority of states in other instances. Having said this, it must ultimately be concluded that the Russian intervention into Georgia was contrary to international law. Going beyond this conclusion, this final section explores the implications that the Russian intervention, and the particular self-defence claim advanced to justify it, have for future international legal practice and international order more generally.

The Caucasus conflict represents the first time that Russia (or its predecessor, the Soviet Union) has explicitly employed the protection of nationals abroad argument.[92] This indicates the possibility of a growing acceptance of the concept. Previous invocation of this version of self-defence has predominantly come from states such as the United States, the United Kingdom, France, Belgium and Israel. That Russia, a powerful state of a different sort, has employed the protection of nationals abroad for the first time may encourage other powerful non-western states to use such a claim to justify international uses of force. The seeds for this already exist. For example, the Chinese Foreign Ministry indicated that China would be willing to use force to protect ethnic Chinese in Indonesia during the widespread anti-Chinese riots of 1998.[93] China quickly backed away from this position at the time, but China's stance in 1998 demonstrates the potential that could now be sparked by the Russian precedent set ten years later. Of course, this is merely speculative: it is impossible to know whether other geopolitically comparable states will follow Russia's lead. The general international condemnation that greeted the Russian claim in 2008 may have the opposite effect.

In any event, an increase in the use of the protection of nationals abroad claim would not necessarily be a negative development. There are arguable benefits to the right to protect nationals abroad being supported by more (and more politically and geographically diverse) state practice, particularly given the continued growth of transnational terrorism and its implications for the safety of individuals in territories other than their own. However, this argument can only hold if the protection of nationals abroad claim is strictly regulated by the requirements of necessity and proportionality. It can equally be argued that – given the abuse of the concept that has clearly occurred in the existing practice – it is evident that states that make the claim do not adhere to necessity and proportionality in this way, and, as such, an increase in its invocation will only be detrimental for world order.

It has already been noted that the aspect of the Russian claim relating to the protection of peacekeepers has the potential to have a destabilising effect on peacekeeping operations generally. This is on the basis that it could make states less willing to co-operate with peacekeeping missions, for fear of inadvertently providing a legal basis for a full-scale military intervention.[94] In addition, the unique employment of the protection of nationals abroad argument based upon the 'manufacture of nationals' has practical implications for international stability. This is because the possibility of a state unilaterally 'creating' a group of nationals, which can then be defended through military force, only increases the scope for states to abuse the protection of nationals abroad concept, and should certainly be resisted.

Indeed, it is possible that the 2008 conflict is already being employed as an undesirable precedent by Russia itself. It has been suggested that one implication of the conflict is that Russia would take it as an indication that it could adopt a more generally militarist foreign policy.[95] More specifically, concern has been raised about whether the Georgian intervention – and the protection of nationals abroad legal claim employed by Russia – would 'stoke up unrest in pro-Russian parts of the Ukraine... [notably] the Crimean peninsula and especially Sevastopol'.[96] Reports indicate that Russia has begun to employ a policy of distributing Russian passports to individuals in the Ukrainian city, many of the residents of which have historic ties with Russia.[97] Admittedly, it seems unlikely that this would, or could, be used as the basis for any kind of forcible intervention into the Ukraine. Nonetheless, the fact that Russia has expanded its policy of distributing passports to individuals in pro-Russian regions in other states – given that this *did* form the key justification for its use of force in Georgia – has implications for the security of numerous states in what would once have been called the 'Soviet sphere of influence'.

The seemingly disingenuous application of the protection of nationals abroad concept by Russia in 2008, and the possibility that it could employ this type of claim again in relation to other states will (rightly) strengthen the view of those who reject this manifestation of the self-defence as one particularly open to abuse. As Iqbal and Hassan have stated, '[a]lthough Russia has not created a new doctrine it has set a dangerous precedent liberalising the standard of international law self-defence. The danger being that states may predictably abuse liberalised standards.'[98] Equally, such a strengthening of a position that *rejects* the protection of nationals abroad would be concerning for the growing number of states, particularly those faced with the threat of transnational terrorism, for which genuine – and arguably valid – situations where there is a need to protect nationals abroad occur and will continue to occur.

Finally, the Russian intervention into Georgia can be seen as another in a long line of examples of states in the UN era that have claimed self-defence but have then gone beyond the bounds of the customary international law requirement of proportionality. In the view of the present author, this criterion is the most crucial element for lawful self-defence, in that it acts as the greatest restraint against the abuse of the right while retaining its functionality.[99]

In this respect, the Russian claim in the context of the conflict in the Caucasus is not especially damaging to the international rule of law in itself. Nonetheless, it should be seen as part of a cumulative erosion of the fundamental proportionality criterion in customary international law. That the Russian intervention adds to the weight of this disregard in state practice for the need for a proportional response in self-defence is ultimately perhaps more concerning than the unique aspects of the protection of nationals abroad concept – and the implications of the 'manufacture of nationals' and the notion of forcibly protecting peacekeepers – that formed the basis of Russian justification.

Notes

1. This point is made by N.N. Petro (2009) 'The Legal Case for Russian Intervention in Georgia', *Fordham International Law Journal*, 32, 1524.
2. It is worth noting that – in contrast to the timeline indicated by Russia – Georgia claimed that Russian forces first entered Georgian territory on 7 August 2008 and not the following day. See the article written by the Georgian President for the *Wall Street Journal*: M. Saakashvili, 'Georgia Acted in Self-Defence', *Wall Street Journal* (2 December 2008), online: http://online.wsj.com/article/SB122817723737570713.html.
3. UN Doc. S/2008/545.
4. See Q. Peel, 'Russia's Reversal: Where Next for Humanitarian Intervention?', *The Financial Times* (22 August 2008), online: http://www.ft.com/cms/s/0/e06e25fc-7076–11dd-b514–0000779fd18c.html?nclick_check=1; A. Cassese, 'The Wolf that Ate Georgia', *Project Syndicate* (2008), online: http://www.project-syndicate.org/print_commentary/cassese5/English; and G. Evans, 'Putin Twists UN Policy', *The Australian* (2 September 2008), online: http://www.theaustralian.news.com.au/story/0,,24278542–17062,00.html.
5. This chapter is not the place to discuss the concept of unilateral humanitarian intervention. There is a vast amount of literature on the subject; a good starting point is J.L. Holzgrefe and R.O. Keohane (eds) (2003) *Humanitarian Intervention: Ethical, Legal and Political Dilemmas* (Cambridge: Cambridge University Press).

6. See 'Russia Recognises Georgian Rebels', *BBC News* (26 August 2008), online: http://news.bbc.co.uk/1/hi/in_depth/7582181.stm for the claim of 'genocide' made by President Medvedev; and 'Sergey Lavrov: Georgia Carries out Ethnic Cleansing of South Ossetia', *Kommersant* (8 August 2008), online: http://www.kommersant.com/p-13041/r_530/Sergey_Lavrov_lashed_out_georgia for Foreign Minister Lavrov's position.

7. For example, such a legal claim would be a complete reversal of the Russian position with regard to NATO action in Kosovo in 1999. See Peel, *supra* note 4.

8. The Report of the Independent International Fact-Finding Mission on the Conflict in Georgia (IIFFMCG) (30 September 2009), online: http://www. ceiig.ch/Report.html.

9. *Ibid.*, Volume II, 284. See also Volume I, 24.

10. UN Doc. S/2008/545.

11. 'Russia Scales Down Georgia Toll', *BBC News* (20 August 2008), online: http://news.bbc.co.uk/1/hi/world/europe/7572635.stm.

12. See, for example, Human Rights Watch, 'Up in Flames: Humanitarian Law Violations and Human Victims in the Conflict Over South Ossetia' (2009), 74, online: http://www.hrw.org/en/reports/2009/01/22/flames-0; and the Council of Europe, Parliamentary Assembly, 'The Consequences of the War Between Russia and Georgia', Res. 1633 (2008), online: http://assembly.coe. int/Main.asp?link=/Documents/AdoptedText/ta08/ERES1633.htm.

13. The scale of the violation of the human rights being responded to forms part of almost all summaries of the requirements for unilateral humanitarian intervention (for those who view it as being potentially lawful). A classic example is the criteria set out by R.B. Lillich (1967–1968) 'Forcible Self-Help by States to Protect Human Rights', *Iowa Law Review*, 53, 347–351. Of course, the legal concept of 'genocide' itself does not require a large-scale action *per se* (as pointed out by Petro, *supra* note 1, 1537–1538), although it would be similarly difficult to argue that the legal conditions for the commission of genocide were present in the 2008 Caucasus conflict.

14. J. Gardam (2004) *Necessity, Proportionality and the Use of Force by States* (Cambridge: Cambridge University Press), particularly at p. 6 and p. 11.

15. J.A. Green (2006) 'Docking the *Caroline*: Understanding the Relevance of the Formula in Contemporary Customary International Law Concerning Self-Defence', *Cardozo Journal of International and Comparative Law*, 14, 450–457.

16. R. Wedgwood (1992) 'Proportionality and Necessity in American National Security Decision Making', *American Society of International Law Proceedings*, 86, 59.

17. See *Military and Paramilitary Activities in and Against Nicaragua (Nicaragua v United States of America)* merits [1986] I.C.J. Rep. 14, para. 191; and *Case Concerning Oil Platforms (Islamic Republic of Iran v United States of America)* merits [2003] I.C.J. Rep. 161, para. 51.

18. J.A. Green (2009) *The International Court of Justice and Self-Defence in International Law* (Oxford: Hart Publishing), particularly pp. 31–42.

19. I. Brownlie (1963) *International Law and the Use of Force by States* (Oxford: Oxford University Press), pp. 278–279.

20. As were noted in the Introduction to this volume.

21. See T.W. Waters, 'Russia-Georgia: The Separatist Regions, the Western Response', *The New York Times* (29 August 2008), online: http://topics. blogs.nytimes.com/2008/08/29/russia-georgia-the-separatist-regions-the-western-response/#more-141; and C. Clover *et al*, 'Countdown in the Caucasus: Seven Days that Brought Russia and Georgia to War', *The Financial Times* (26 August 2008), online: http://www.ft.com/cms/s/0/af25400a-739d-11dd-8a66-0000779fd18c.html?nclick_check=1.

22. Y. Dinstein (2005) *War, Aggression and Self-Defence*, 4th edn (Cambridge: Cambridge University Press), p. 178.

23. UN Doc. S/2008/545.

24. This definition is adapted from the one given in A.C. Arend and R.J. Beck (1993), *International Law and the Use of Force* (London: Routledge), p. 94.

25. There is a wealth of literature on the protection of nationals abroad. Key texts include: T.C. Wingfield (1999–2000) 'Forcible Protection of Nationals Abroad', *Dickinson Law Review*, 104, 447; N. Ronzitti (1985) *Rescuing Nationals Abroad through Military Coercion and Intervention on the Grounds of Humanity* (Dordrecht: Martinus Nijhoff); D.W. Bowett (1986) 'The Use of Force for the Protection of Nationals Abroad' in A. Cassese (ed.) *The Current Legal Regulation of the Use of Force* (Dordrecht: Martinus Nijhoff), p. 39; R.B. Lillich (T.C. Wingfield and J.E. Meyen, eds) (2002) 'Lillich on the Forcible Protection of Nationals Abroad', *International Law Studies Series, US Naval War College*, 77, i; T. Ruys (2008) 'The "Protection of Nationals" Doctrine Revisited', *Journal of Conflict and Security Law*, 13, 233; and R.J. Zedalis (1990) 'Protection of Nationals Abroad: Is Consent the Basis of Legal Obligation?', *Texas International Law Journal*, 25, 209.

26. Bowett, *ibid.*, 40.

27. Zedalis, *supra* note 25, 221–229.

28. D.J. Gordon (1977) 'Use of Force for the Protection of Nationals Abroad: The Entebbe Incident', *Case Western Reserve Journal of International Law*, 9, 131–132.

29. Wingfield, *supra* note 25, 440–441; and Arend and Beck *supra* note 24, 94.

30. T. Gazzini (2005) *The Changing Rules on the Use of Force in International Law* (Manchester: Manchester University Press), p. 170.

31. C. Gray (2008) *International Law and the Use of Force*, 3rd edn (Oxford: Oxford University Press), p. 157.

32. M. Iqbal and S. Hassan (2008) 'Armed and Ready', *New Law Journal*, 158, 1277. It is also notable that two judges of the ICJ appeared to take this view in regard to the ill-fated attempt by the United States to rescue hostages in Tehran in April 1980. See *United States Diplomatic and Consular Staff in Tehran (United States v Iran)* merits [1980] I.C.J. Rep. 3, dissenting opinion of Judge Morozov, 56–57; and dissenting opinion of Judge Tarazi, 64–65. However, in arguing that the United States had not suffered an armed attack against it, neither judge was particularly clear as to whether this was because of issues of gravity, or because attacks on nationals abroad could *never* constitute an armed attack. It is also worth noting that the majority merits decision took no position on this point (as the Court concluded the American intervention was not a matter before it), see 43–44 of the judgment.

33. Ronzitti, *supra* note 25, 12; Arend and Beck, *supra* note 24, 106 and 110; and J. Quigley (1990) 'The Legality of the United States Invasion of Panama', *Yale Journal of International Law*, 15, 287.
34. A. Randelzhofer (2002) 'Article 51' in B. Simma (ed.), *The Charter of the United Nations: A Commentary, Vol I*, 2nd edn (Oxford: Oxford University Press), pp. 798–799.
35. Ruys, *supra* note 25, 259–263; Ronzitti, *supra* note 25, 62–64; and J. Allain (2004) 'The True Challenge to the United Nations System of the Use of Force: The Failures of Kosovo and Iraq and the Emergence of the African Union', *Max Planck Yearbook of United Nations Law*, 8, 243.
36. Brownlie, *supra* note 19, 301. It is notable that this objection is, understandably, advanced most strongly in the developing world, see Quigley, *supra* note 33, 293.
37. Dinstein, *supra* note 22, 175.
38. See *Oil Platforms, supra* note 17, para. 72.
39. T.J. Farer (1990) 'Panama: Beyond the Charter Paradigm', *American Journal of International Law*, 84, 505.
40. UN Doc. S/2008/545.
41. See *supra* note 11; and also A. Nußberger (2009) 'The War between Russia and Georgia – Consequences and Unresolved Questions', *Göttingen Journal of International Law*, 1, 359–360; and A. Dworkin (2008) 'The Georgian Conflict and International Law', *Crimes of War Project*, online: http://www.crimesofwar.org/onnews/news-georgia.html.
42. Specifically based on *Oil Platforms, supra* note 17, para. 72. On this, see Green, *supra* note 18, 38–41.
43. A very good recent summary is provided by Ruys, *supra* note 25, 238–263.
44. See Statement Presented to the United States House Committee on Foreign Affairs by Deputy Secretary of State, K.W. Dam, 2 November 1983, reproduced in M.N. Leich (ed.) (1984) 'Contemporary Practice of the United States Relating to International Law', *American Journal of International Law*, 78, 200, especially 203–204.
45. This is well evidenced by a resolution of the General Assembly, which condemned the American intervention and labelled it 'a flagrant violation of international law'. GA Res. 38/7, 1983.
46. A good example of the state response to the intervention with regard to the question of proportionality is the statement made by the representative of Zimbabwe in the Security Council, see UN Doc. S/PV.2491, 5.
47. M.J. Levitin (1986) 'The Law of Force and the Force of Law: Grenada, the Falklands, and Humanitarian Intervention', *Harvard International Law Journal*, 27, 650.
48. UN Doc. S/PV.2899, 31–37; and the letter dated 21 December 1989 from President Bush to Congress, extract in R. Wedgwood (1991) 'The Use of Armed Force in International Affairs: Self-Defence and the Panama Invasion', *Columbia Journal of Transnational Law*, 29, 609.
49. Again, a General Assembly resolution condemned the action as being 'a flagrant violation of international law'. GA Res. 44/240, 1989. See also, *inter alia*, the statements of Nicaragua, UN Doc. S/PV.2899, 3–17; and Peru, UN Doc. S/PV.2900, 34–37.
50. See, for example, the statement of Finland in the Security Council, UN Doc. S/PV.2900, 14–15. It is worth noting that a minority of states argued that

the intervention was unlawful because no armed attack had occurred, on the basis that the threat to American nationals in Panama was not grave enough to constitute an armed attack; see, for example, the view of the Soviet Union, UN Doc. S/PV.2899, 17–21. Of course, this position was equally not a rejection of the concept of the protection of nationals abroad justification in principle.

51. See generally UN Docs. S/PV.1939–1943.
52. See, for example, the position of Cuba, UN Doc. S/PV.1943, 11.
53. See, for example, the view taken by Panama, UN Doc. S/PV.1942, 4; and by India, UN Doc. S/PV.1942, 17.
54. See the statements made by Mauritania (on behalf of a group of African states), UN Doc. S/PV. 1939, 26; and Mauritius, UN Doc. S/PV.1940, 6.
55. Examples include the view taken by the United States, UN Doc. S/PV.1941, 8; France, UN Doc. S/PV.1943, 7; and Mauritius, UN Doc. S/PV.1940, 6.
56. For example, the United States was careful to point out that the 'Israeli military action was limited to the sole objective of extricating the passengers and crew and it terminated when that objective was accomplished.' UN Doc. S/PV.1941, 8.
57. Farer, *supra* note 39, 505. In the quoted passage, Farer was specifically referencing the Grenada intervention of 1983, though it is notable that in the same article he takes the view that one can argue for the lawfulness of the protection of nationals abroad concept, but not the Panama intervention of 1989 (for the same reason). See also V.P. Nanda (1990) 'The Validity of United States Intervention in Panama Under International Law', 84 *American Journal of International Law*, 494, 496–497.
58. This conclusion is well set out by Ruys, *supra* note 25, 261, although he goes on to question it given that there is practice that suggests a *principled* rejection of the protection of nationals concept by some states.
59. Bowett, *supra* note 25, 46.
60. Indeed, it has been said that proportionality is the 'key' to resolving the debate over the protection of nationals abroad, Wingfield, *supra* note 25, 465.
61. Some have argued that Georgia did withdraw its consent to the presence of the peacekeepers, based upon a number of resolutions of the Georgian Parliament (passed in 2005 and 2006), which called for the revocation of consent. See N.M. Shanahan Cutts (2007–2009) 'Enemies through the Gates: Russian Violations of International Law in the Georgia/Abkhazia Conflict', *Case Western Reserve Journal of International Law*, 40, 302–304; and C.P.M. Waters (2008) 'Russia, Georgia and the Use of Force', *Jurist*, Forum, online: http://jurist.law.pitt.edu/forumy/2008/08/russia-georgia-and-use-of-force. php. In contrast, others have taken the opposite view, based on the fact that the President of Georgia's National Security Council stated in 2008 that the government itself had no intention of withdrawing consent. See Petro, *supra* note 1, 1529.
62. See A.-M. Slaughter, 'Russia in Violation of UN Charter, Says International Law Expert' *Eurasia Insight*, EurasiaNet, (21 August 2008), online: http:// www.eurasianet.org/departments/insight/articles/pp082108a.shtml.
63. IIFFMCG Report, *supra* note 8, Volume I, 23. See also Volume II, 268.
64. See Lillich, *supra* note 25, 107.

65. A. Umland, 'A Shield of a Passport: Moscow Uses Russian Citizenship as a Tool for Recollecting the Empire's Lands', *Global Politician* (26 August 2008), online: http://www.globalpolitician.com/25140-russia.

66. S. Walker, 'South Ossetia: Russian, Georgian...Independent?', *Open Democracy* (15 November 2006), online: http://www.opendemocracy.net/democracy-caucasus/south_ossetia_4100.jsp.

67. D. McElroy, 'South Ossetian Police Tell Georgians to Take a Russian Passport, or Leave Their Homes', *The Telegraph* (30 August 2008), online: http://www.telegraph.co.uk/news/worldnews/europe/georgia/2651836/South-Ossetian-police-tell-Georgians-to-take-a-Russian-passport-or-leave-their-homes.html.

68. The IIFFMCG Report also noted this possibility of coercion, and the factual uncertainty surrounding it. The Report ultimately concluded, though, that the conferral of Russian nationality '*generally* occurred on a voluntary basis', IIFFMCG Report, *supra* note 8, Volume II, 168 (emphasis added).

69. This was certainly Georgia's claim, see Saakashvili, *supra* note 2. A number of commentators have also taken this view, see Cassese, *supra* note 4; McElroy, *supra* note 67; Waters, *supra* note 61; Umland, *supra* note 65; and A. Blomfield, 'Russia Distributing Passports in the Crimea', *The Telegraph* (17 August 2008), online: http://www.telegraph.co.uk/news/worldnews/europe/ukraine/2575421/Russia-distributing-passports-in-the-Crimea.html.

70. Umland, *ibid.*

71. This point was made by Shanahan Cutts, *supra* note 61, 301, *prior* to the August 2008 conflict, implying that this demonstrated that Russia was establishing a pretext for intervention (specifically into Abkhazia).

72. Shanahan Cutts, *ibid.*, 301.

73. *Nottebohm* case (*Liechtenstein v Guatemala*) merits [1955] I.C.J. Rep. 4, 22–24.

74. IIFFMCG Report, *supra* note 8, Volume II, 288–289.

75. See *supra* note 16 and accompanying text.

76. Evans, *supra* note 4.

77. UN Doc. S/2008/545.

78. Slaughter, *supra* note 62; Waters, *supra* note 61; Evans, *supra* note 4; Dworkin, *supra* note 41; T.M. Franck (2008) 'On Proportionality of Countermeasures in International Law', *American Journal of International Law*, 102, 734; and Nußberger, *supra* note 41, 362–363.

79. See Waters, *supra* note 21; and Petro, *supra* note 1, 1532–1533 and 1543–1544.

80. See the televised statement of President George W. Bush, video link, BBC News (11 August 2008), online: http://news.bbc.co.uk/2/hi/europe/7554507.stm.

81. See statements made by German Chancellor Angela Merkel, *Deutsche Welle* (15 August 2008), online: http://www.dw-world.de/dw/article/0,2144,3567243,00.html.

82. UN Doc. S/PV.5961, 6.

83. 'Foreign Secretary Deplores Continued Fighting in Georgia', *Foreign and Commonwealth Office*, press release (9 August 2008), online: http://www.fco.gov.uk/resources/en/press-release/2008/august/georgia-statement-080809.

84. UN Doc. S/PV.5953, 15.

85. 'NATO Chief Deplores "Disproportionate" Force in Georgia', *The Age* (11 August 2008), online: http://www.theage.com.au/world/nato-chief-deplores-disproportionate-force-in-georgia-20080811–3t3z.html.

86. UN Doc. A/62/972.

87. IIFFMCG Report, *supra* note 8, Volume I, 24–25 and Volume II, 274–275.

88. See C. Henderson and J.A. Green (2010) 'The *Jus ad Bellum* and Entities Short of Statehood in the Report on the Conflict in Georgia', *International and Comparative Law Quarterly*, 59, particularly at 131–134; and Dworkin, *supra* note 41.

89. Definition of Aggression, annexed to GA Res. 3314, 1974.

90. See Henderson and Green, *supra* note 88, 134; and Petro, *supra* note 1, 1526–1528.

91. See in general, Human Rights Watch, Report, *supra* note 12.

92. Though it is worth noting that in 1993, just after the fall of the Soviet Union, Russian ministers did state that if necessary they would use force to protect ethnic Russians in former Soviet republics. However, this was not put into practice and such rhetoric was quickly dropped. See Gray, *supra* note 31, 157.

93. A.L. Smith, 'From Latent Threat to Possible Partner: Indonesia's China Debate', *Asia-Pacific Centre for Security Studies*, 6 (December 2003), online: http://www.apcss.org/Publications/SAS/ChinaDebate/ChinaDebate_SmithIndo.pdf.

94. See *supra* note 64 and accompanying text.

95. C. King (2008) 'The Five-Day War: Managing Moscow After the Georgia Crisis', *Foreign Affairs*, 87, 7.

96. R. Müllerson, 'The World After the Russia-Georgia War', *Open Democracy* (15 September 2008), online: http://www.opendemocracy.net/article/the-world-after-the-russia-georgia-war.

97. Blomfield, *supra* note 69.

98. Iqbal and Hassan, *supra* note 32, 1277.

99. Green, *supra* note 18, 137.

4

The International Court of Justice and the Provisional Measures Order in the *Georgia v Russian Federation* Case

Sandy Ghandhi

Introduction

On 12 August 2008, Georgia filed an Application instituting proceedings against the Russian Federation for violation of the International Convention on the Elimination of All Forms of Racial Discrimination 1966 (CERD). On 14 August, referring to Article 41 of the Statute of the International Court of Justice (ICJ) and to Articles 73, 74 and 75 of the Rules of Court, Georgia submitted a Request for the Indication of Provisional Measures in order to preserve its rights under CERD 'to protect its citizens against violent discriminatory acts by Russian armed forces, acting in concert with separatist militia and foreign mercenaries', including 'unlawful attacks against civilians and civilian objects, murder, forced displacement, denial of humanitarian assistance, and extensive pillage and destruction of towns and villages, in South Ossetia and neighbouring regions of Georgia, and in Abkhazia and neighbouring regions, under Russian occupation'. On 25 August, as a result of 'the rapidly changing circumstances in Abkhazia and South Ossetia', Georgia submitted an Amended Request for the Indication of Provisional Measures of Protection pending the Court's determination of the case on the merits. The Amended Request sought to prevent irreparable harm to the rights of ethnic Georgians under Articles 2 and 5 of CERD to be secure in their persons and to be protected against violence or bodily harm in the areas of Georgian territory under the effective control of the Russian Federation; it sought also to prevent irreparable injury to the right of return of ethnic Georgians under Article 5 of CERD. Public hearings were held from 8 to 10 September in the presence of both parties. The Court delivered its Order on 15 October 2008.

The essence of Georgia's claim was that: (1) 'the Russian Federation, acting through its organs, agents, persons and entities exercising elements of governmental authority, and through South Ossetian and Abkhaz separatist forces under its direction and control, has practised, sponsored and supported racial discrimination through attacks against, and mass expulsion of, ethnic Georgians, as well as other ethnic groups, in the South Ossetia and Abkhazia regions of the Republic of Georgia'; (2) the Russian Federation seeks to consolidate changes in the entire ethnic composition of South Ossetia and Abkhazia resulting from its actions 'by preventing the return to South Ossetia and Abkhazia of forcibly displaced ethnic Georgian citizens and by undermining Georgia's capacity to exercise jurisdiction in this part of its territory'; and (3) '[t]he changed demographic situation in South Ossetia and Abkhazia is intended to provide the foundation for the unlawful assertion of independence from Georgia by the *de facto* South Ossetian and Abkhaz separatist authorities.'[1]

Origins of the dispute

On 10 November 1989, the Regional Public Council of the South Ossetian Autonomous District (which formed part of the Georgian Soviet Socialist Republic) formally requested the Georgian Supreme Soviet to upgrade the status of the District to 'Autonomous Republic'. After the refusal of the Georgian Supreme Soviet to do so, the Regional Public Council of the South Ossetian Autonomous District re-named the District the 'Soviet Republic of South Ossetia' on 28 November 1990, and scheduled elections for a new Supreme Council to be held on 9 December 1990. On 11 December 1990, the Georgian Supreme Soviet declared the 9 December elections illegitimate, annulled the results and abolished the Autonomous District of South Ossetia and its Regional Public Council. Following these events, violent conflict broke out. Throughout 1991, coinciding with Georgia's Declaration of Independence on 9 April 1991, over 1000 people were killed in the fighting in South Ossetia. In addition, during this period, some 23,000 ethnic Georgians were forced to flee South Ossetia and settle in other parts of Georgia. As far as the origins of the conflict in Abkhazia were concerned, following the dissolution of the Soviet Union in December 1991, 'Abkhaz separatists under the leadership of Vladislav Ardzinba sought to secede from the Republic of Georgia, including by the use of force.'[2]

History of the conflict

Georgia contended that the Russian Federation had violated its obligations under CERD during three distinct phases of its interventions in South Ossetia and Abkhazia in the period from 1990 to August 2008. It was claimed that the first phase of the intervention in South Ossetia took place between 1990 and 1992 and in Abkhazia between 1991 and 1994. It was alleged that during this first phase 'the Russian Federation provided essential support to South Ossetian and Abkhaz separatists in their attacks against, and mass expulsion of, virtually the entire population of South Ossetia and Abkhazia' and that support from the Russian Federation included 'the provision of weapons and supplies and the recruitment of mercenaries to support separatist forces in both regions, and in the case of Abkhazia, the deployment of Russian armed forces directly to assist military operations conducted by the separatists'.[3] Hostilities came to an end formally in South Ossetia on 24 June 1992 following the Agreement on the Principles of the Settlement of the Georgian–Ossetian Conflict signed by Georgia, the South Ossetian separatist forces and the Russian Federation, and in Abkhazia on 14 May 1994 following the signing of the Moscow Agreement on a Ceasefire and Separation of Forces by Georgia, the Abkhaz separatists and the Russian Federation. Both agreements provided for the creation of joint peacekeeping forces that, according to Georgia, were 'dominated by ostensibly neutral Russian peacekeepers'.[4]

Georgia alleged that the signature of these agreements, which 'formalized the Russian Federation's dual status as a party to those conflicts and as an ostensible peacekeeper and facilitator of negotiations' marked the second phase of the 'Russian Federation's intervention' in South Ossetia and Abkhazia. A whole raft of allegations were made against the Russian Federation during this second phase: (1) that 'by implementing discriminatory policies in South Ossetia and Abkhazia under cover of its peacekeeping mandate, the Russian Federation had sought to consolidate the forced displacement of the ethnic Georgian and other populations that resulted from "ethnic cleansing" from 1991 to 1994'; (2) that the Russian Federation had supported the claims for independence from Georgia by both sets of separatists, and achieving that goal necessarily implied the expulsion of ethnic Georgians and other populations from their homes and a denial of their right to return to their homes in Georgia; (3) that as part of its policy of racial discrimination, the Russian Federation had consistently frustrated the return of internally displaced persons (IDPs) since the conflicts of 1991–1994, thereby making forced demographic changes more likely to become permanent; (4) that the Russian Federation had conferred its citizenship on almost all the non-ethnic Georgian population of the separatist regions, and harassed and intimidated those ethnic Georgians who had refused to renounce their Georgian citizenship; (5) that the Russian Federation had given far-reaching and unprecedented support to the *de facto* separatist authorities in implementation of discriminatory policies against ethnic Georgians, which had the effect both of denying the right of self-determination of ethnic Georgians remaining in the separatist regions and of preventing Georgia from implementing its obligations under CERD by assuming control over its territory; (6) that the Russian Federation had escalated tensions by taking steps to recognise the independence of the separatist regions; and (7) that since April 2008 there had been a surge in Russian military activities in both regions, which was accompanied by a campaign of discrimination against ethnic Georgians.[5]

It was alleged that the third phase of the Russian Federation's intervention in the separatist regions began with the Russian invasion of Georgian territory on 8 August 2008. However, on 7 August 2008, Georgia admitted that its forces had launched a strictly limited operation into territory held by South Ossetian separatist forces with the intention of terminating the persistent shelling of ethnic Georgian villages in South Ossetia. It was alleged that the Russian Federation responded with a full-scale invasion of Georgian territory by occupying more than half of the country.[6]

Jurisdiction

The Court commenced its consideration of the jurisdictional issues by remarking that on a request for the indication of provisional measures, the Court need not finally satisfy itself, before deciding whether or not to indicate such measures, that it had jurisdiction on the merits of the case, but it may not indicate them unless the provisions invoked by the Applicant appear, *prima facie*, to afford a basis on which the jurisdiction of the Court might be founded.[7] At this stage of the proceedings, Georgia sought to found the jurisdiction of the Court solely on the compromissory clause contained in Article 22 of CERD.[8] Thus the Court had to proceed to an examination of Article 22 CERD to determine if it provided a *prima facie* basis for jurisdiction to rule on the merits such as would permit the Court, if it considered that the circumstances so warranted, to indicate provisional measures.[9]

Article 22 CERD provides that:

> Any dispute between two or more State Parties with respect to the interpretation or application of this Convention, which is not settled by negotiation or by the procedures expressly provided for in this Convention, shall, at the request of any of the parties to the dispute, be referred to the International Court of Justice for decision, unless the disputants agree to another mode of settlement.

Both Georgia and the Russian Federation are parties to CERD; Georgia deposited its instrument of accession on 2 June 1999 without reservation; the Soviet Union deposited its instrument of ratification on 4 February 1969 with a reservation to Article 22; by a communication received by the Secretary-General of the United Nations (UN) as depositary on 8 March 1989, the government of the Soviet Union notified the Secretary-General that it had decided to withdraw its reservation relating to Article 22; accordingly, the Russian Federation, as the state continuing legal personality of the Soviet Union, is a party to CERD without reservation.

After reciting in full the texts of Articles 1(1) (the definitional article), and Articles 2 and 5 (substantive provisions), particular violations of which were invoked by Georgia in the present proceedings, the Court proceeded to deal with the first disputed issue of the territorial application of CERD. Georgia claimed that CERD does not include any limitation on its territorial application and that accordingly, 'Russia's obligations under [CERD] extend to acts and omissions attributable to Russia which have their locus within Georgia's territory and in particular in Abkhazia and South Ossetia.'[10] By contrast, the Russian Federation claimed that the provisions of CERD could not be applied extraterritorially, and that in particular Articles 2 and 5 of CERD cannot govern a state's conduct outside its own borders.[11]

In a remarkably brief statement, the Court observed that there was no restriction of a general nature in CERD relating to its territorial application. Furthermore, it noted that neither Articles 2 nor 5 of CERD (violations of which were alleged by Georgia) contain a specific territorial limitation. Accordingly, the Court found that these provisions of CERD appear to apply, like other provisions of that nature, to the actions of a state party when it acts beyond its territory.[12] Interestingly, the joint dissenting opinion attached to the Court's Order was completely silent on this point, presumably indicating concurrence with the view of the Court.

This articulation by the Court of the extraterritorial application of CERD is rather peremptory and lacks a detailed analysis. In addition, it ignores the structural differences between 'general' international human rights treaties such as the International Covenant on Civil and Political Rights 1966 (ICCPR) and 'issue specific' human rights treaties (such as CERD) dealing with race discrimination. The nature of the two types of treaty is entirely different. It is true that Articles 2 and 5 of CERD contain no territorial limitation. However, Article 3 states expressly that 'States Parties particularly condemn racial segregation and *apartheid* and undertake to prevent, prohibit and eradicate all practices of this nature in territories under their jurisdiction.' The clear limitation to territorial jurisdiction established in this article is a reflection of the appreciation of the drafters of this Convention that a state can only prevent acts of racial discrimination within its own domestic territory, assuming that such territory is under its control. The more limited nature of a 'specific' human rights treaty warranted a more limited application.

It must be remembered also that CERD was the first of the major international human rights treaties subsequent to the adoption of the Universal Declaration of Human Rights in 1948. Given the historical setting of CERD, it is rather unlikely that the drafters were contemplating anything other than a strictly territorial jurisdiction. Indeed, there is nothing in the *travaux préparatoires* of CERD to indicate that the drafters intended the document to impose obligations on states parties to prevent racial discrimination anywhere outside of their territorial jurisdiction. Of course, the same could be said about the converse situation, as the Court itself argued. However, a general reading of the debates as a whole provides a sense that the overall thrust of the discussions related only to the intra-territorial prohibition of discrimination. By contrast, there is no explicit reference to any possibility of the Convention having extraterritorial effect. The reason is apparent: the drafters did not even envisage such a possibility. Indeed, there are frequent references to the eradication by states parties of practices taking place 'in the territories subject to their jurisdiction'.[13]

Overall, it is plain that the drafters had in mind each state's responsibility to enforce, and adhere to, the Conventional norms within its own borders. This interpretation is supported by the background to the adoption of CERD. The Convention was adopted in a response to a proliferation of wanton acts of 'swastika-daubing' and 'other manifestations of anti-Semitism and other forms of racial and national hatred and religious and racial prejudices of a similar nature' that occurred in many states during the winter of 1959–1960.[14] It is manifest that states can take effective action only in their own territories to eliminate such evils. Furthermore, in its General Recommendations, the Committee on Elimination of Racial Discrimination has consistently used expressions that highlight the strictly territorial nature of the obligations: 'on whose territories' and 'in their respective territories' in General Recommendation No II;[15] 'all persons living in a given State' in General Recommendation No XX;[16] and, 'on the presence within their territory' and 'on their territory' in General Recommendation XXIV.[17] It is submitted that it was not intended that CERD should apply extraterritorially.

The second jurisdictional issue was whether there existed a dispute within the meaning of Article 22 CERD. Georgia claimed its Application concerned the interpretation and application of provisions of CERD (particularly Articles 2 and 5). The Russian Federation maintained that the dispute related essentially to the use of force, principles of non-intervention and self-determination and to violations of international humanitarian law (IHL). Thus, there was a difference of opinion between the parties on the issue of whether the events that occurred in South Ossetia and Abkhazia (particularly after 8 August 2008) gave rise to legal rights and obligations under CERD. The Court had to determine *prima facie* whether such a dispute existed.[18]

Georgia alleged that: (1) events in South Ossetia and Abkhazia have involved racial discrimination of ethnic Georgians living in these regions in violation of the provisions of Articles 2 and 5 of CERD; (2) displaced ethnic Georgians who have been expelled from South Ossetia and Abkhazia, have not been permitted to return to their place of residence in contravention of Article 5 of CERD; and (3) ethnic Georgians have been subject to violent attacks in South Ossetia since the ceasefire on 10 August in breach of Article 5 of CERD. By contrast, the Russian Federation asserted that the facts related exclusively to the use of force, IHL and territorial integrity, and therefore did not fall within the scope of CERD.[19]

The Court held that as the parties disagreed on the applicability of Articles 2 and 5 of CERD in the context of events in South Ossetia and Abkhazia, there consequently appeared to be a dispute between them as to the interpretation and application of CERD. Furthermore, the acts alleged to have occurred by Georgia, appeared capable of contravening rights provided for by CERD, even if certain of these alleged acts might be covered also by other rules of international law, including

IHL. Accordingly at this stage, that was enough to establish the existence of a dispute between the parties capable of falling within the provisions of CERD, a necessary prerequisite for the Court to have *prima facie* jurisdiction under Article 22 of CERD.[20]

The joint dissenting opinion challenged the finding of the Court on this issue. The opinion articulates the perfectly orthodox view that a dispute must exist prior to the seisin of the Court. First, the dissenting judges asked the question whether: 'the violent acts which Georgia imputes to Russia [are] likely to "com[e] within the provisions" of CERD, to reprise the terminology which the Court employed to decline jurisdiction *prima facie* in its Order of 2 June 1999 on the *Legality of Use of Force (Yugoslavia v Belgium) (Provisional Measures, Order of 2 June 1999, ICJ Reports 1999 (I), p 138, para 41)*?' The opinion argued that Russia's armed activities after 8 August could not, in and of themselves, constitute acts of racial discrimination in the sense of Article 1 of CERD unless it was proven that they were *aimed* at establishing a 'distinction, exclusion, restriction or preference based on race, colour, descent, or national or ethnic origin'. It was argued that the circumstances of the armed confrontation arising on 7/8 August were such that this could not be the case, and that it was difficult to consider that the armed acts in question, in and of themselves (whether committed by Russia and Georgia) fell within the provisions of CERD.[21] Why the need for the *'aim'* of establishing racially based discrimination is relevant is not immediately apparent. Whether or not these acts had this *'aim'* is surely immaterial, if the acts indeed had the *effects* alleged of widespread breaches of CERD? Similarly, the armed acts may not 'in and of themselves' have fallen within the terms of CERD, but their *consequences* did.

Second, the joint dissenting opinion criticised the Court for concluding that a dispute appeared to exist as to the interpretation and applicability of CERD because the opposing parties had manifested a disagreement over the applicability of Articles 2 and 5 of the Convention; the dissentients considered that this elevated an argument expounded during oral proceedings into evidence of a dispute between the parties.[22] Surely, the whole point about pleadings, whether oral or written, is to ensure that a dispute has crystallised between the opposing parties? And, this is exactly what happened here: thus, a dispute did exist.

Third, the joint dissenting opinion criticised the assertion by the Court that 'the acts alleged by Georgia appear to be capable of contravening rights provided for by CERD, even if certain of these alleged acts might also be covered by other rules of international law, including humanitarian law'.[23] The basis of this criticism is unclear. If it is meant to suggest an artificial watertight division between international human rights law and IHL, it is plainly misconceived. In sum, the arguments advanced by the joint dissenting opinion lack convincing reasoning. It is asserted that the Court was right to find that a 'dispute' existed as to the application of interpretation of provisions of CERD.

The third disputed issue between the parties was whether the procedural conditions laid down in Article 22 had been satisfied; the Court needed to ascertain the fulfilment of these conditions before deciding if it had *prima facie* jurisdiction to deal with the case, and accordingly, also had the power to indicate provisional measures if it found that the circumstances so required. Article 22 provides that a dispute relating to the interpretation or application of CERD may be referred to the Court if it 'is not settled by negotiation or by the procedure expressly provided for in this Convention'. Georgia claimed that 'this phrase was descriptive of the fact that that a dispute has not so been settled and does not represent conditions to be exhausted before the Court can be seized of the dispute'.[24] In addition, Georgia claimed that 'bilateral discussions and negotiations relating to the issues which form the subject-matter of the Convention have been held between the Parties'.[25] For its part, the Russian Federation submitted that: (1) 'pursuant to Article 22 of CERD, prior negotiations or recourse to the procedures under CERD constitute an indispensable precondition for the seisin of the Court'; (2) no negotiations had been held between the parties on issues relating to CERD; and (3) nor had Georgia brought any such issues to the attention of the Committee on the Elimination of Racial Discrimination in accordance with the procedures envisaged in CERD.[26]

The Court observed that: (1) the structure of Article 22 of CERD was not identical to provisions in certain other instruments which required that a period of time should have elapsed or that arbitration should have been attempted before initiation of proceedings before the Court; (2) the phrase 'any dispute...which is not settled by negotiation or by the procedure expressly provided for in this Convention' did not, on its plain meaning, suggest that formal negotiations in the framework of the Convention or recourse to the procedure referred to in Article 22 of CERD constitute preconditions to be fulfilled before the seisin of the Court; (3) however, Article 22 suggested that some attempt should have been made by the claimant party to initiate with the respondent party, discussions on issues that would fall under CERD; (4) it was clear from the case file that such issues had been raised in bilateral contacts between the parties, and, that these issues had not been resolved by negotiation prior to filing of the Application; that in several representations to the UN Security Council in the days before the filing of the Application, those same issues were raised by Georgia and commented upon by the Russian Federation; accordingly, the Russian Federation was made aware of Georgia's position in that regard; the fact that CERD had not been mentioned specifically in a bilateral or multilateral context was not an obstacle to the seisin of the Court under Article 22 of CERD; and (5) neither party claimed that the dispute had been brought to the attention of the Committee on Elimination of Racial Discrimination under the inter-state procedure detailed in Articles 11–13.[27]

The joint dissenting opinion dismissed the interpretation of the Court detailed in point (2) above on the issue of whether (assuming there was a dispute likely to fall within the provisions of CERD that existed between Georgia and Russia before the seisin of the Court) it had not been settled by 'negotiation'. First, the opinion remarked that the Court's interpretation would amount to denying any useful scope to the provision for 'negotiation' in Article 22 of CERD. Second, the opinion remarked that although the Court had referred to bilateral contacts between the parties and certain representations made to the Security Council, nowhere in these had Georgia accused Russia of racial discrimination. Third, the opinion suggested that 'for the condition of prior negotiation to be fulfilled, it suffices for an attempt to have been made and for it to have become clear at some point that there was no chance of success. In any event, it is clear that when negotiation is expressly provided for by a treaty, the Court cannot ignore this prior condition without explanation; nor can the Court dispose of this condition merely by observing that the question has not been resolved by negotiation.'[28] In substance, the joint dissenting opinion argues that the Court at least should have asked itself whether negotiations had been opened and whether they were likely to yield a result, but it did not do so. It is suggested that in fact the Court broadly adopted this approach in its articulation in point (4) above, without perhaps expressly stating that the dispute had reached the point where it obviously could not be settled by negotiation.

The joint dissenting opinion considered next whether the alternative criterion in Article 22 of CERD had been satisfied: that the dispute had not been settled by 'the procedures expressly provided for in this Convention'.[29] The opinion rejected the Court's summary disposal of the issue, characterising it as 'puzzling', because it neither accepted the ordinary meaning of Article 22 nor its object and purpose which (the opinion claimed) was to encourage the maximum number of states

parties to submit to the jurisdiction of the Court, with the assurance
that the procedures provided for in the Convention would be exhausted
first. Neither did the Court's interpretation refer to the *travaux préparatoires* for this article drafted by the Third Committee of the General
Assembly. The opinion also made the point that the Court could
have considered that the gravity of the situation when armed conflict
erupted on 7/8 August did not allow for resort to these procedures, but
remarked that that would have shown little confidence in the rapid
response procedure developed by the Committee on Elimination of
Racial Discrimination in 1993 to allow it to intervene quickly and effectively in cases of possible violations of the Convention.[30] This writer has
considerable sympathy with the view that the point of Article 22 was
to ensure the exhaustion of both negotiation and all internal to CERD
methods of dispute resolution before a referral to the Court. However,
it is clear now that this interpretation may have been flawed. Neither
the Court's Order nor the joint dissenting opinion refers to Article 16
of the Convention. This is unfortunate as it seems to hold the key to
unlocking the correct interpretation of Article 22. Article 16 is worth
setting out in full:

> The provisions of this Convention concerning the settlement of
> disputes or complaints shall be applied without prejudice to other
> procedures for settling disputes or complaints in the field of dis-
> crimination laid down in the constituent instruments of, or in
> conventions adopted by, the United Nations and its specialized
> agencies, and shall not prevent the States Parties from having
> recourse to other procedures for settling a dispute in accordance
> with general or special international agreements in force between
> them.

The final clause of this provision is sufficiently wide and elastic to
suggest that exhaustion of the intra-treaty procedure specified in Article
22 is not a prerequisite of referral to the Court for resolution. Thus, it
seems that the Court reached the right decision on this issue, albeit for
a different reason.

Having disposed of all the objections to jurisdiction, the Court considered that *prima facie* it had jurisdiction under Article 22 of CERD to
deal with the case to the extent that the subject matter of the dispute
related to the 'interpretation or application' of CERD. Thus, the Court
could proceed to address the Request for the Indication of Provisional
Measures.[31]

Provisional measures order

The Court began its consideration of this issue by articulating three basic principles underlying the indication of provisional measures. First, the power of the Court to indicate provisional measures under Article 41 of the Statute of the Court has as its objective the preservation of the respective rights of the parties pending the decision of the Court, in order to ensure that irreparable prejudice shall not be caused to rights that are the subject of dispute in judicial proceedings.[32] Second, it follows that the Court must be concerned to preserve by such measures the rights that may subsequently be adjudged to belong to either the Applicant or Respondent.[33] Third, therefore, a link must be established between the alleged rights, the protection of which is the subject of the provisional measures being sought, and the subject of the proceedings before the Court on the merits of the case.[34]

After consideration of the arguments of the parties, the Court noted that Articles 2 and 5 of CERD are intended to protect individuals from racial discrimination by obliging states parties to undertake certain measures specified therein.[35] Furthermore, states parties to CERD had the right to demand compliance by a state party with specific obligations incumbent upon it pursuant to those provisions. Accordingly, there was a correlation between respect for individual rights, the obligations of states parties under CERD and the right of states parties to seek compliance therewith. The Court concluded that the rights that Georgia invoked in its Request for the Indication of Provisional Measures had a sufficient connection with the merits of the case it had brought, for the purposes of the present proceedings. Consequently, the Court considered that its attention must be focussed now upon the rights thus claimed in its consideration of Georgia's request for the indication of provisional measures.[36]

Having established the existence of the basis on which its jurisdiction might be founded, the Court warned that it ought not to indicate measures for the protection of any disputed rights other than those that might ultimately form the basis of a judgment in the exercise of that jurisdiction. Accordingly, the Court resolved to confine its examination of the measures requested by Georgia, and of the grounds asserted for the request for such measures, to those who appear to fall within the scope of CERD.[37]

Since the power of the Court to indicate provisional measures could be exercised only if there was 'urgency' in the sense that there was a real risk that action prejudicial to the rights of either party might be taken prior to the Court's final decision on the merits,[38] the Court had to consider also whether such 'urgency' existed in the current proceedings.

On the issues of 'irreparable prejudice' and 'urgency', Georgia argued that the conduct of the Russian Federation in South Ossetia, Abkhazia and adjacent regions necessitated the urgent indication of provisional measures because ethnic Georgians in those areas were 'at imminent risk of violent expulsion, death or personal injury, hostage-taking and unlawful detention, and damage to or loss of their homes and other property' and 'in addition, the prospects for the return of those ethnic Georgians who [had] already been forced to flee [were] rapidly deteriorating'.[39] Georgia introduced evidence to support these claims from the reports of international and non-governmental organisations and witness statements, purporting to show the 'on going, widespread and systematic abuses of rights of ethnic Georgians under the Convention' in South Ossetia, Abkhazia and other parts of Georgia occupied then by Russian forces.[40] Georgia claimed that 'the widespread violations of the rights of ethnic Georgians under the Convention grew even worse after military engagements ceased, that they have continued unabated since then, and that they are continuing still'.[41] Georgia claimed that 'the risk of irreparable prejudice to the rights at issue in this case is not only imminent [but] already happening'.[42]

In rebuttal, the Russian Federation claimed that the criteria of Article 41 were not met in the instant case and that Georgia had not established that any rights against Russia under Articles 2 and 5 of CERD were exposed to 'serious risk' of irreparable damage. In support, the Russian Federation pointed to: (1) the statements of Georgian Ministers, decisions and international agreements to which Georgia is a party, in which its role and the role of its peacekeeping forces are consented to and recognised as beneficial in the period characterised by Georgia as the 'first and second phases of Russia's intervention in South Ossetia and Abkhazia'; (2) that the facts that can be relied upon with reasonable certainty militate against the existence of a serious risk to the rights pleaded by Georgia because, first, deaths and mass displacements of persons of *all* ethnicities had taken place, and second, because since the cessation of hostilities, civilians of all ethnicities were returning to some of the conflict zones; in addition the Russian Foreign Minister in discussions with the UN High Commissioner for Refugees on 15 August agreed on the principle of the non-discriminatory nature of the right of return for all civilians forced to flee; (3) that the issue of 'urgency' could be established only on events subsequent to 7 August as before that date Georgia had never raised violations of CERD with Russia;

(4) events subsequent to that date did not support an 'urgent' situation: the ceasefire came into effect on 12 August, and the six principles for the peaceful settlement of the conflict had been adopted by the presidents of Russia and France on the same day, and signed on 13–16 August 2008 by the president of Georgia and the leaders of South Ossetia and Abkhazia in the presence of the Organization for Security and Co-operation in Europe (OSCE) and the European Union (EU), thus terminating all armed actions; (5) 'the case on urgency in relation to Abkhazia [was] built almost exclusively on inference, and that [this was] not a sound basis for a provisional measures award'; and (6) a number of other initiatives were being taken at the highest levels to deal precisely with the problem put before the Court: from 8 September EU monitors were deployed into the buffer-zones around South Ossetia and Abkhazia; Russian peacekeeping troops would withdraw 10 days later; UN and OSCE observers would carry out their mandates; the issues of security, stability and refugees were being discussed at the highest political levels; in short, there was no ongoing worsening crisis.[43]

Before addressing the issues of 'irreparable prejudice' and 'urgency' the Court explained that: (1) it was not called upon, for the purpose of its decision on the Request for the Indication of Provisional Measures, to establish the existence of breaches of CERD, but to determine whether the circumstances require the indication of provisional measures for the protection of rights under CERD; (2) it could not at this stage make definitive findings of fact nor findings of attribution; and (3) the right of each party to submit arguments in respect of the merits remained unaffected by the Court's decision on the Request for the Indication of Provisional Measures.[44]

On these issues, the Court asserted that the rights in question in these proceedings – in particular those stipulated in Article 5(b) and (d)(i) of CERD – are of such a nature that prejudice to them could be irreparable in three senses: (1) violations of the right to security of person and of the right to protection by the state against violence or bodily harm (Article 5(b)) could involve potential loss of life or bodily injury and could therefore cause irreparable prejudice; (2) violations of the right to freedom of movement and residence within a state's borders (Article 5(d)(i)) could also cause irreparable prejudice in situations where the persons concerned are exposed to privation, hardship, anguish and even danger to life and health; and (3) individuals forced to leave their own place of residence and deprived of their right to return could, depending on the circumstances, be subject to a serious risk of irreparable prejudice.[45] The Court then indicated the importance of assessing contemporary conditions in this context: the exceptional and complex situation on the ground in South Ossetia, Abkhazia and adjacent areas together with uncertainties as to where the lines of authority lay. The Court then extended several considerations that affected its decision on these issues: (1) the ethnic Georgian population in the areas affected by the recent conflict remained vulnerable; (2) the situation in South Ossetia, Abkhazia and the adjacent areas in Georgia was unstable and could change rapidly; (3) given the ongoing tension and in the absence of an overall settlement to the conflict in this region, ethnic Ossetian and Abkhaz populations remained vulnerable also; (4) the problem of refugees and internally displaced persons in the region was being addressed presently, but was not completely resolved; and (5) in light of the above factors, there remained an imminent risk that the rights in issue in this case (Article 5(b) and (d)(i)) might suffer irreparable prejudice in respect of the various ethnic groups (Georgian, South Ossetian and Abkhaz).[46] The Court was thus able to conclude that it was satisfied that the indication of measures was required for the protection of rights under CERD. However, the Court remarked that it had the power under its Statute, on a request for provisional measures, to indicate measures that were in whole or partly other than those requested, or measures that were addressed to the party that itself had made the request. The Court pointed out that Article 75(2) of the Rules of Court refers expressly to this power of the Court, and that the Court had exercised this power on several previous occasions.[47]

Having found that that the indication of provisional measures was required in the current proceedings, the Court considered the terms of the provisional measures requested by Georgia. The Court found that, in the circumstances of the case, the measures to be indicated were not identical to those requested by Georgia: in particular, the Court considered it appropriate in all the circumstances of the case to indicate measures addressed to *both* parties.[48]

Finally, before indicating the precise provisional measures, the Court reaffirmed that its orders on provisional measures under Article 41 of the Statute have binding effect.[49] Accordingly, such orders create international legal obligations that both parties are required to comply with.[50]

The joint dissenting opinion denied that the first necessary condition of 'irreparable harm' existed even if *prima facie* jurisdiction were established. The opinion remarks that: (1) nowhere does the Court demonstrate the existence of any risk of 'irreparable harm' to Georgia's rights under CERD; referring to the statement in the Order of the Court that 'the rights in question in these proceedings…are of such nature that prejudice to them could be irreparable' (Order of the Court, para 142), the opinion declares that this 'appears to suggest that certain rights may automatically fulfil the irreparable harm criterion, without analysing the real facts on the ground or the actual threat against the said rights';[51] (2) with regard to the 'expulsions', they could not in and of themselves be considered to constitute 'irreparable harm', since the Court, if it arrived at the merits stage of the case, could always order that the expelled individuals be allowed to return to their homes and be granted appropriate compensation; and (3) it was even harder to claim that 'irreparable harm' to the rights in dispute when the appropriate organs of the UN had reported that thousands of persons had had returned to their homes in Abkhazia and South Ossetia, and when the ceasefire agreement of 12 August 2008 provided that negotiations would begin soon in Geneva on 15 October 2008 between the parties in respect, *inter alia*, of the progressive return of displaced persons.[52]

This criticism of the dissenting judges is not altogether convincing as it is not thought that the Court was categorising certain rights as satisfying automatically the 'irreparable harm' criterion, but actually specifying concretely that in cases of death or personal injury such a criterion would be satisfied. Nor was the Court stating that in cases of 'expulsions' that would satisfy the criterion automatically *per se*; it explained that in the case of 'expulsions', this could also result in danger to life or bodily injury.

The joint dissenting opinion dismisses peremptorily the second necessary condition of 'urgency' found by the Court. The opinion states quite categorically that there was no situation of 'urgency' because after the conclusion of the ceasefire agreement and the return of troops of both states to their positions before 7 August 2008, EU observers had been deployed to monitor the ceasefire and observers from the UN Mission in Georgia and those from the OSCE would continue with their missions in Abkhazia and South Ossetia.

It is suggested that these considerations for denying the 'urgency' of the situation simply fail to take account of the reality of the situation on the ground, where all ethnic groups continued to be under threat of violent attacks and expulsion from their homes at the hands of various armed militia for an indefinite period of time after the ceasefire. In any event, the OSCE observers were withdrawn by 23 December 2008 after Russia rejected plans to extend their mandate, although a 200 strong contingent of the EU's Monitoring Mission is on the ground on the Georgian side of the unrecognised border. Furthermore, as Anneke

Smit highlights in Chapter 6 of this volume, the reality is that internally displaced ethnic Georgians are unlikely to return to their homes in Abkhazia or South Ossetia, irrespective of any possibility of compensation, not least because their homes have been destroyed. Indeed, of the $4.5 billion pledged by international donors to help re-build Georgian infrastructure at a conference at Brussels on 22 October 2008, the UN and World Bank have estimated that Georgia would need $3.5 billion over the next three years to help the tens of thousands forced to flee from their own homes (and living in camps now) and to repair infrastructure.[53] In sum, the evidence of all official and media reports is that the situation was still extremely volatile and dangerous at the moment of the Court's delivery of its Provisional Measures Order. As such, it would seem that the criterion of 'urgency' was satisfied.

The order of the court

By a majority of eight votes to seven in each case,[54] the Court indicated the following provisional measures:

1. Both parties, within South Ossetia and Abkhazia and adjacent areas in Georgia, shall: (1) refrain from any act of racial discrimination against persons, groups of persons or institutions; (2) abstain from sponsoring, defending or supporting racial discrimination by any persons or organisations; (3) do all in their power, whenever and wherever possible, to ensure, without distinction as to national or ethnic origin (i) security of persons; (ii) the right of persons to freedom of movement and residence within the border of the State; (iii) the protection of the property of displaced persons and of refugees; (4) do all in their power to ensure that public authorities and public institutions under their control or influence do not engage in acts of racial discrimination against persons, groups of persons or institutions;
2. Both parties shall facilitate, and refrain from placing any impediment to, humanitarian assistance in support of the rights to which the local population are entitled under the International Convention on the Elimination of All Forms of Racial Discrimination;
3. Each party shall refrain from any action which might prejudice the rights of the other party in respect of whatever judgment the Court may render in the case, or which might aggravate or extend the dispute before the Court or make it more difficult to resolve;
4. Each party shall inform the Court as to its compliance with the above provisional measures.

Extraterritoriality of CERD in the Context of other international human rights treaties

The really challenging finding of the Court was on the extraterritorial application of CERD. The Court's argument is not fully convincing for the reasons stated above, especially in the light of the background to the Convention, its history and the *travaux préparatoires*. It is considered that obligations undertaken by states parties to CERD were understood by the drafters to be strictly territorial in scope. Neither is the Court's comparison of CERD with other international human rights instruments – such as the ICCPR – particularly apt.[55] These treaties are entirely dissimilar: one is an 'issue specific' human rights treaty, whereas the ICCPR is a 'general' human rights treaty where other considerations *may* apply.

Even the Court's suggestion that other human rights treaties, such as the ICCPR, apply to 'the actions of a State party when it acts beyond its territory'[56] is somewhat controversial. The pronouncements of the Human Rights Committee and the practice of states seem to reflect diametrically opposed appreciations of the territorial scope of the ICCPR. In General Comment No. 31 [80] Nature of the General Legal Obligation Imposed on states parties to the Covenant, the Human Rights Committee states that:

States parties are required by Article 2, paragraph 1, to respect and to ensure the Covenant rights to all persons who may be within their territory and to all persons subject to their jurisdiction. This means that a State party must respect and ensure the rights laid down in the Covenant to anyone within the power or effective control of that State party, even if not situated within the territory of a State party. As indicated in General Comment 15 adopted at the twenty-seventh session (1986), the enjoyment of Covenant rights is not limited to citizens of States parties, but must also be available to all individuals, regardless of nationality or statelessness, such as asylum seekers, migrant workers and other persons who may find themselves in the territory or subject to the jurisdiction of the State party. The principle also applies to those within the power or effective control of the forces of a State party acting outside its territory, regardless of the circumstances in which such power or effective control was obtained, such as forces constituting a national contingent of a State party assigned to an international peace-keeping or peace-enforcement operation.[57]

Recent examples of the practice of states parties to the ICCPR are completely contradictory to the above General Comment. In the United Kingdom's Sixth Periodic Report to the Human Rights Committee, the government states:

> In paragraph 10 of its general comment No. 31, the Committee has suggested that there may be circumstances in which the ICCPR has effect outside the territory of a State Party. The Government considers the Covenant can only have such effect in very exceptional cases. The Government has noted the Committee's statement that the obligations of the ICCPR extend to persons 'within the power or effective control of the forces of State Party acting outside its territory'. Although the language adopted by the Committee may be too sweeping and general, the Government is prepared to accept, as it has in relation to the application of the [European Convention on Human Rights], that, in these circumstances, its obligations under the ICCPR can in principle apply to persons who are taken into custody by British forces and held in British-run military detention facilities outside the UK.[58]

In its List of Issues to be taken up in connection with the United Kingdom's Sixth Periodic Report, the Human Rights Committee requested the United Kingdom to 'indicate how the provisions of the Covenant are applied to persons who are taken into custody in British-run military detention facilities outside the United Kingdom and/or killed by British armed forces abroad'.[59] In relation to this issue, the United Kingdom responded that whereas it 'reserve[d] the UK's position as to the extent to which the Covenant applies outside of the territory of the UK', it confirmed that the standards of conduct and physical treatment of prisoners required of United Kingdom forces were in accordance with relevant international law and United Kingdom military law, which applied to United Kingdom forces at all times, wherever in the world they were operating, and that these explicitly forbade the torture of (and other comparable actions against) detainees.[60]

At the oral examination of the United Kingdom's Sixth Periodic Report in Geneva, Ms Akiwumi, a member of the United Kingdom's delegation declared:

> The human rights obligations of the United Kingdom were primarily territorial obligations owed by the Government to the people. It followed that the Covenant could only have effect outside the territory

of the United Kingdom in very exceptional circumstances. While obligations under the Covenant, could, in principle, apply to persons taken into custody by United Kingdom forces and held in military detention facilities outside the country, any such decision would have to be made in the light of the prevailing facts and circumstances.[61]

In its Concluding Observations on the United Kingdom's Sixth Periodic Report, the Committee declared that it was 'disturbed about the State party's statement that its obligations under the Covenant can apply only to persons who are taken into custody by the armed forces and held in British-run detention facilities outside the UK *in exceptional circumstances*'. The Committee recommended that the 'State party should state clearly that the Covenant applies to all individuals who are subject to its jurisdiction or control.'[62] The record of all these proceedings shows unequivocally that the United Kingdom is not prepared to accept the extraterritoriality of the ICCPR, except in the very limited circumstances of British-run detention centres outside the United Kingdom territory.

The position of the government of the United States is, if anything, even more unequivocal. In its Concluding Observations on the Second and Third Periodic Reports of the United States, the Human Rights Committee requested the state party to provide information relating to selected recommendations within one year. Most of these requests for information on follow-up to its recommendations concerned matters outside of the territory of the United States, for example: 'secret detention', 'interrogation techniques', investigations into allegations of abuse, and 'transfer, rendition, extradition, expulsion or refoulement' of detainees 'in facilities outside [the United States] territory'.[63] In its Comments on the Concluding Observations of the Human Rights Committee, the United States reaffirmed categorically its long-standing position that the Covenant did not apply extraterritorially. The United States declared that states parties are required to ensure the rights in the Covenant only to individuals who are (1) within the territory of a state party; *and* (2) subject to that state party's jurisdiction. In the view of the United States government, its position on this matter was supported by the plain text of Article 2 and the *travaux préparatoires* of the ICCPR. The United States stated that ever since Eleanor Roosevelt successfully proposed the language that was adopted as part of Article 2 providing that the Covenant does not apply outside the territory of a state party, the United States had interpreted the treaty in that manner.[64] The United States stated further that its views on this matter were detailed exhaustively in Annex 1 of the United States Periodic Report to the Committee and discussed at length during the oral examination of the report in July 2006.[65] Accordingly, the United States respectfully disagreed with the view of the Committee that the Covenant applied extraterritorially.[66] The position of the United States is thus clear.

In stating that other human rights treaties – such as the ICCPR – apply to 'actions of a State party when it acts beyond its territory', the Court was relying clearly on its earlier jurisprudence. In its *Wall* advisory opinion,[67] the Court considered whether the ICCPR, *inter alia*, applied outside the territories of states parties, and if so, in what circumstances. Article 2(1) of the ICCPR uses the expression '[e]ach State Party to the present Covenant undertakes to respect and to ensure to all individuals within its own territory and subject to its jurisdiction ...' The Court commented that the provision could be interpreted as covering only individuals who are both present within a state's territory and subject to that state's jurisdiction; or, it could be construed as covering both individuals present within a state's territory and those outside that territory but subject to that state's jurisdiction.[68] The Court observed that whereas the jurisdiction of a state was primarily territorial, it could sometimes be exercised outside national territory. The Court commented that, given the object and purpose of the ICCPR, it would seem natural that, even when such was the case, states parties to the ICCPR should be bound to comply with its provisions.[69] The Court then characterised the jurisprudence of the Human Rights Committee under the right of individual communication as being consistent with its view. The Court commented that the Committee had found that the Covenant applied where the state exercised its jurisdiction on foreign territory, observing that the Committee had ruled on the lawfulness of acts by Uruguay in cases of arrests carried out by Uruguayan agents in Brazil and Argentina (*López Burgos v Uruguay*, communication no. 52/79 and *Lilian Celiberti de Casariego v Uruguay*, communication no. 56/79). The Court observed that the Committee had decided to the same effect in the case of confiscation of a passport by a Uruguayan consulate in Germany (*Montero v Uruguay*, communication no. 106/81).[70]

It should be observed that in all these cases, there was a clear nexus of *nationality* between the applicant and the state party concerned. Thus, these cases decided by the Human Rights Committee do not support any very wide application of the extraterritoriality of the ICCPR. In fact, the cases cited are very limited exceptions where the HRC has refused to permit states parties to exclude any governmental responsibility for conduct occurring beyond its national boundaries; such cases include only situations where the state party has refused to renew the passport of one of its own nationals abroad or where agents of the state party have violated the rights of its own nationals abroad in some other way, for example by kidnapping them and then clandestinely returning them to the territory of the state party. The rationale for these exceptions is to prevent states parties from breaching the ICCPR rights of its nationals abroad when it could not do so at home on its own territory.[71] As Professor Tomuschat made clear in his individual concurring opinion in both the *López Burgos* and *Celiberti de Casariego* communications, the formulation adopted by the drafters was intended to deal with objective difficulties that could affect the implementation of the ICCPR in specific situations. Professor Tomuschat instanced the example of a state party generally being unable to ensure the effective enjoyment of ICCPR rights to its *citizens* abroad because it could rely only on the limited device of diplomatic protection. Professor Tomuschat stated explicitly that:

> Instances of occupation of foreign territory offer another example of situations which the drafters of the Covenant had in mind when they confined the obligations of State Parties to their own territory. All these factual patterns have in common, however, that they provide plausible grounds for denying the protection of the Covenant. It may be concluded, therefore, that it was the intention of the drafters, whose sovereign decision cannot be challenged, to restrict the territorial scope of the Covenant in view of such situations where enforcing the Covenant would be likely to encounter exceptional obstacles. Never was it envisaged, however, to grant to States parties unfettered discretionary power to carry out wilful and deliberate attacks against the freedom and personal integrity [of] their *citizens* living abroad.[72]

The Court then examined the *travaux préparatoires* of Article 2(1) of the ICCPR, which the Court characterised as confirming the Committee's interpretation of that provision. The Court considered that the drafting history showed that the drafters did not intend to allow states to escape from their obligations when they exercise jurisdiction outside their national territory; the drafters only intended to prevent persons residing abroad from asserting, *vis-à-vis* their state of origin, rights that did not fall within the competence of that state but of that of the state of residence.[73]

A careful examination of the drafting history of the provision in question leads to a conclusion that is at some variance with the interpretation placed on it by the Court. The examples that were given in support of the argument that a state should not be relieved of its obligation under the Covenant to persons who remained within its jurisdiction merely because they were not within its territory included: (1) states parties would have to recognise the right of *their nationals* to join associations within their territories even when they were abroad; (2) there might also be a contradiction between the obligation laid down in Article 2(1) and that laid down in some of the other Articles, particularly Article 12(2)(b), which provided that anyone should be free to enter his *own country*; and (3) on the other hand, it was contended that it was not possible for a state to protect the rights of persons subject to its jurisdiction, when they were outside its territory; in such cases action would be possible only through diplomatic channels; although the word 'nationals' was not used in this latter example, it is clear that the concept being adverted to here was the diplomatic protection of nationals abroad.[74] In the Third Committee, some representatives expressed misgivings regarding the words 'within its territory and ...' and suggestions were made that the words be deleted and the term 'jurisdiction' be qualified to show that the guarantee extended to individuals subject to the territorial and personal jurisdiction of the state. Again, although it is not made explicit, clearly envisaged is the nexus of *nationality* of the state party concerned. In addition, it was felt that the addition of the words 'within its territory' could restrict the exercise of certain rights, such as the right of the individual to have free access to the courts of his state of *nationality*.[75] Ultimately, at the request of the representatives of China and France, a separate vote was taken on the words 'within its territory and' in Article 2(1) and adopted by 55 votes to 10, with 19 abstentions.[76] It is here argued that the Court's appreciation of the *travaux préparatoires* was simply wrong. It is clear that the drafters were only prepared to envisage extraterritorial application where there was a manifest link of 'nationality' of the state party by an individual claiming a violation of Covenant rights.

The Court examined then the history of the dialogue between Israel and the Human Rights Committee under the compulsory reporting procedure of the ICCPR. The Court pointed out that in 1998 when Israel was preparing its Report to the Committee, it had to examine the issue of whether 'individuals resident in the occupied territories were indeed subject to Israel's jurisdiction' for the purposes of the ICCPR.[77] Israel adopted the position that 'the Covenant and similar instruments did not apply directly to the current situation in the occupied territories'.[78] In its Concluding Observations after examination of the Israeli report, the Human Rights Committee referred to Israel's long-standing presence in the occupied territories, its ambivalent attitude towards their future status as well as effective exercise of jurisdiction by Israeli security forces therein.[79] In 2003, in response to Israel's consistent position that the ICCPR did not apply to the West Bank and Gaza, the Committee concluded that:

> In the current circumstances, the provisions of the Covenant apply to the benefit of the population of the Occupied Territories, for all conduct by the state party's authorities or agents in those territories that affect the enjoyment of rights enshrined in the Covenant and fall within the ambit of state responsibility of Israel under the principles of public international law.[80]

It was concluded by the Court that the ICCPR was applicable in respect of acts done by a state in the exercise of its jurisdiction outside its own territory.[81] It should be observed that later in this part of the discussion in its advisory opinion, the Court concluded that it considered that the construction of the wall and its associated regime impeded the liberty of movement of the inhabitants of the Occupied Palestinian Territory (with the exception of Israeli citizens and those assimilated thereto) as guaranteed under Article 12(1) of the ICCPR.[82] Bearing in mind the terminology of this provision, could it be argued that the Court considered the Occupied Territories to fall within the territory of Israel? Some credence can be attached to such an interpretation as the Court observed that 'the territories occupied by Israel have for over 37 years been subject to its territorial jurisdiction as occupying Power'.[83] If so, it seems to conflict with its direct finding in paragraph 111 of its opinion (above), that the ICCPR applied extraterritorially.

The Court considered also the issue of extraterritorial application of the ICCPR, *inter alia*, in the *Democratic Republic of Congo v Uganda*.[84] In this case, the Court concluded that Uganda was the occupying Power in Ituri at the relevant time, and as such it was under an obligation, according to Article 43 of the Hague Regulations of 1907 to take all measures in its power to restore, and to ensure, as far as possible, public order and safety in the occupied area, while respecting (unless absolutely prevented) the laws in force in the Democratic Republic of the Congo (DRC). In this case, 'this obligation comprised the duty to secure respect for the applicable rules of international human rights law and IHL, to protect the inhabitants of the occupied territory against acts of violence, and not to tolerate such violence by any third party'.[85] The

Court noted that Uganda had responsibility at all times for all actions and omissions of its own military forces in the territory of the DRC in breach of its obligations under the rules of international human rights law and IHL, which were relevant and applicable in the specific situation.[86] Then the Court, having established that the conduct of the Uganda Peoples' Defence Forces (UPDF) and of the officers and soldiers of the UPDF was attributable to Uganda, examined whether this conduct constituted a breach of Uganda's international obligations. In this regard, the Court had to determine which rules and principles of international human rights law and IHL were relevant.[87] The Court cited with approval the principle articulated in its earlier *Wall* advisory opinion that international human rights instruments were applicable 'in respect of acts done by a state in the exercise of its jurisdiction outside its territory', particularly in occupied territories.[88] The Court considered that the ICCPR, *inter alia*, was applicable in the present case as part of the corpus of international human rights law and IHL.[89] Subsequently, the Court found that the acts committed by the UPDF and officers and soldiers of the UPDF violated various international instruments, including Articles 6(1) and 7 of the ICCPR.[90] Accordingly, the Court concluded that Uganda was internationally responsible for violations of international human rights law and IHL committed by the UPDF and by its members in the territory of the DRC and for failing to comply with its obligations as an occupying Power in Ituri in respect of violations of international human rights law and IHL in the occupied territory.[91] In essence, this judgment does not extend any further cogent reasoning for imposing an extraterritorial obligation on states parties to the ICCPR, beyond what was stated by the Court in its *Wall* advisory opinion.

Conclusions

Despite the arguments advanced in the joint dissenting opinion, generally the Court's findings on the issues in dispute between the parties are fairly uncontroversial. It might have been thought that the reference in Article 22 to 'procedures expressly provided for in this Covenant' imposed a precondition that had to be fulfilled before the seisin of the Court. Indeed, that was the view until recently of this author. However, it appears that the terms of Article 16 are sufficiently wide and flexible to outflank this perceived limitation on the seisin of the Court.

The major, questionable finding by the Court of the extraterritorial application of CERD is much harder to justify either textually, by the practice of states parties to CERD, or by analogy with other existing international human rights treaties, such as the ICCPR. Doubtless the Court was motivated by the laudable objective of saving lives in making this finding. One can imagine easily a Court composed of judges such as President Higgins and Judges Buergenthal and Simma with their powerful and substantial human rights law expertise coming to such a conclusion.[92] Nevertheless, the jurisprudential justification was uncertain. However, it may be true to say that in this case the end pragmatic objective of saving lives justified the means.

Afterword

It is manifest that the Russian Federation continues to be in breach of the ceasefire agreement brokered by President Sarkozy that required all sides to withdraw to positions held before the fighting broke out. The evidence points to continued Russian occupation of the Akhalgori district of South Ossetia, which was actually under Georgian control before fighting broke out, where most of those living in the town and its surrounding villages were ethnic Georgians. This district continues to be in the firm grip of separatist forces backed by Russian military apparatus.[93] On 30 April 2009, at a ceremony in the Kremlin, Russia assumed formal control of the borders of South Ossetia and Abkhazia in an agreement signed between President Medvedev and the leaders of Georgia's two breakaway regions, again in clear contravention of the ceasefire. Effectively, these agreements hand power to Russia to defend the *de facto* borders of South Ossetia and Abkhazia with Georgia, including Abkhazia's Black Sea coastal waters.[94]

It is pertinent to ask what impact the Order of the Court has had on the disputing states. The circumstances of the dispute, the roots of which go back to late 1989/early 1990, are extremely complicated. Accordingly, it is not very easy to assess the impact of the Court's Order on the actions of both the Russian Federation and Georgia. Of course, the Court did order the parties to inform it of the measures they have taken to comply with the Order.[95] The Russian Federation has generally been very careful to comply with such orders of international tribunals. Thus, there is no reason to suppose that Russia will act any differently in this instance. It is entirely possible that the Court's Order may have had a substantial impact in saving the lives of all ethnic groups, principally Georgians, enmeshed in the struggle of the breakaway regions for secession. In the wider context of the role of the ICJ in influencing the conflict, it is important to note that the object of the Court's

Provisional Measures Order was to save innocent lives. The terms of the Order, which focus in large measure on humanitarian issues, make that clear. Indeed, it should be recalled that on 15 August 2008, acting in accordance with powers conferred on her by Article 72, paragraph 4 of the Rules of Court, President Higgins addressed an urgent communication to the parties calling on them 'to act in such a way as will enable any order the Court may take on the request for provisional measures to have appropriate effects'.[96] It can be claimed that this humanitarian objective was in some measure achieved. Clearly, the Court was able to exert some influence over the conduct of the parties to the dispute. However, the limits to the power of the Court to restrain both states from resorting to the use of military force are obvious. Certainly, the reality is that in the instance of this conflict, it was political processes that brokered the cessation of hostilities, but nevertheless the Court played a significant part in the de-escalation of the dispute in the Caucasus.

That the political realities on the ground are vastly different today than they were at the genesis of the 2008 conflict in the Caucasus is manifest. On 15 June 2009, the Security Council failed to extend the presence of the United Nations Observer Mission in Georgia (UNOMIG) after Russia vetoed a technical roll-over for the nearly 16-year-old operation. China, Libya, Uganda and Vietnam abstained on the vote on the text, which would have extended the Mission (entrusted with overseeing the ceasefire accord between the government and Abkhaz separatists in the country's north western region) for two more weeks until 30 June. As a result, Secretary-General Ban Ki-moon instructed his special representative to take all measures required to cease UNOMIG's operations, with effect from 16 June and consulted with his advisers on the immediate next steps. Explaining Russia's veto, Ambassador Vitaly Churkin stated that 'there's no sense in extending it since it is built on old realities. ... Developing a new UN mission mandate would have allowed us to quickly put in place practical co-operation of all interested parties to strengthen security and to restore trust. ... However, our Western partners did not accept this approach.'[97] It is clear that the Mission had contributed to the overall security of the local population and that a revised security regime is needed to ensure long-term stability. It is important to recall that UNOMIG's area of responsibility in Abkhazia consisted of a security zone (where no military presence was permitted), a restricted weapons zone (where no heavy weapons could be introduced), and the Kodori Valley. It had no jurisdiction in South Ossetia.[98]

The volatility of the situation remains to this day. On 29 June 2009, Russian launched massive military exercises (the 'Caucasus 2009' manoeuvres) in a show of force. 8500 troops, 200 tanks, 450 armoured vehicles and 250 artillery pieces poured into the disputed areas in exercises due to last until 6 July when President Obama was to arrive in Moscow for his first official visit to Russia. Soldiers based in the breakaway regions of Abkhazia and South Ossetia also participated as did elements of the Russian Black Sea fleet, the air force and elite airborne troops.[99] A tense situation of uncertainty is very likely to prevail for a long period of time to come. The processes of international law are likely to be called on again before this dispute is resolved finally.

Notes

I am grateful to the Leverhulme Trust for the stimulus and support provided by the Reading-based 'Liberal Way of War' Programme. This chapter builds on an earlier article, J.C. Barker and S. Ghandhi (2009) 'International Court of Justice Application of the *International Convention on the Elimination of All Forms of Racial Discrimination* (*Georgia v Russian Federation*) Provisional Measures Order of 15 October 2009', *International and Comparative Law Quarterly*, 58, 713–725.

1. *Case Concerning Application of the International Convention on the Elimination of All Forms of Racial Discrimination* (*Georgia v Russian Federation*), *Request for the Indication of Provisional Measures*, Order of 15 October 2008, para. 3, International Court of Justice, online: http://www.icj-cij.org/docket/files/140/14801.pdf.
2. *Ibid.*, paras. 4–5. For a detailed examination of facts about the events of August 2008 together with comprehensive coverage of the background to those events, see S.E. Cornell and S.F. Starr (2009) *The Guns of August 2008* (New York: M.E. Sharpe).
3. *Georgia v Russian Federation, ibid.*, para. 7.
4. *Ibid.*, para. 8.
5. *Ibid.*, paras. 9–16.
6. *Ibid.*, paras. 17–18. There is some evidence to suggest that the events that triggered the conflict originated with the shelling by Georgia of Tskhinvali, the South Ossetian capital, in the evening of 7/8 August 2008; this is corroborated by the Report of the Independent International Fact-Finding Mission on the Conflict in Georgia (IIFFMCG) (30 September 2009), Volume I, para. 14, online: http://ceiig.ch/Report.html.
7. *Georgia v Russian Federation, ibid.*, para. 85.
8. 660 U.N.T.S. 195.
9. *Georgia v Russian Federation, supra* note 1, para. 86.
10. *Ibid.*, para. 108.
11. *Ibid.*
12. *Ibid.*, para. 109.
13. See, for example, UN Doc. A/6181, Report of the Third Committee, Annexes, Vol III, (Agenda Item 58), 20th Session, 15. At p. 20 of this report the

words 'subject to their jurisdiction' were replaced by 'under their jurisdiction' following a proposal by a number of states (including Argentina and Brazil), presumably to emphasise the territorial nature of the obligations undertaken.

14. See E. Schwelb (1966) 'The International Convention on the Elimination of All Forms of Racial Discrimination', *International and Comparative Law Quarterly*, 15, 996.
15. UN Doc. A/8718.
16. UN Doc. A/51/18.
17. UN Doc. A/54/18, Annex V.
18. *Georgia v Russian Federation, supra* note 1, para. 110.
19. *Ibid.*, para. 111.
20. *Ibid.*, para. 112.
21. *Ibid.*, joint dissenting opinion, paras. 8–9.
22. *Ibid.*, joint dissenting opinion, para. 10.
23. *Ibid.*, joint dissenting opinion.
24. *Ibid.*, para. 113.
25. *Ibid.*
26. *Ibid.*
27. *Ibid.*, paras. 115–116.
28. *Ibid.*, joint dissenting opinion, para. 13. See also cited in support in the opinion: *Mavrommatis Palestine Concessions, Judgment No 2* (1924) P.C.I.J. (Ser. A) No. 2, 3 suggesting that the point must have been reached where there can be no doubt that '*the dispute cannot be settled by negotiation*'.
29. See text of Article 22 CERD recited in full in the main text following *supra* note 9.
30. UN Doc A/48/18, Annex III, *Georgia v Russian Federation*, joint dissenting opinion, para. 18.
31. *Ibid.*, para. 117.
32. *LaGrand (Germany v United States of America)*, Provisional Measures, Order of 3 March 1999, [1999] I.C.J. Rep. (I), pp. 14–15, para. 22; Article 41(1) of the ICJ's Statute reads: '[t]he Court shall have the power to indicate, if it considers that circumstances so require, any provisional measures which ought to be taken to preserve the respective rights of either party'. The Rules of Court may be found on the Court's website, online: http://www.icj-cij.org. There has been copious literature on this provision and the similar provision in the Statute of the Permanent Court of International Justice. See, in particular, H. Thirlway (2001) 'The Law and Procedure of the International Court of Justice 1960–1989', *British Yearbook of International Law*, 72, 37, particularly pp. 111–126; and S. Oda (1996) 'Provisional Measures: The Practice of the International Court of Justice' in V. Lowe and M. Fitzmaurice (eds) *Fifty Years of the International Court of Justice: Essays in Honour of Robert Jennings* (Cambridge: Cambridge University Press), p. 542.
33. See *Application of the Convention on the Prevention and Punishment of the Crime of Genocide (Bosnia and Herzegovina v Yugoslavia (Serbia and Montenegro)*, Provisional Measures, Order of 8 April 1993, [1993] I.C.J. Rep., p. 19, para. 34; and *Land and Maritime Boundary Between Cameroon and Nigeria (Cameroon v Nigeria)*, Provisional Measures, Order of 15 March 1996, [1996] I.C.J. Rep. (I), p. 22, para. 35.

34. *Georgia v Russian Federation, supra* note 1, para. 118.
35. The Court did not consider it appropriate, in the present phase, for it to pronounce on the issue of whether Articles 2 and 5 of CERD imply a duty to prevent racial discrimination by other actors; in support of its contention that the required connection between the rights that Georgia sought to protect by its Request for the indication of provisional measures and the subject matter of the proceedings on the merits did not exist, the Russian Federation had argued that nowhere in the provisions of Articles 2 and 5 of CERD 'do states undertake to prevent breaches of the Convention' and thus there was 'no duty to prevent racial discrimination by other actors'; according to the Russian Federation, 'owing to this fact, a duty to prevent racial discrimination – or specific, positive measures said to flow from such a duty – cannot form the subject of the proceedings on the merits'; and therefore 'any related right cannot be protected by the indication of provisional measures'. *Ibid.*, para. 125.
36. *Ibid.*, para. 126.
37. *Ibid.*, para. 127. Cf. *Application of the Convention on the Prevention and Punishment of the Crime of Genocide (Bosnia and Herzegovina) v Yugoslavia (Serbia and Montenegro)*, Provisional Measures, Order of 8 April 1993, [1993] I.C.J. Rep., p. 19.
38. *Georgia v Russian Federation, ibid.*, para.129. See *Passage through the Great Belt (Finland v Denmark)*, Provisional Measures, Order of 29 July 1991, [1991] I.C.J. Rep., p. 17, para. 23; *Certain Criminal Proceedings in France (Republic of the Congo v France)*, Provisional Measures, Order of 17 June 2003, [2003] I.C.J. Rep., p. 107, para. 22; and *Pulp Mills on the River Uruguay (Argentina v Uruguay)*, Preliminary Objections, Order of 23 January 2007, p. 11, para. 32, International Court of Justice, online: http://www.icj-cij.org/docket/index.php?p1=3&p2=3&code=au&case=135&k=88.
39. *Georgia v Russian Federation, ibid.*, para. 130.
40. *Ibid.*, para. 131.
41. *Ibid.*, para. 132.
42. *Ibid.*, para. 133.
43. *Ibid.*, paras. 134–140.
44. *Ibid.*, para. 141.
45. *Ibid.*, para. 142.
46. *Ibid.*, para. 143.
47. *Ibid.* para. 145. The joint dissenting opinion agreed that the Court had the power to indicate provisional measures exceeding those requested or to decide *proprio moto*, see para. 2. See also *Armed Activities on the Territory of the Congo (Democratic Republic of the Congo v Uganda)*, Provisional Measures, Order of 1 July 2000, [2000] I.C.J. Rep., p. 128, para. 43; *Land and Maritime Boundary between Cameroon and Nigeria (Cameroon v Nigeria)*, Provisional Measures, Order of 15 March 1996, [1996] I.C.J. Rep. (I), p. 24, para. 48; and *Application of the Convention on the Prevention and Punishment of the Crime of Genocide (Bosnia and Herzegovina v Yugoslavia (Serbia and Montenegro)*, Provisional Measures, Order of 8 April 1993, [1993] I.C.J. Rep., p. 22, para. 46.
48. *Ibid.*, para. 146. Whereas Judge *ad hoc* Gaja voted in favour of all the provisional measures; he declared that he could not share the view of the Court

that the conditions existed for addressing the provisional measures also to Georgia. He remarked that: (1) the Russian Federation had not even alleged that in Abkhazia, South Ossetia or adjacent areas the conduct of Georgian authorities or of individuals, groups or institutions under their control or influence might cause the risk of irreparable harm to rights conferred under CERD; (2) nor had the Court, in para. 143, given an adequate explanation when appraising the risk; and (3) in the present factual situation it seemed unlikely that the applicant state could be responsible for violations of rights under CERD that might occur in the relevant areas: even before the recent events, the Committee on Elimination of Racial Discrimination had found that Georgia had experienced 'difficulty in exercising its jurisdiction with regard to the protection of human rights and the implementation of the Convention in [Abkhazia and South Ossetia]', CERD/C/GEO/CO/3, para. 4, 27 March 2007.

49. *Ibid*. para. 147. The joint dissenting opinion observed, at para. 2, that because of the binding nature of these pronouncements, the Court had to be extra vigilant in concluding whether the required conditions for their indication had been met. See also *LaGrand* (*Germany v United States of America*) merits [2001] I.C.J. Rep., p. 506, para. 109.

50. *Ibid*. para. 147. See also *Armed Activities on the Territory of the Congo* (*Democratic Republic of the Congo v Uganda*) merits [2005] I.C.J. Rep. 116, para. 263.

51. *Georgia v Russian Federation, ibid.*, joint dissenting opinion, para. 21.

52. *Ibid.*

53. D. Charter, 'World Steps in with $4.5 Billion for War-Ravaged Georgia', *The Times* (23 October 2008), p. 38.

54. In favour: President Higgins, Judges Buergenthal, Owada, Simma, Abraham, Keith, Sepulveda-Amor, Judge *ad hoc* Gaja; against: Vice-President Al-Khasawneh, Judges Ranjeva, Shi, Koroma, Tomka, Bennouna, Shotnikov.

55. 999 U.N.T.S. 171.

56. *Georgia v Russian Federation, supra* note 1, para. 109.

57. CCPR/C/21/Rev.1/Add.13, para. 10, adopted on 29 March 2004.

58. CCPR/C/GBR/6, para. 59 (b), dated 18 May 2007.

59. CCPR/C/GBR/Q/6, para. 12, dated 13 November 2007.

60. CCPR/C/GBR/Q/6/Add.1, para. 98, dated 18 June 2007.

61. Human Rights Committee, 93rd Session, Summary Record of the 2542nd Meeting, para. 36 (8 July 2008), CCPR/C/SR.2542, dated 21 July 2008; subsequently, in its Initial Response to the Concluding Observations of the Human Rights Committee, the United Kingdom added that '[t]he UK, therefore, considers that the ICCPR applies within a state's territory'.

62. CCPR/C/GBR/CO/6, para. 14, dated 30 July 2008.

63. CCPR/C/USA/CO/Rev.1, dated 18 December 2006. In para. 10, the Human Rights Committee noted with concern the restrictive interpretation made by the state party of its obligations under the Covenant, as a result of its position that the Covenant does not apply with respect to individuals under its jurisdiction but outside its territory despite the contrary opinions and established jurisprudence of the Committee and the International Court of Justice. The Committee recommended that the state party should acknowledge the applicability of the Covenant with respect to individuals under its jurisdiction but outside its territory.

64. See, for example, the statement by Eleanor Roosevelt, Summary Record of the 138th Meeting, UN ESCOR Human Rights Commission, 6th Session, 138th Meeting, UN Doc E/CN.4/SR.138 (1950), para. 10. The United States stated that this interpretation was conveyed also to the Human Rights Committee in 1995 by Conrad Harper, the Legal Adviser of the United States Department of State. In response to a question posed by the Committee, Mr Harper stated: 'Article 2 of the Covenant expressly stated that each state party undertook to respect and to ensure the rights recognized to all individuals within its territory and subject to its jurisdiction'; that dual requirement restricted the scope of the Covenant to persons under United States jurisdiction and within United States territory; that during the drafting history, the words 'within its territory' had been debated and were added by vote, with the clear understanding that such wording would limit the obligations to within a state party's territory: Summary Record of the 1405th meeting (United States of America, UN ESCOR Human Rights Commission, 53rd Session, 1504th Meeting, paras. 7 and 20) CCPR/C/SR 1405 (1995).

65. Second and Third Periodic Reports of the United States to the UN Committee on Human Rights, Annex 1 (21 October 2005), online: http://www.state.gov/g/drl/rls/55504.htm. See also: CCPR/C/USA/3, dated 28 November 2005.

66. CCPR/USA/CO/3/Rev.1/Add.1.

67. *Advisory Opinion in Legal Consequences of the Construction of a Wall in the Occupied Palestinian Territory* [2004] I.C.J. Rep., p.136.

68. *Ibid.*, para. 108.

69. *Ibid.*, para. 109. The Court did not elaborate on the 'object' and 'purpose' of the ICCPR in any way. In General Comment No. 24 [52] Issues Relating to Reservations made upon Ratification or Accession to the Covenant or the Optional Protocols thereto, or in Relation to Declarations under Article 41 of the Covenant, the Human Rights Committee states that '[t]he object and purpose of the Covenant is to create legally binding standards for human rights by defining certain civil and political rights and placing them in a framework of obligations which are legally binding for those states which ratify; and to provide an efficacious supervisory machinery for the obligations undertaken', CCPR/C/21/Rev.1/Add.6, para. 7, adopted on 4 November 1994. It is interesting to observe that in *Banković and Others v Belgium and Others*, Admissibility Decision of the Grand Chamber of the European Court of Human Rights, no. 52207/99, [2001] E.C.H.R. 890, that the Court rejected the so-called 'living instrument' approach to jurisdictional Article 1 of the European Convention on Human Rights.

70. *Wall* opinion, *ibid.*

71. Other passport cases decided by the Human Rights Committee include: *Vidal Martins v Uruguay*, GAOR, 37th Session, Supp. No. 40, UN Doc. A/37/40, Report of the Human Rights Committee, 157; *Lichtensztejn v Uruguay*, GAOR, 38th Session, Supp. No. 40 UN Doc. A/38/40, Report of the Human Rights Committee, 166; *Varela Nuñez v Uruguay*, GAOR, 38th Session, Supp. No. 40 UN Doc. A/38/40, report of the Human Rights Committee, 225; and *MMQ v Uruguay*, Vol II Selected Decisions of the Human Rights Committee, 8.

72. GAOR, 36th Session, Supp. No. 40 UN Doc. A/36/40, Report of the Human Rights Committee, 184, 189 (emphasis added). Professor Tomuschat has expanded his views on extraterritoriality of the ICCPR in his 2008 book titled *Human Rights: Between Idealism and Realism*, 2nd edn (Oxford: Oxford University Press), pp. 129–132. The author of this chapter himself drew attention to these cases of the Human Rights Committee as long ago as 1986: see P.R. Ghandhi (1986) 'The Human Rights Committee and the Right of Individual Communication', *British Yearbook of International Law*, 57, pp. 201 and 220–224. See also P.R. Ghandhi (1998) *The Human Rights Committee and the Right of Individual Communication: Law and Practice* (Aldershot: Ashgate), pp. 128–131. These cases are considered also in the illuminating article by M.J. Dennis and A.M. Surena (2008, no. 6) 'Application of the International Covenant on Civil and Political Rights in Times of Armed Conflict and Military Occupation: The Gap Between Legal Theory and State Practice', *European Human Rights Law Review*, 714, in which the authors point out that the complete absence of the use by states parties of the right to derogate under Article 4 of the ICCPR in respect of overseas military activity further supports their conclusion that that instrument was not intended to apply extraterritorially. See on extraterritoriality of human rights treaties generally: T. Meron (1995) 'Extraterritoriality of Human Rights Treaties', *American Journal of International Law*, 89, 79; M.J. Dennis (2005) 'Application of Human Rights Treaties Extraterritorially in Times of Armed Conflict and Military Occupation', *American Journal of International Law*, 99, 119; R. Wilde (2005) 'Legal "Black Hole"? Extraterritorial State Action and International Treaty Law on Civil and Political Rights', *Michigan Journal of International Law*, 26, 739; F. Coomans and M.T. Kamminga (eds) (2004) *Extraterritorial Application of Human Rights Treaties* (Antwerp: Oxford: Intersentia); and M. Gondek (2009) *The Reach of Human Rights in a Globalising World: Extraterritorial Application of Human Rights Treaties* (Antwerp: Oxford: Portland: Intersentia). See further still on the extraterritorial application of the European Convention on Human Rights, the case of *Banković and Others v Belgium and Others*, *supra* note 69; and compare it with the case of *Issa and Others v Turkey*, no. 31821/96, Judgment of Chamber of the European Court of Human Rights (19 October 2004), advancing a much broader proposition than the Grand Chamber in *Banković*. See yet further for the extraterritorial scope of the Human Rights Act 1998, the case of *Al-Skeini and Others v Secretary of State for Defence* [2007] UKHL 26, especially the judgment of Lord Rodger of Earlsferry, paras. 65–84, in which he analyses critically the decisions of the Human Rights Committee and which this writer is wholly in agreement with. Note that Lord Rodger's analysis was adopted by the Court of Appeal in *Secretary of State for Defence v The Queen on the Application of Mrs Catherine Smith* [2009] EWCA Civ 441.
73. *Wall* opinion, *supra* note 67. The Court referred to the discussion of the preliminary draft in the Commission on Human Rights: E/CN.4/SR.194, para. 46, Official Records of the General Assembly, 10th Session, Annexes, UN Doc. A/2929 (1955), Part II, Chap V, para. 4.
74. Commission on Human Rights, 5th Session (1949), 6th Session (1950), 8th Session (1952), UN Doc. A/2929, Chap V, para. 4.

75. Third Committee, 18th Session (1963), UN Doc. A/5655, para. 18.
76. Third Committee, 18th Session (1963), UN Doc. A/5655, para. 29.
77. CCPR/C/SR.1675, para. 21; and *Wall* opinion, *supra* note 67, para. 110.
78. CCPR/C/SR.1675, para. 27; and *Wall* opinion, *ibid.*, para. 110.
79. CCPR/C/79/Add.93, para. 10; and *Wall* opinion, *ibid.*, para. 110.
80. CCPR/CO/78/ISR, para. 11; and *Wall* opinion, *ibid.*, para. 110.
81. *Wall* opinion, *ibid.*, para. 111.
82. *Ibid.*, para. 134. Article 12(1) reads: 'Everyone lawfully within the territory of a state, shall, within that territory, have the right to liberty of movement and freedom to choose his residence.'
83. *Ibid.*, para. 112.
84. *Democratic Republic of Congo v Uganda, supra* note 50.
85. *Ibid.*, para. 178.
86. *Ibid.*, para. 180.
87. *Ibid.*, para. 215.
88. *Ibid.*, para. 216, citing paras. 107–13 of the *Wall* opinion, *supra* note 67.
89. *Ibid.*, para. 217.
90. *Ibid.*, para. 219.
91. *Ibid.*, para. 220.
92. For the contribution of the Court to the development of human rights law, see S.R.S. Bedi (2007) *The Development of Human Rights Law by the Judges of the International Court of Justice* (Oxford: Hart Publishing).
93. T. Halpin, 'Moscow's Military Occupation Continues Despite Peace Deal', *The Times* (11 April 2009), online: http://www.timesonline.co.uk/tol/news/world/europe/article6074566.ece.
94. T. Halpin, 'Peace Pact Rift After NATO Expels Two in Spy Row', *The Times* (1 May 2009), p. 39.
95. The Court cannot confirm nor deny whether it has received information from the parties on compliance; such information is always confidential (both the fact of submission and the content), and therefore is not ordinarily placed on the Court's website.
96. *Georgia v Russian Federation, supra* note 1, para. 37.
97. 'Russia Vetoes Extension of UN Mission in Georgia,' *UN News Centre* (15 June 2009), online: http://www.un.org/apps/news/story.asp?NewsID=31151&Cr=georgia&Cr1.
98. *Ibid.*
99. P. Pank 'Fear of Second Invasion Casts a Shadow Over Frontline Villages', *The Times*, (25 June 2009), pp. 34–35; and T. Halpin, 'Moscow "Provokes" the Enemy in its Backyard with Huge Military Exercises', *The Times* (30 June 2009), p. 28.

5
Georgia, Russia and the Crisis of the Council of Europe: Inter-State Applications, Individual Complaints, and the Future of the Strasbourg Model of Human Rights Litigation

Bill Bowring

Introduction

The Report of the Independent International Fact-Finding Mission on the Conflict in Georgia (IIFFMCG) appeared in September 2009, in three volumes.[1] With a certain degree of hubris, the Report asserts that the 'successful political action' of the French President, acting on behalf of the European Union (EU) 'stood in contrast to the failure of the international community, including the [United Nations] Security Council...'[2]

Neither Russia nor Georgia are members of the European Union, but both are members of the Council of Europe (CoE), Russia since 1996 and Georgia since 1999. Both have ratified the European Convention on Human Rights (ECHR) and there are judges from each state at the European Court of Human Rights (ECtHR).[3] While the European Union is primarily an engine of economic integration, the 'three pillars' of the CoE are the rule of law, pluralistic democracy and the protection of individual human rights.[4]

It is noteworthy therefore that while the Report makes cursory reference to the CoE – as one of a list of 'other interested parties',[5] as one of a list of 'international and regional organisations'[6] and as a contributor, with the Organization for Security and Co-operation in Europe (OSCE) to a 'political culture of co-operativeness', through 'relevant documents adopted in the framework' of the CoE[7] – the 'Observations' that conclude the first volume of the Report make no mention of the CoE at all.

In the view of the author of this chapter, this is a surprising and an unfortunate omission.[8] The authors of the IIFFMCG Report are not alone, however. Charles King[9] in his authoritative analysis for *Foreign Affairs* also ignores the CoE. Oksana Antonenko, writing in *Survival*, makes no mention of the CoE either.[10] It is intended that this chapter will establish beyond question the vital importance of the CoE not only as part of the context for the 2008 conflict, but also as the locus of a wide range of conflict prevention and conflict resolution mechanisms.

This chapter will start, therefore, with a presentation of the Council of Europe. Next, the inter-state cases brought by Georgia against Russia at the ECtHR will be introduced and the procedure analysed. The third section will examine the individual complaints currently lodged at Strasbourg against both Russia and Georgia. Fourth, there will be a look at the acute problems posed by Russia for the Strasbourg Court. Fifth, there will be an examination of the CoE mechanisms for the protection of minorities and of linguistic diversity.

The Council of Europe

Even though the CoE now includes 47 states, and has a population of around 811 million people from Iceland to the Bering Straits, it had a much more limited significance at its inception than it now enjoys.

Brownlie and Goodwin-Gill have correctly stated that the Council of Europe was 'an organization created in 1949 as a sort of social and ideological counterpart to the military aspects of European co-operation represented by the North Atlantic Treaty Organisation. [It] was inspired partly by interest in the promotion of European unity, and partly by the political desire for solidarity in the face of the ideology of communism.'[11] In other words, the Western European states wished to demonstrate that they were as serious about the 'first generation' of rights – civil and political rights – as the Soviet Union and its allies undoubtedly were with regard to the 'second generation' of social and economic rights. After all, the 'communist' states guaranteed the rights to work, pensions, social security, health care, education and so on not only in their constitutions, but also in practice. This provided the legitimacy of the 'communist' order, and is one of the reasons why the Soviet Union collapsed, indeed rotted away, rather than being overthrown. It also explains the continuing nostalgia especially in Russia, among the older generations, for the late Soviet way of life.

The Council of Europe had its origins in May 1948, when 1000 delegates met at the Hague Conference.[12] This has been called 'The Congress of Europe'. A series of resolutions were adopted at the end of the Conference. These called, amongst other things, for the creation of an economic and political union to guarantee security, economic independence and social progress; for the establishment of a consultative assembly elected by national parliaments; for the drafting of a European charter of human rights; and for the setting up of a court to enforce its decisions. The last of these was the most revolutionary. There was no precedent in international law for an international court with the power to interfere in the internal affairs of states and to render obligatory judgments.

The Soviet Union could not have accepted or indeed tolerated such interference at the time. It was always an early signatory to United Nations (UN) human rights instruments. For example, it ratified the International Covenant on Civil and Political Rights 1966 (ICCPR) in 1973, in contrast to the United States that finally ratified in 1992, albeit with a series of reservations.[13] However, the Soviet Union was even more resistant to outside interference than the United States. Its thoroughly positivistic approach to international law placed state sovereignty and the right to non-interference at the centre of its commitment.[14]

According to Steven Greer and Andrew Williams, the original consensus in the CoE was that:

> ...the Convention's main modus operandi should be complaints made to an independent judicial tribunal by states against each other (the 'inter-state' process). At its inception, therefore, the Convention was much more about protecting the democratic identity of Member States through the medium of human rights...than it was about providing individuals with redress for human rights violations...[15]

This was of course fully consistent with the CoE's intended purpose as a bulwark against communism.

Thus, recognition of the right of individual petition did not become a requirement of membership of the system until the 1990s, after the collapse of communism. Greer has also pointed out that the original raison d'être for the Convention has undergone a profound transformation since its inception in the Cold War: 'it now provides an "abstract constitutional identity" for the entire continent, especially for the former communist states ...'[16]

Russia's accession to the Council of Europe

There can be no question of the importance for the Russian Federation of its accession to the Council of Europe on 28 February 1996, or its ratification of the European Convention of Human Rights on 5 May 1998.[17] To many observers, the Council of Europe's invitation to Russia and the political decisions to accede and to ratify were a great surprise.[18] As noted above, the Soviet Union had considered that the principles of state sovereignty and non-interference in internal affairs were the two cornerstones of international law, but even the communists and nationalists in the Russian parliament voted in favour. Russia was now accepting an unprecedented degree of external supervision and intervention, with the prospect of compulsory judgments and the payment of large sums of compensation.

It was perhaps even more surprising that the Council of Europe was prepared to accept Russia, given that the First Chechen War (1994–1997) was in full swing. However, Germany in particular considered that its own vital interests demanded that Russia be 'inside the tent'.

The road to ratification had been opened by the publication of the *Conception of Judicial Reform* on 24 October 1991 (after several years work) by Sergei Pashin, Sergei Vitsin[19] and others, and the enactment on 22 November 1991 of the *Declaration of the Rights and Freedoms of the Person and Citizen* by the Supreme Soviet of the RSFSR. The dissolution, by force, of the Supreme Soviet and suspension of the Constitutional Court, and the tearing up of the existing Constitution by President Yeltsin in October 1993, appeared to throw the whole process of reform into doubt. But the new Constitution of the Russian Federation, adopted by (dubious) referendum on 12 December 1993, contained many human rights provisions taken straight from the ECHR and the relevant UN instruments.

An initial challenge to the renewed Constitutional Court was presented by the First Chechen War (1994–1997). On 31 July 1995, the Constitutional Court of the Russian Federation delivered its decision on the constitutionality of President Yeltsin's decrees sending Federal forces into Chechnya.[20] The complaint was lodged by a number of the Duma, and one of the key witnesses was the first Ombudsman for Human Rights of the Russian Federation, Sergei Kovalyov, who up until he witnessed for himself the ferocity of Russia's attack on its own citizens, had been one of Yeltsin's staunchest supporters.[21] The Court held, not surprisingly, that the President was entitled to use force in order to preserve Russia's territorial integrity.

The Court did however – and very much unexpectedly – consider the consequences of Russia's participation in the 1977 Additional Protocol II relating to the Protection of Victims of Non-International Armed Conflicts[22] to the Geneva Conventions of 1949.[23] As Gaeta pointed out:

> The Court determined that at the international level the provisions of Protocol II were binding on both parties to the armed conflict and that the actions of the Russian armed forces in the conduct of the Chechen conflict violated Russia's international obligations under Additional Protocol II to the 1949 Geneva Conventions. Nonetheless, the Court sought to excuse this non-compliance because Protocol II had not been incorporated into the Russian legal system.[24]

Despite an order of the Court to the effect that all necessary changes should be made to legislation and practice, incorporation has still not taken place. And Chechnya was *de facto* independent for two years, from 1997 to 1999, although it was not recognised by any state.

On 25 January 1996, despite the First Chechen War, and after fierce debate, the Parliamentary Assembly of the CoE (PACE) voted by a two thirds majority to admit Russia, and on 21 February 1996 the Russian State Duma approved, by 204 votes to 18.[25] Vladimir Lukin, then Chair of the Duma's International Affairs Committee, and now the Human Rights Ombudsman, assured deputies that the benefits of Council membership would more than justify the €12 million a year dues.[26] The upper house, the Federation Council, unanimously agreed.

When, on 28 February 1996, the Russian Foreign Minister signed the ECHR and other CoE treaties, he did so pursuant to the long list of obligations accepted by Russia, set out in PACE Opinion 193 (1996) of 25 January 1996.[27] In February 1998, the Duma once again voted overwhelmingly to ratify the ECHR, and it entered into force for Russia on 1 November 1998. Russia thus complied in full with one of the most important of the obligations that it accepted on accession to the CoE. Indeed, Russia has satisfied most of its obligations, including the transfer of the penitentiary system from the Ministry of the Interior to the Ministry of Justice, in 1998, and enactment of new judicial procedural laws.

In an important step, on 10 October 2003 the Plenum of the Supreme Court of the Russian Federation adopted, after consultation with the Constitutional Court justices, and the Russian judge at Strasbourg, the excellent and thoroughly independent Anatoly

Kovler, a resolution '[o]n application by courts of general jurisdiction of the commonly recognized principles and norms of the international law and the international treaties of the Russian Federation.'[28] Russia has a 'monist' approach to international law, so that a treaty ratified by Russia is automatically part of Russian law, taking priority over domestic legislation. Therefore, the resolution contains the following, at paragraph 10:

> The Russian Federation, as a Member State of the Convention on Protection of Human Rights and Basic Freedoms recognises the jurisdiction of the European Court on Human Rights as mandatory with respect to interpretation and application of the Convention and Protocols thereof in the event of an assumed breach by the Russian Federation of provisions of these treaty acts when the assumed breach has taken place after their entry into force in respect to the Russian Federation (Article 1 of the Federal Law 'On Ratification of the Convention on Protection of Human Rights and Basic Freedoms and Protocols Thereof' No 54-FZ of 30 March, 1998). That is why the application by courts of the said Convention should take into account the practice of the European Court on Human Rights to avoid any violation of the Convention on Human Rights and Basic Freedoms.

At the time of writing, the *opredeleniye* (determination) of the Constitutional Court of 19 November 2009, in response to a request from the Supreme Court, has finally rendered it impossible that the death penalty could be restored. This is because Russia signed Protocol 6 to the ECHR, abolishing the death penalty on 16 April 1997, although it has not yet ratified it.[29] The Court based its reasoning in part on the obligation imposed on it by Article 18 of the 1969 Vienna Convention on the Law of Treaties: '[a] State is obliged to refrain from acts which would defeat the object and purpose of a treaty when...it has signed the treaty...'[30]

This is all very positive: however, it is a different story when it comes to protection by Russia of individual human rights under the ECHR, as will be shown below.

Inter-state cases

First, however, we return to the question of inter-state complaints.

It is especially regrettable that the IIFFMCG Report makes no mention of the first of two inter-state complaints made by Georgia to the European Court of Human Rights against Russia.

This first inter-state complaint was filed on 26 March 2007[31] and concerned Russia's mass deportations of Georgians in the autumn of 2006. As was noted at the time, this was the first inter-state complaint between members of the former Soviet Union.[32]

On 30 June 2009, the Chamber of the European Court of Human Rights held by a majority that Georgia's complaint was admissible. The case concerned the events following the arrest in Tbilisi on 27 September 2006 of four Russian service personnel on suspicion of espionage against Georgia. Georgia maintained that Russia's actions had amounted to an administrative practice, namely the practice of the official authorities giving rise to specific and continuing breaches of the ECHR under the following provisions: Article 3 (prohibition of inhuman and degrading treatment and punishment), Article 5 (right to liberty), Article 8 (right to respect for private and family life), Article 13 (right to an effective remedy), Article 14 (prohibition of discrimination), Article 18 (limitation on the use of restrictions on rights) of the Convention; Articles 1 (protection of property) and 2 (right to education) of Protocol No. 1; Article 4 (prohibition of collective expulsion of aliens) of Protocol No. 4 and Article 1 (procedural safeguards relating to expulsion of aliens) of Protocol No. 7.[33]

These breaches were said to have derived, in particular, from widespread arrests and detention of the Georgian immigrant population in the Russian Federation creating a generalised threat to security of the person and multiple, arbitrary interferences with the right to liberty. The Georgian Government also complained of the conditions in which 'at least 2,380 Georgians' had been detained. It asserted that the collective expulsion of Georgians from the Russian Federation had involved a systematic and arbitrary interference with these persons' legitimate right to remain in Russia – a right duly evidenced by regular documents – as well as with the requirements of due process and statutory appeal process.[34]

It was important that Georgia was asking the Court to find that there had been an 'administrative practice' on the part of Russia, rather than to find violations in individual cases. According to the former Commission's 1983 judgment in *France, Norway, Denmark, Sweden and the Netherlands v Turkey*,[35] an administrative practice involves two distinct elements: a repetition of acts and official tolerance. The usual rule as to exhaustion of domestic remedies does not apply, as decided in the 1978 case: *Ireland v United Kingdom*,[36] the 1996 case: *Cyprus v Turkey*,[37] and the 1999 case: *Denmark v Turkey*.[38]

Now, Georgia has launched a second inter-state complaint against Russia. On 12 August 2008, upon the request of the Georgian authorities, the European Court of Human Rights indicated interim measures to Russia and Georgia under Rule 39 of the Court[39] – basically, to keep the peace pending the determination of the complaint.

It is clear that although there have been relatively few inter-state complaints in the history of the ECHR, there has been a significant development of the law. Writing in 1988, Scott Leckie wrote[40] that:

> ...it still remains highly unlikely that the inter-state complaint procedure will be utilized with frequency in the near future. This procedure is still seen as a hostile and quite drastic response by a state desiring to address human rights questions in another state. Therefore, it continues to be viewed with skepticism and apprehension of its economic or political repercussions.[41]

Leckie also pointed out that:

> Within the European system, Article 24 concerning inter-state complaints has been interpreted to mean that a state using this procedure is not to be regarded as exercising a right of action for the purpose of enforcing its own rights, but rather as bringing before the Commission an alleged violation of the public order of Europe.[42]

By the time Leckie was writing, in 1988, 18 complaints had been brought before the former Commission on Human Rights on the basis of Article 24, concerning six distinct situations. The cases that had been examined were: *Greece v United Kingdom* (May 1956 and July 1957), arising out of Britain's suppression of the EOKA movement in Cyprus; *Netherlands v Greece* (five complaints, September 1967, March 1968, and April 1970), arising out of the rule of the colonels in Greece; *Ireland v United Kingdom* (two complaints, December 1971 and March 1972), arising out of the United Kingdom's response to the conflict in Northern Ireland; *Cyprus v Turkey* (three complaints, September 1974, March 1975, and September 1977), arising out of the Turkish occupation of Northern Cyprus in July 1974; *Denmark, France, the Netherlands, Norway and Sweden v Turkey* (five complaints, June 1982), arising out of the military rule in Turkey.[43] Only one of these cases, *Ireland v United Kingdom*, went to the Court.[44] This was the notorious case of the 'five techniques' used by the British forces to obtain information from detainees, condemned by the Commission of Human Rights as torture, and by the Court as 'inhuman and degrading treatment' contrary to Article 3.

Some years after Leckie wrote his authoritative survey, which compared the ECHR inter-state mechanism with the other international
and regional systems, there was a path-breaking judgment of the court.
On 10 May 2001 the ECtHR delivered a historic judgment[45] in which it
found Turkey responsible for committing grave and continuing violations in Cyprus of a number of human rights under the ECHR.[46]

The Court found (as summarised by Loukis Loukaidis, a judge of the
ECtHR):[47]

- a continuing violation of Article 8 of the Convention by reason of the
  refusal to allow the return of any Greek-Cypriot displaced persons –
  exceeding 211,000 – to their homes in northern Cyprus;
- a continuing violation of Article 1 of Protocol No. 1 by virtue of the
  fact that Greek-Cypriot owners of property in northern Cyprus –
  again exceeding 211,000 – were being denied access to and control,
  use and enjoyment of their property as well as any compensation for
  the interference with their property rights;
- a continuing violation of Article 2 of the Convention on account of
  the Turkish authorities' failure to conduct an effective investigation
  into the whereabouts and fate of Greek-Cypriot missing persons who
  disappeared in 1974 in life-threatening circumstances and of Article 5
  by virtue of the failure to investigate the fate of the Greek-Cypriot
  missing persons in respect of whom there was an arguable claim that
  they were in Turkish custody at the time of their disappearance;
- a continuing violation of Article 3 of the Convention in respect of
  the relatives of the Greek-Cypriot missing persons on account of
  their agony resulting from the silence of the respondent state as to
  the fate of the missing persons.

It is immediately apparent that this judgment is highly relevant to
the first of Georgia's inter-state complaints against Russia.

Individual complaints

International armed conflict between two member states of the CoE
is unprecedented. But many cases have come to the ECtHR arising out
of internal armed conflict: in Cyprus under British rule; in the Turkish
occupation of North Cyprus; in Northern Ireland; in the Basque
Country; in south-eastern Turkey with the Kurds; and in Chechnya.
Violence arising out of internal conflicts is by no means foreign to the
Court.

Russia poses an ever increasing problem for the Strasbourg Court. It has in recent years been losing some high-profile cases in the Court. In May 2004, in *Gusinskiy v Russia*[48] the Court held that Russia had acted in bad faith in using the criminal justice system to force a commercial deal, by arresting a TV magnate. In July 2004, in *Ilascu and Others v Moldova and Russia*[49] the majority of the Grand Chamber of the Court found that Russia rendered support to Transdniestria, which broke away from Moldova, amounting to 'effective control'. The first six Chechen applicants against Russia won their applications to Strasbourg in February 2005.[50] In April 2005, in *Shamayev and 12 Others v Russia and Georgia*,[51] the Court condemned Russia for deliberately refusing to co-operate with it despite diplomatic assurances; and in October 2002, the Court had given 'interim measures' indicating to Georgia that Chechens who had fled to Georgia should not be extradited to Russia pending the Court's consideration.

Finally, in *Aleksanyan v Russia*,[52] the applicant, who was held in pre-trial detention, was seriously ill with AIDS. The Court on several occasions issued 'interim measures' ordering Russia to permit him to receive treatment, but Russia ignored the order on three occasions. In the circumstances, the Court held that the Russian Government had failed to honour its commitments under Article 34 of the Convention: 'The High Contracting Parties undertake not to hinder in any way the effective exercise of [the right of petition].'

Moreover, Russia is now a major contributor to the current crisis of the Court. This can be shown by a comparison between 2006 and 2008. In 2006, 10,569 (out of a total of 50,500) complaints were made against Russia, of which 380 were referred to the Russian government, and 151 were found to be admissible. There were 102 judgments against Russia (out of 1,498 against all Council of Europe states). In 2008 there were 269 judgments against Russia, and 825 cases were communicated to the government.[53] By the end of 2006, of 89,887 cases pending before the Court, about 20% concerned Russia, 12% Romania and 10% Turkey.[54] In 2008 Russia was again the leader, with 27,250 pending before a judicial formation, 28.0% of the total.[55]

A September 2006 report of the Committee on Legal Affairs and Human Rights (CLAHR) of PACE observed that 'after the prompt reactions to the first European Court's judgments, the execution process has slowed down in the adoption of further legislative and other reforms to solve important structural problems ...' This diplomatic language expressed the problems of Russia's relationship with the Court. Such frosty relations between Russia and the Court were simply not sustainable, since at stake is the very authority, and the integrity, of the Strasbourg enforcement mechanism. CLAHR went on in February 2007 to analyse in depth the failure of Russia (and other states, especially Turkey) to co-operate with the Court.[56]

In an unusual move, PACE passed a further follow-up resolution on 2 October 2007. This stated, in part:

> Illicit pressure has also been brought to bear on lawyers who defend applicants before the Court and who assist victims of human rights violations in exhausting domestic remedies before applying to the Court. Such pressure has included trumped-up criminal charges, discriminatory tax inspections and threats of prosecution for 'abuse of office'. Similar pressure has been brought to bear on NGOs who assist applicants in preparing their cases. Such acts of intimidation have prevented alleged victims of violations from bringing their applications to the Court, or led them to withdraw their applications. They concern mostly, but not exclusively, applicants from the North Caucasus region of the Russian Federation ...[57]

Such public criticism of a Council of Europe member state was without precedent.

Individual complaints following the conflict

One of Russia's responses to the aftermath of the August 2008 conflict was the initiation of a large number of individual complaints against Georgia. A 'Public Commission for Investigation of War Crimes in South Ossetia and Help for the Suffering Civilian Population' was established with its own website.[58] On 28 April 2009, the Rapporteurs for the CoE's Monitoring Committee wrote:

> On 16 January 2009, the ECtHR announced that it would urgently examine seven applications of South Ossetians against Georgia, which it considers to be representative of the over 3,300 similar applications that have been filed with it. These cases have now been communicated to the Georgian Government under Rule 54, paragraph 2.b of the Rules of Court.
>
> In addition, the Georgian nongovernmental human rights organisation 'The 42nd Article of the Constitution' has assisted Georgian citizens in filing applications with the Court against Russia in relation to the war. On 18 March 2009, the CoE's Special Rapporteurs

were informed by the Court that over 100 cases had been filed against Russia, involving approximately 600 Georgian applicants.[59]

The ECtHR has also been dealing with many cases arising both out of the internal armed conflict in Chechnya, and also Saakashvili's first act after the 'Rose Revolution', the suppression in May 2004 of the autonomy in the southern region, adjoining Turkey, of Adjara, and the deposing of its president, Abashidze.

On 12 February 2009, the European Human Rights Advocacy Centre (EHRAC)[60] and the Georgian Young Lawyers Association (GYLA)[61] announced that they had jointly lodged 32 groups of cases with the European Court of Human Rights on behalf of 135 Georgian citizens who allege that Russia committed a number of serious violations of the ECHR during the August 2008 armed conflict between Russia and Georgia.

The applications, which originate from Gori and the surrounding villages, including a number of villages within South Ossetia and also Tskhinvali, primarily concern instances of shelling and air attacks on villages, allegedly by Russian armed forces, resulting in the destruction of property and the killing or injuring of civilians and the deliberate burning and looting of villagers' houses by Russian soldiers or Ossetian militia.

In one case, on behalf of eight villagers from Kekhvi, it is alleged that the village was shelled from the surrounding Ossetian villages on 6 and 7 August and attacked by air by Russian helicopters and planes on 8 and 9 August. The applicants state that Russian armed forces entered the village on 9 August. From 11 August a group of people wearing military uniforms looted and burned the villagers' houses, including those of the applicants. One applicant also alleges that her mother was killed by shrapnel during the shelling of the village.

In a number of cases the applicants complain about being illegally detained by Russian soldiers. One applicant states that on 13 August 2008 he was detained near his home village of Eredvi by three men in military uniforms who spoke Russian. He alleges that they took him to Tskhinvali in a small tank and detained him there for about 22 days in the basement of a building. He was not given food or water and was drugged and beaten daily.

A number of applicants also complain about not being able to go back to their homes, such that they are now internally displaced persons (IDPs).[62]

These important cases have to date been lodged by way of introductory letters, and the full applications must be submitted to the Court by the end of 2009.

The Council of Europe and minorities: The FCNM and Languages Charter

The Council of Europe is not only a mechanism for the protection of individual human rights. Since the bloody falling apart of the former Yugoslavia, and the collapse of the Soviet Union in 1991, it has evolved the most sophisticated mechanisms in the world for the protection of national minorities and of linguistic diversity.

The right of peoples to self-determination is not only *jus cogens*, as Robert McCorquodale and Kristin Hausler note in Chapter 2 of this volume (where they also explain the strict limitations placed upon exercise of the right in international law). It is also a human right, the first and most fundamental of the rights of the 'third generation', the rights of interdependence. In the current author's own recent book, the right of peoples to self-determination is described as the 'revolutionary kernel of international law'.[63] And the Caucasus region, North and South, contains a seething mass of competing claims to self-determination. These claims have been exacerbated by the 'parade of sovereignties' – a multitude of claims to sovereignty by territorial entities within the Soviet Union that preceded and followed the collapse of the Soviet Union at the end of 1991.

There are various markers that define and distinguish the various claimants, but the most potent is that of language. The Russian language, written in Cyrillic script, needs no further introduction. The Georgian language, a member of the very small South Caucasian group, is written in a beautiful and ornate script, *mkhedruli* ('military') whose 33 letters correspond to the sounds of the language, but bear no relation to Latin or Cyrillic or indeed any other script.[64] To complicate matters, while ethnic Georgians comprise (according to the 2002 census) 83.8% of the total population of the country (excluding Abkhazia and South Ossetia), there are also significant minorities: Azeri 6.5%, Armenian 5.7%, Russian 1.5%, other 2.5%.[65] Although this is changing, these minorities do not have a command of the state language, Georgian. The language of inter-ethnic communication tends to be Russian.

The Abkhaz language is one of the family of Caucasian languages, very different from Georgian or its dialects, with a Cyrillic script.[66] Ossetian on the other hand is an East Iranian language, related for example to Pashto, and also written in a modified Cyrillic script.[67] These four languages bear absolutely no relation to each other and are mutually incomprehensible.

As already mentioned, in a process that began in the 1980s, but was greatly accelerated following the demise of the former Yugoslavia and the former Soviet Union, and the bloody conflicts unleashed, CoE has developed sophisticated and increasingly influential instruments and mechanisms for the preservation and development of linguistic diversity, and for the protection of national minorities. These are encapsulated in two binding treaties, the 1992 European Charter on Regional or Minority Languages (Languages Charter)[68] and the 1994 Framework Convention for the Protection of National Minorities (FCNM)[69]. Both these treaties require states parties to undertake regular reporting on compliance, and the respective treaty bodies have by now developed a rich body of explanation, interpretation and progressive development, drawing from the examination of states' periodical reports.

The FCNM

Russia and Georgia have both subscribed to the protection of national minorities. Russia signed the FCNM on 28 February 1996 and ratified it on 21 August 1996. The FCNM came into force for Russia on 1 December 1998. Georgia signed the FCNM on 21 January 2000 and ratified it on 22 December 2005. The FCNM came into force for Georgia on 1 April 2006.

Russia has now submitted two periodical reports under the FCNM, on 8 March 2000 and 26 April 2005. Its third report is due on 1 December 2009.[70] The Second Opinion of the FCNM's Advisory Committee was published on 2 May 2007[71] after Russia had been given the opportunity to comment. This Opinion (paragraph 308) raised the following concern:

> The situation of persons belonging to national minorities in the Northern Caucasus is particularly disturbing, with incidents of violence and intolerance reported in a number of regions. Selective impunity reported in the investigation of human rights violations in Chechnya and other parts of the Northern Caucasus continues to hinder efforts to build a society based on the rule of law and negatively affects the protection of national minorities.

Georgia submitted its first State Report on 16 July 2007 (the next is due on 1 April 2012). The Advisory Committee published its Opinion on Georgia on 10 October 2009, following Georgia's comments.[72] In paragraph 8, the Committee observed that it:

> ...would first like to highlight the fact that it is faced with an unprecedented situation, i.e. the consequences of a recent armed conflict

between two States Parties to the Framework Convention, which took place after their ratification of the Convention. This situation is contrary to the spirit and letter of the Framework Convention, whose Preamble provides that one of the purposes of the Convention is to contribute to stability and peace in Europe and to promote international co-operation without prejudice to the territorial integrity of each State.

The Committee noted with concern, at paragraph 216, that for Georgia:

Participation of persons belonging to national minorities in the country's cultural, social and economic life and in public affairs remains limited, and many of them are isolated from Georgian society. Their inadequate command of the Georgian language is one of several factors accounting for their marginalisation.

The Languages Charter

Russia signed the Languages Charter on 10 May 2001, and, with the assistance of the EU and the Council of Europe, is now in the process of formulating an Instrument of Ratification – a complex process in view of Russia's enormous size and ethnic and linguistic variety, with 83 subjects of the Federation, and as many as 150 ethnic groups.

Georgia has not so far signed the Languages Charter.[73] As Jonathan Wheatley points out, '[o]n being formally admitted to the Council of Europe (CoE) in April 1999, Georgia pledged to sign and ratify the European Charter for Regional or Minority Languages (ECRML) within a year of its accession. However, ten years after joining the CoE, Georgia has still neither signed nor ratified the Charter.' One of the chief reasons for this delay, as he shows, is that '[l]anguage is a highly politicised issue and Georgian as a language is bestowed with almost sacred status as a wellspring of the Georgian nation.'[74] He concludes that:

In most countries that have already ratified the ECRML, the official language or languages is known by virtually all, if not all citizens. In Georgia, however, the lack of knowledge of the state language has impeded the integration of members of national minorities and has led to fears that the lack of a notion of 'we, the people' may impede the consolidation of statehood.[75]

It would not be utopian to hope that further constructive engagement by Georgia with the Languages Charter would in the long run also assist in coming to better terms with Abkhazia and South Ossetia.

Concern by the Council of Europe

Finally, this section highlights the fact that the CoE has engaged with the conflict and its aftermath in a great deal more depth and more consistently than has the EU – even if there has not been so much publicity.

On 2 October 2008, the Parliamentary Assembly adopted Resolution 1633 (2008) on the consequences of the conflict between Georgia and Russia. In this resolution, the Assembly strongly condemned the outbreak of war between two of its member states and considered that, during the conflict and its immediate aftermath, both states had violated human rights and humanitarian law principles, as well as the Statute of the Council of Europe and specific accession commitments.[76]

On 28 January 2009, the Parliamentary Assembly adopted Resolution 1647 (2009) on the Implementation of Resolution 1633 (2008). In this resolution, the Assembly fully reaffirmed its position taken in Resolution 1633 (2008) with regard to the consequences of the conflict, including its opinion that *both* member states had violated human rights and principles of humanitarian law, as well as the Statute of the Council of Europe and specific accession commitments.[77]

The Parliamentary Assembly's Committee on the Honouring of Obligations and Commitments by Member States of the Council of Europe (Monitoring Committee) has also been taking a close interest. It appointed two Rapporteurs, Mr Luc van den Brande (Belgium, Group of the European People's Party), and Mr Mátyás Eörsi (Hungary, Alliance of Liberals and Democrats for Europe). On 29 April 2009, they provided an information report on the follow-up given by Georgia and Russia to Resolution 1647 (2009).[78]

On 9 September 2009, the Rapporteurs published a further report, 'The War Between Georgia and Russia: One Year After'.[79] They were obliged to note that '[w]hile Georgia has complied with most, albeit not all, demands of the Assembly, Russia has not complied with most of the key demands placed upon it.' They concluded that '[i]t therefore considers that Russia's non-compliance with its demands underscores its lack of political will to address the consequences of the war in a manner incumbent on a member state of the Council of Europe.'

The Rapporteurs concluded: 'We therefore consider it inevitable that the Monitoring Committee challenges the credentials of the Russian delegation at the opening of the January 2010 part-session, if the Russian authorities have not:

- given unrestricted access for EU monitors to both South Ossetia and Abkhazia;
- granted freedom of movement for Georgian civilians across the ABL [Administrative Boundary Lines] and lifted restrictions, including on the point of entry, on the access to the two regions for international and humanitarian organisations as well as humanitarian aid to South Ossetia and Abkhazia;
- formally and effectively recognised the right of return of all IDPs from the 2008 hostilities to their original place of residence in South Ossetia and Abkhazia;
- initiated a credible investigation into the alleged ethnic cleansing, by the South Ossetian forces allied to it, and/or by civilians under its *de facto* jurisdiction and control.'[80]

This firm line, if adopted by PACE, could prove a considerable embarrassment for Russia.

On 29 September 2009, at its 30th Sitting, the Assembly adopted Resolution 1683 (2009).[81] Paragraph 11 of the resolution contains a stinging rebuke to Russia:

The Assembly is fully aware of Russia's argument that its non-compliance with the Assembly demands is the result of its diverging position with regard to the status of the two regions. The Assembly underscores that most of its demands have no relation to the status of the two regions and therefore can not understand that Russia failed to comply even with these demands. It therefore considers that Russia's non-compliance with its demands underscores its lack of political will to address the consequences of the war in a manner incumbent on a member state of the Council of Europe. In addition, the Assembly deeply regrets that the leadership of both the State Duma and the Council of the Federation, as well as the members of the Russian delegation to the Assembly have publicly opposed the demands of the Assembly and dismissed the possibility for Russian compliance with them.

PACE asked its Monitoring Committee to observe the follow-up given by Georgia and Russia to the PACE demands, and to propose any further action to be taken by the Assembly as required by the situation, in particular with regard to compliance.

Conclusion

This chapter concludes as it started: in the light of the membership of both Georgia and Russia in the Council of Europe, and the very close engagement of the Council and its institutions and mechanisms in the aftermath of the conflict, it is simply inexplicable that the expert report commissioned by the European Union should, in effect, ignore all of this. Of course, Russia's membership may be more and more thrown into question. On the other hand, both states appear firmly committed to continuing in the organisation; witness, for example, the resources committed by Russia to engagement with the FCNM and the Languages Charter, the fact that in every case it pays the damages awarded against it, and the belated abolition of the death penalty. Finally, it should be noted that one of the reasons for Russia's application to join the CoE, and its acceptance of such a degree of interference from the ECtHR, was the opportunity to engage, following the collapse of the Soviet Union, with a new space in which to exert influence.[82] Hopefully, the 2008 conflict in the Caucasus will prove to have been an aberration, in a process in which both Russia and Georgia have made significant changes within the dynamic of the Council of Europe.

Notes

1. The Report of the Independent International Fact-Finding Mission on the Conflict in Georgia (IIFFMCG) (30 September 2009), online: http://www.ceiig.ch/Report.html. The IIFFMCG was established by European Union Council Decision 2008/901/CFSP of 2 December 2008 concerning an independent international fact-finding mission on the conflict in Georgia, Official Journal of the European Union 323/66.
2. IIFFMCG Report, *ibid.*, Volume I, 11.
3. The author is well acquainted both with the Russian judge, Anatoly Kovler, an academic legal anthropologist who lectured for years as a visitor to the Sorbonne, speaks perfect French and is a highly independent judge, very often voting against Russia; and the Georgian judge, the youthful Nona Tsotsoria, with her background in United States-funded NGOs, and rapid promotion to Deputy Prosecutor General following the 'Rose Revolution'.
4. See Council of Europe, online: http://www.coe.int/aboutCoe/index.asp?page=nosObjectifs&l=en.
5. IIFFMCG Report, *supra* note 1, Volume I, 7.
6. *Ibid.*, 8.
7. *Ibid.*, 32.

8. The author has some experience in the region. He has been a regular visitor to Russia since 1983, in (North) Ossetia in 1986. In 2003, he founded the European Human Rights Advocacy Centre (EHRAC), which represents over one hundred Chechen applicants in their complaints against Russia at the EctHR and is now chair of EHRAC. The first six applicants against Russia, whose relatives were killed and property destroyed in late 1999 and early 2000 won their cases in 2005. EHRAC, in partnership with the Georgian Young Lawyers Association (GYLA), is helping to represent applicants who complain of violation of their rights by Georgia. EHRAC and GYLA are now working together on cases against Russia arising out of the August 2008 war. He has also visited Georgia on many occasions since 1986, when he was also in Abkhazia. Very shortly before the August 2008 war, he was in Tbilisi training the staff of the Georgian Public Defender (or human rights ombudsman), Sozar Subari, an outspoken critic of the human rights abuses of the regime of Mikhail Saakashvili.

9. C. King (2008) 'The Five-Day War: Managing Moscow After the Georgia Crisis', *Foreign Affairs*, 87, 2–11.

10. O. Antonenko (2008) 'A War with No Winners', *Survival*, 50, 5, 22–36.

11. I. Brownlie and G. Goodwin-Gill (2006) *Basic Documents on Human Rights*, 5th edn (Oxford: Oxford University Press), p. 609.

12. Council of Europe, online: http://www.coe.int/T/E/Com/About_Coe/1000delegates.asp.

13. See International Covenant on Civil and Political Rights, United Nations Treaty Series, online: http://treaties.un.org/Pages/ViewDetails.aspx?src=TREATY&mtdsg_no=IV-4&chapter=4&lang=en.

14. On this see B. Bowring (2008) 'Positivism Versus Self-Determination: The Contradictions of Soviet International Law' in S. Marks (ed.) *International Law on the Left: Re-Examining Marxist Legacies* (Cambridge: Cambridge University Press), pp.133–168.

15. S. Greer and A. Williams (2009) 'Human Rights in the Council of Europe and the EU: Towards 'Individual', 'Constitutional' or 'Institutional' Justice?', *European Law Journal*, 15, 4, 462–481, 464.

16. S. Greer (2006) *The European Convention on Human Rights: Achievements, Problems and Prospects* (Cambridge: Cambridge University Press), pp. 170–171.

17. The date of deposition of the Instrument of Ratification at Strasbourg.

18. See B. Bowring (1997) 'Russia's Accession to the Council of Europe and Human Rights: Compliance or Cross-Purposes?', *European Human Rights Law Review*, 6, 629; and B. Bowring (2000) 'Russia's Accession to the Council of Europe and Human Rights: Four Years On', *European Human Law Review*, 4, 362.

19. Now professor, indeed a general, in the University of the Ministry of the Interior, in Moscow.

20. An unofficial English translation of this judgment was published by the European Commission for Democracy through Law (Venice Commission) of the Council of Europe, CDL-INF (96) 1.

21. See B. Bowring (1998) 'Sergei Kovalyov: The First Russian Human Rights Ombudsman – and the Last?' in R. Müllerson, M. Fitzmaurice and M. Adenas (eds) *Constitutional Reform and International Law in Central and Eastern Europe* (London: Kluwer Law International), pp. 235–256.

22. 12 December 1977, 1125 U.N.T.S. 609.
23. The Russian Federation is a party to the 1949 Geneva Conventions. The Soviet Union ratified both the 1977 Additional Protocols on 29 September 1989 to become effective on 29 March 1990. The Russian Federation deposited a notification of continuation on 13 January 1992.
24. P. Gaeta (1996) 'The Armed Conflict in Chechnya Before the Russian Constitutional Court', *European Journal of International Law*, 7, 563.
25. Federal Law No.19 – F3. The text is set out in S.A. Glotov (1996) *Pravo Soveta Evropy i Rossii [The Law of the Council of Europe and Russia]* (Rostov on Don), p.118.
26. S. Parish, *OMRI Daily Digest* (22 February 1996). Lukin is now the Human Rights Ombudsman.
27. See *ibid.*, pp.82–89.
28. In English on the Supreme Court's website, online: http://www.supcourt.ru/EN/resolution.htm.
29. N 1344-O-P (19 November 2009), online: http://www.yuristyonline.ru/index.php?topic=4695.msg15625.
30. 23 May 1969, 1155 U.N.T.S. 331.
31. N. Khutsidze, 'Georgia Brings Russia to European Court over Deportations' *Civil Georgia* (27 March 2007), online: http://www.civil.ge/eng/article.php?id=14868.
32. C. Bigg, 'Georgia: Tbilisi Lodges Suit Against Russia At Human Rights Court' *Radio Free Europe/Radio Liberty* (2 April 2007), online: http://www.rferl.org/content/article/1075638.html.
33. Court Press Release No.543 (3 July 2007).
34. See *ibid.*
35. Nos. 9940–9944/82 (6 December 1983), 35 Eur. Comm'n H.R. D.R. 143, para. 19.
36. No. 5310/71 (18 January 1978), 25 E.C.H.R. (Ser. A), para. 159.
37. No. 25781/94 (28 June 1996), 86A Eur. Comm'n H.R. D.R. 10.
38. No. 34382/97, (8 June 1999), European Court of Human Rights, online: http://cmiskp.echr.coe.int/tkp197/view.asp?item=1&portal=hbkm&action=html&highlight=&sessionid=44337556&skin=hudoc-en.
39. Doc. 11876 (28 April 2009), Follow-up given by Georgia and Russia to Resolution 1647 (2009), Information Report Committee on the Honouring of Obligations and Commitments by Member States of the Council of Europe (Monitoring Committee), Council of Europe, online: http://assembly.coe.int/Documents/WorkingDocs/Doc09/EDOC11876.pdf.
40. S. Leckie (1988) 'The Inter-State Complaint Procedure in International Human Rights Law: Hopeful Prospects or Wishful Thinking?', *Human Rights Quarterly*, 10, 2, 249–303.
41. *Ibid.*, 299.
42. *Ibid.*, 257.
43. *Ibid.*, 272.
44. *Ireland v United Kingdom, supra* note 36, 90–91.
45. *Cyprus v Turkey* merits, no. 25781/94, (10 May 2001), European Court of Human Rights, online: http://cmiskp.echr.coe.int/tkp197/view.asp?item=1&portal=hbkm&action=html&highlight=&sessionid=44337556&skin=hudoc-en.
46. L. Loucaides (2002) 'The Judgment of the European Court of Human Rights in the Case of *Cyprus v Turkey*', *Leiden Journal of International Law*, 15,

225–236. See also L. Loucaides (2004) 'The Protection of the Right to Property in Occupied Territories', *International and Comparative Law Quarterly*, 53, 670–690.

47. Loucaides (2002), *ibid.*, 226.
48. No. 70276/01, (19 May 2004), European Court of Human Rights, online: http://cmiskp.echr.coe.int/tkp197/view.asp?item=8&portal=hbkm&action= html&highlight=&sessionid=44337556&skin=hudoc-en.
49. No. 48787/99, (8 July 2004), European Court of Human Rights, online: http://cmiskp.echr.coe.int/tkp197/view.asp?item=1&portal=hbkm&action= html&highlight=&sessionid=44337556&skin=hudoc-en.
50. These applicants were represented, from 2000, by the author and his colleagues from the European Human Rights Advocacy Centre, which he founded, in partnership with the Russian human rights NGO 'Memorial', with EU funding, in 2002.
51. No. 36378/02, (12 April 2005), [2005] E.C.H.R. 233.
52. No. 46468/06, (22 December 2008), European Court of Human Rights, online: http://cmiskp.echr.coe.int/tkp197/view.asp?item=2&portal=hbkm& action=html&highlight=Aleksanyan%20%7C%20v.%20%7C%20Russia&se ssionid=44337556&skin=hudoc-en; final judgment on 5 June 2009 following rejection of Russia's request for a hearing by the Grand Chamber.
53. Analysis of Statistics, European Court of Human Rights, online: http://www. echr.coe.int/NR/rdonlyres/55E4E440–6ADB-4121–9CEB-355E527600BD/0/ Analysisofstatistics2008.pdf.
54. See Annual Survey of Activity for 2006, European Court of Human Rights, online: http://www.echr.CouncilofEurope.int/NR/rdonlyres/69564084– 9825-430B-9150-A9137DD22737/0/Survey_2006.pdf.
55. Analysis of Statistics, *supra* note 53.
56. See Doc. 11183 (9 February 2007), Report of the CLAHR, PACE, *Member States' Duty to Co-Operate with the European Court of Human Rights.*
57. PACE Resolution 1571 (2007), Council of Europe, online: http://assembly. coe.int/Main.asp?link=/Documents/AdoptedText/ta07/ERES1571.htm#1.
58. 'Public Commission for the Investigation of War Crimes in South Ossetia and Help for the Suffering Civilian Population', online: http://www. osetinfo.ru.
59. Doc. 12010 (14 September 2009), 'The War Between Georgia and Russia: One Year After, Report – Committee on the Honouring of Obligations and Commitments by Member States of the Council of Europe', Co-Rapporteurs: Mr Luc van den Brande, Belgium, Group of the European People's Party and Mr Mátyás Eörsi, Hungary, Alliance of Liberals and Democrats for Europe, Council of Europe, online: http://www.reliefweb.int/rw/rwb.nsf/db900SID/ SNAA-7WF5CL?OpenDocument.
60. EHRAC is based in London, and was founded by the author in 2003 with a grant of €1 million from the European Commission. See EHRAC, online: www.londonmet.ac.uk/ehrac.
61. The largest human rights NGO in Georgia. See Georgian Young Lawyers Association, online: http://www.gyla.ge/index.php?lang=en.
62. Press release, EHRAC (12 February 2009), online: http://www.londonmet. ac.uk/londonmet/library/k13142_3.pdf.

63. B. Bowring (2008) *The Degradation of the International Legal Order? The Rehabilitation of Law and the Possibility of Politics* (Abingdon: Routledge Cavendish), Chapter 1, pp. 9–38.

64. See *Ethnologue*, online: http://www.ethnologue.com/show_language.asp?code=kat.

65. See CIA World Factbook, online: https://www.cia.gov/library/publications/the-world-factbook/geos/gg.html.

66. See *Ethnologue*, online: http://www.ethnologue.com/show_language.asp?code=osshttp://www.ethnologue.com/show_language.asp?code=abk; and 'Abkhaz Worried by Language Law', *Institute for War & Peace Reporting* (20 December 2007), online: http://iwpr.net/?p=crs&s=f&o=341580&apc_state=henpcrs.

67. See *Ethnologue*, online: http://www.ethnologue.com/show_language.asp?code=oss.

68. Council of Europe, online: http://conventions.coe.int/Treaty/EN/Treaties/html/148.htm.

69. Council of Europe, online: http://conventions.coe.int/Treaty/EN/Treaties/Html/157.htm.

70. Council of Europe, online: http://www.coe.int/t/dghl/monitoring/minorities/3_FCNMdocs/Table_en.asp#Russian_Federation.

71. ACFC/OP/II(2006)004

72. Council of Europe, online: http://www.coe.int/t/dghl/monitoring/minorities/3_FCNMdocs/Table_en.asp#Georgia.

73. The author has been engaged as an expert by the CoE in round table meetings with Georgian civil society in Tbilisi to discuss ratification of the Languages Charter.

74. J. Wheatley, *Georgia and the European Charter for Regional or Minority Languages* ECMI Working Paper # 42 (June 2009), p. 4, online: www.ecmi.de/37/2009/06/18/Working-Paper-42.php.

75. *Ibid.*, 38.

76. Doc. 11800 (26 January 2009), Implementation of Resolution 1633 (2008) on the Consequences of the War Between Georgia and Russia, Council of Europe, online: http://assembly.coe.int/Main.asp?link=/Documents/WorkingDocs/Doc09/EDOC11800.htm.

77. Doc. 11876, *supra* note 39.

78. *Ibid.*

79. Doc. 12010, *supra* note 59.

80. *Ibid.*, para. 72.

81. Council of Europe, online: http://assembly.coe.int/Mainf.asp?link=/Documents/AdoptedText/ta09/ERES1683.htm.

82. See Bowring (1997), *supra* note 18.

6

A 'Sea of Tiny Houses': Novel Approaches to Ending Forced Displacement Following the 2008 Russia–Georgia Conflict

Anneke Smit

Introduction

The approach of both domestic Georgian authorities and international organisations to solving the displacement crisis created by the 2008 Russia–Georgia conflict charted a new path.[1] It was radically different than approaches taken in the early 1990s when Georgia was faced with mass displacements following the secessionist conflicts in South Ossetia and Abkhazia. In particular, the expectation that a prompt return to homes of origin would be the preferred durable solution to the displacement was quickly abandoned for a sizeable number of internally displaced persons (IDPs) forced to leave their homes during the 2008 conflict. In its place, the two other theoretically accepted – but much less widely used – durable solutions to displacement (local integration and resettlement) have been embraced with unprecedented speed and vigour, with both funding and logistical support in place to implement such plans.

In part, the flexible and novel approach taken to the assistance of IDPs from the 2008 Russia–Georgia conflict has been facilitated by developments brewing in international refugee law and policy in the last several years.[2] At the same time, the pre-existing circumstances in this geopolitical context, onto which the 2008 displacement crisis was superimposed, have necessitated more radical approaches to ending the displacement than have been attempted in other recent displacement situations, in which such approaches have been far less readily accepted by the international community and/or state actors, as well as the displaced themselves.

The need for pragmatic responses to a large, and in all likelihood protracted, displacement crisis in Georgia has accelerated a trend in approaches to refugee and IDP protection.

The extent to which this durable solutions template will now transfer to other conflicts remains to be seen. While there are unique aspects of the displacement from the Russia–Georgia conflict which distinguish this situation from others, this chapter will argue that the approach taken in Georgia has pushed the international community to a level of flexibility in approaching the solution of displacement situations that is likely to continue to impact refugee law and policy. Further, it is argued that while such a development is a positive one in principle, in order for such a paradigm to be compliant with the 'international rule of law', a fuller and more transparent framework for determining appropriate durable solutions in a given displacement context is required.

The Refugee/IDP situation in Georgia

The conflicts over South Ossetia in both the early 1990s and 2008 saw the creation of hundreds of thousands of refugees and IDPs. The 1991–1992 conflict produced a population of more than 60,000 long-term refugees and IDPs, about 10,000 of whom are ethnic Georgians displaced from South Ossetia and displaced to Georgia proper (the others were ethnic Ossetians from Georgia proper who took refuge in South Ossetia or North Ossetia). The conflict over Abkhazia at about the same time produced approximately 250,000 ethnic Georgian IDPs from that region. A small proportion of IDPs from these conflicts found refuge with family members or friends and a very few managed to purchase their own housing. However, the vast majority of these IDPs have been housed in collective centres since the conflicts. These are primarily publicly-owned buildings – former hotels, hospitals, community centres and schools, for example – over which IDPs have no ownership rights. The centres are squalid, cramped and offer either little or no private or family space. Georgian legislation has provided for some humanitarian assistance over the years, in particular a monthly stipend of a few Lari and occasional bread deliveries.[3] International humanitarian efforts have also, somewhat sporadically, provided food and other essentials. There have been gradual expansions over the years in the rights explicitly extended to IDPs – for example the right to vote and the right to employment – and in the publicising of these rights.[4] However such efforts have been limited and clearly have taken a back seat to the stated goal of returning Georgian IDPs to their homes in South Ossetia and Abkhazia. Importantly, other rights extended to the Georgian population as a whole, for example the right to privatise land and/or housing in the early and mid-1990s, have been denied IDPs.[5]

Throughout the period of displacement since the early 1990s the language of return has been used continually by both Georgian politicians and representatives of international organisations to assure IDPs that they will, some day, return to their homes of origin. Yet over almost two decades of forced displacement in Georgia it has become clear to many observers that no widespread return of ethnic Georgians to South Ossetia or Abkhazia will take place. In late 2004, a United Nations Development Programme (UNDP) Working Group – finally moving away from the rhetoric of return – explicitly recognised the need to find a solution to the problem of the displacement of IDPs who were not returning home. It considered the possibility of promoting a 'temporary local integration' that would allow IDPs some benefits of local integration while maintaining the right of return.[6] However this was never implemented. Further, the 'Law of Georgia on Property Restitution and Compensation for the Victims of Conflict in the Former South Ossetian Autonomous District in the Territory of Georgia', which entered into force on 1 January 2007, formally enunciated the right to return. Article 5.1 of the Law states that the Law 'recognizes the rights of all forced migrants and other persons to return to their residence'.[7]

By the time the legislation was passed, however, there was little or no expectation that the availability of restitution would actually have the effect of persuading or allowing the displaced to return to their homes. Rather, it was clear to most that the effect would be primarily symbolic.[8] Georgian Deputy Justice Minister Konstantine Vardzelashvili argued that the message of commitment sent by the Law on Restitution 'could help start a positive dialogue between Tbilisi and the separatist government in Tskhinvali'.[9] A leader of a high-profile human rights NGO closely aligned with Saakashvili's government stated, '[t]his process will show a real commitment towards one thing: To give people equal rights in this country and I think that is a very powerful message.'[10] Another Georgian human rights activist involved in the drafting of the Law asked, 'how can there be trust if there are no concrete steps?'[11] A Georgian political analyst stated, '[t]he future will show the results. Restitution is an obligation and a question of dignity for us.'[12] Meanwhile, aggressive privatisation efforts in 2004 by the Georgian government of Mikhail Saakashvili led to the sale of some collective centres, most visibly the

Hotel Iveria in the centre of Tbilisi, which was sold to German investors for a reported $2.3 million USD.[13] IDPs were given little notice of their eviction and compensation was limited (approximately $7,000 per household, which in many cases consisted of numerous family members) and insufficient in the 2005 real estate market to purchase anything in the neighbourhoods in which they had resided for more than a decade, requiring yet another upheaval in their lives.

The displacement crisis of the 2008 conflict arose in the context of this ongoing state of affairs. As in the earlier crisis, at the beginning of the 2008 displacement most of the approximately 138,000 IDPs[14] from South Ossetia and the Gori region were housed in collective centres; some, like before, found refuge with relatives. However, while in the early 1990s and in the years following it had been possible for Georgian authorities and international organisations to continue to assure IDPs that return would occur, and to encourage IDPs to wait patiently in collective centres until that was possible, the 2008 IDPs had only to look at their predecessors to understand the risks of waiting it out until return was deemed safe and assistance provided. As early as 25 August 2008, as soon as there was a ceasefire in the conflict, many IDPs, in particular those from areas in Georgia proper neighbouring South Ossetia (such as Gori), began spontaneously to return to their homes, with the majority of IDPs returning within months of the initial displacement.

For a still significant number of IDPs, however, a prompt return was simply not possible. This was due to lack of security, extensive damage to – and destruction of – property during the conflict, and ongoing Russian and Ossetian control of many areas of South Ossetia, among other factors. The Report of the Independent International Fact-Finding Mission on the Conflict in Georgia (IIFFMCG) estimates that approximately 38,000 IDPs fall into this category.[15] In a striking contrast to the earlier conflict, rather than a 'wait and see' approach to return, the IDPs who did not return promptly were quickly branded 'unlikely to return' at least for an extended period of time, by domestic and international actors.[16] In fact, the IIFFMCG Report suggests that rather than further returns taking place, as late as September 2009 Georgian families were continuing to leave areas such as Akhalgori in South Ossetia.[17]

International refugee law principles on durable solutions

The United Nations High Commissioner for Refugees (UNHCR) has long acknowledged three possible durable solutions to forced displacement.

They are: return to home of origin, local integration in area of refuge and resettlement in another area or state. While traditionally existing in the realm of policy rather than law, the durable solutions trilogy is well-entrenched. However, despite the consistent recognition of the validity of all three durable solutions, clear policy preferences by the international community for one solution or another have been evident at all points since the coming into force of the foundational international instrument on the rights of refugees, the 1951 Convention Relating to the Status of Refugees.[18]

The possibility for refugees to return to their homes was not mentioned at all in the Refugee Convention: the focus was primarily on the rights of post-war refugees, for whom there were few expectations of return.[19] A 1950 report of the United Nations (UN) Secretary-General further indicated that local integration, rather than return, was envisaged as the primary durable solution:

> The refugees will lead an independent life in the countries which have given them shelter. … They will be integrated in the economic system of the countries of asylum and will themselves provide for their own needs and those of their families. This will be a phase of the settlement and assimilation of the refugees. Unless the refugee consents to repatriation, the final result of that phase will be his integration in the national community which has given him shelter.[20]

Indeed, for years following, return was hardly considered,[21] with local integration and resettlement continuing to be treated as the preferred solutions to displacement.

However, particularly since the early 1990s, both policy and practice have heavily favoured return as the preferred durable solution. This has occurred for a variety of reasons ranging from the economic burdens on – and security concerns of – host states, to the perceived preferences of the displaced themselves.[22]

Further, while discussions of refugees' access to durable solutions have traditionally been couched in the language of policy rather than rights, return has received different treatment in this regard. Recent developments at international law provide stronger support for, and evidence of, the existence of a right of return. The prevailing view, exemplified by Rosand's writing on the Bosnia and Kosovo crises, seems to be that there now exists a customary international law right of return.[23] Durable solutions for IDPs have been treated similarly. For example, while stopping short of enunciating a right of return for IDPs, Principle 28 of the non-binding 1999 Guiding Principles on Internal Displacement enunciates the obligation of competent authorities to establish conditions and provide the means for IDPs to return voluntarily.[24]

Correspondingly, as housing and property restitution mechanisms have been created with increasing regularity in the post-conflict sphere, restitution 'in kind' – the return of one's actual pre-conflict property – has consistently been prioritised over compensation, again reflecting a preference for return over local integration or resettlement. Kosovo's Housing and Property Claims Commission (HPCC) and Bosnia-Herzegovina's Commission for Real Property Claims (CRPC) are two examples of internationally sponsored programmes clearly prioritising return and restitution in kind, both in the rhetoric of their foundational documents and in the remedy available (only restitution in kind – compensation has not been offered as a remedy). In so doing, in principle at least, the international community prioritises the durable solution of return over local integration and resettlement. The non-binding Pinheiro Principles: United Nations Principles on Housing and Property Restitution for Displaced Persons, passed by the UN Subcommittee on the Promotion and Protection of Human Rights in 2005, state at principle 2.1 that 'states shall demonstrably prioritise restitution of pre-conflict housing' over other remedies for property deprivations including compensation.[25] It is not clear that a customary international law right to return specifically to one's pre-conflict *property* has yet crystallised, but there are strong signs that one is developing.[26]

Yet in conflict after conflict – the most recent one in Georgia included – the same patterns of non-return occur even when legal and humanitarian assistance is provided to refugees and IDPs by the international community. It has been seen in a variety of situations in recent years that refugees and IDPs who return home quickly following the end of hostilities, and often even before the international community deems return to be safe, have the best chance of a sustainable return.[27] Albeit in circumstances very different than those in Georgia, this is a lesson the international community also learned in Kosovo. The spontaneous return of upwards of 800,000 Kosovo Albanian refugees immediately following the end of the conflict in 1999 took place before the international community had deemed it safe to return. By contrast, refugees and IDPs displaced for the long term are unlikely to achieve a sustainable return. In a great number of displacement situations, prompt return is not an option. Primarily for security reasons, immediate return was not possible for the majority of the more than 250,000 ethnic Serbs and other ethnic minorities displaced from Kosovo in 1999, and most remain displaced after more than a decade, with hopes of return increasingly fading. As the then-head of the UNHCR mission's Protection section in Georgia stated in 2003, 'either you go back quickly, or you don't go back at all'.[28]

There are also ever stronger and more frequent condemnations of lengthy and widespread 'warehousing' of refugees in camps with limited freedom of movement, access to employment/livelihoods, *et cetera*, as a result of the impossibility of return.[29] Further, while IDPs may enjoy greater freedom of movement (by virtue of having remained in their home state, at least as defined at international law) than refugee groups having crossed an international border, IDPs too may experience a form of warehousing through restrictions on employment and educational opportunities. This type of warehousing may also limit the extent to which significant local integration can take place. Calls for approaches to durable solutions that would reduce these lengthy displacements have been increasing in intensity.[30]

As a result, there is evidence of a slow policy and practice shift back towards supporting local integration, and perhaps also resettlement,[31] as viable durable solutions flowing through the policies of UNHCR and other international actors. UNHCR's 2006 'State of the World's Refugees' report devoted an entire chapter to 'Rethinking Durable Solutions', accepting an important role for each:

> The recognition, on the one hand, that voluntary repatriation is not always possible, and, on the other, that indefinite encampment is unacceptable has led to a profound review of the three durable solutions and how they relate to each other. The need to avoid human degradation while simultaneously safeguarding voluntariness has spurred the development of new methods and approaches.[32]

A September 2009 UNHCR policy document on urban refugees also outlines in more specific terms the importance of gearing the organisation's activities towards the 'early attainment' of durable solutions and states that 'a comprehensive approach will be adopted, recognizing that different refugees may benefit from different solutions'.[33] Slaughter and Crisp call this new focus on the range of durable solutions 'tangible evidence of a new commitment on UNHCR's part to addressing the problem of protracted refugee situations'.[34]

Yet, for all the rhetoric, not all signs point to a more flexible approach to durable solutions. For example, the 2005 Pinheiro Principles are a clearly retrogressive move in this regard, given their almost exclusive focus on return. As Paglione notes, the phrase 'durable solutions' appears only once in the Principles.[35] Given that the Principles are arguably the most important international law instrument on the rights of refugees and IDPs in recent years, this sends a clear message that local integration is still afforded a lesser status than return.

This is the area in which the new Georgian displacement crisis may have made a significant contribution to the development of a more flexible formalised framework, at a time when the rigidity of the Pinheiro Principles was just starting to take root. As discussed above, given circumstances on the ground, the Georgian government and international organisations were forced to depart from the return 'script', instead having to embrace a strikingly different approach. It is a highly visible case study, one which will doubtless be considered when future cases are addressed. As such, the recent Georgian displacement crisis may have helped to create the type of flexible paradigm that this chapter argues is needed. The following section depicts the approach to local integration taken in Georgia following the 2008 conflict.

Local integration and the 2008 Georgian displacement

As described above, for the approximately 38,000 Georgian IDPs who have been unable quickly to return to their homes in South Ossetia following the 2008 conflict, local integration was considered a viable option very early on. There was a clear – and quick – recognition that return will not occur for these IDPs in the near future, if at all. Realistically, any other response would have been nearly impossible to maintain in good faith, more so than almost any other displacement crisis in recent history. In the face of hundreds of thousands of IDPs still displaced after more than 15 years – who have been unable or unwilling to return to South Ossetia under conditions less dire than those now faced[36] – there could be no realistic expectation that prompt return would happen this time.

Both the Georgian state and international agencies seemed quickly to be on board with the assessment that widespread return was unlikely. The Secretary-General of the Norwegian Refugee Council (NRC), one of the lead agencies in providing IDP assistance during and following the conflict, stated on 27 August 2008, only two weeks after the cessation of hostilities: 'We are working to find solutions so that people displaced by the war are able to return home safely. We are also working to find durable solutions for those that are unable or unwilling to return.'[37]

On 13 March 2009 Walter Kälin, the UN Secretary-General's Special Representative on the Human Rights of IDPs, advised the UN Human Rights Council that it was unlikely that the IDPs who remain displaced (both from this and the previous conflict) would return home unless and until a political solution to the conflict and the status of South Ossetia was found. He emphasised the urgent need to facilitate the local integration of both sets of IDPs into Georgian society.[38] Early post-war communications from the Georgian government also reflected its acceptance of the need to secure sustainable living conditions for IDPs in their host communities, rather than focussing solely on return.[39]

The effect of this early recognition was a much-changed approach to IDP assistance this time around. The most notable development has been the creation of at least 37 new settlements for Georgian IDPs. These settlements have been built throughout the country but many are near the capital Tbilisi. Each consists of between several dozen and hundreds of normally identical homes. Facilities are being built to house public services, and bussing arranged to schools, hospitals, and other amenities not yet available in the settlements. The Georgian government has reportedly spent close to $10 million USD building these new settlements, which will house approximately 21,000 people in 7,000 cottages.[40] While the housing is still less than ideal – the houses were built quickly in preparation for winter in 2008 and there have been problems with leaking and damp for example[41] – the physical conditions of the houses seem to be an improvement over the collective centres, and IDPs have ownership certificates for their properties, meaning that the kinds of evictions which took place in some collective centres should not occur in the new settlements.[42]

It is not the first time that states, intergovernmental organisations and NGOs have considered property and infrastructure-focussed programmes to aid local integration in concrete ways. Staying with the South Caucasus, in Georgia – as mentioned above – there was talk in 2005 of regularising property rights in collective centres as a way of facilitating integration of IDPs in the host community and providing security of tenure and a measure of economic stability. Further, a pilot 'housing voucher' project in 2006 in Kutaisi in Georgia allowed selected IDPs to use their allocated voucher amount on the open market.[43] In Azerbaijan the NRC, as part of its Urban Resettlement Programme, constructed new housing for IDPs in Baku who had been living in collective centres for 13 years since they had fled the Nagorno–Karabakh conflict.[44] However the differences following the 2008 conflict were the speed with which it was accepted that there was a need to provide opportunities for local integration or settlement, as well as the scale of the project. Rather than an issue that arises after a decade or more of displacement, the Georgian state and an array of aid agencies came to this conclusion right away, and then set in to find pragmatic solutions. Moreover, unlike earlier pilot projects, this local integration programme was on a large-scale, intended to provide housing for *all* IDPs who desired it.

Of course, the focus on return in Georgia and South Ossetia has not disappeared entirely, nor should it. The International Court of Justice's interim measures order provides the latest enunciation at international law (and seemingly the first by the Court on this subject) of the need to protect the pre-conflict housing and property rights of refugees and IDPs, ordering that both Georgia and Russia shall:

> ...do all in their power, whenever and wherever possible, to ensure, without distinction as to national or ethnic origin...the protection of the property of displaced persons and of refugees.[45]

Likewise, the IIFFMCG Report of September 2009 emphasised that 'under no circumstances should the current question of the status of South Ossetia...be used to hamper or impede the right of IDPs to return'.[46] Indeed, although the report is pragmatic in its acceptance of the impossibility of return of ethnic Georgian IDPs to South Ossetia for the foreseeable future, the above quotation is indicative of the underlying tone of continuing to affirm the right of return.

Relatedly, the language used to describe local integration efforts in Georgia since the 2008 conflict is also equivocal, seemingly so as to allow these efforts to co-exist with the ongoing right of return. Rather than talking about the durable solution of local integration, the language of both international organisations and the Georgian government speaks of accommodating those who are 'displaced for the long term'.[47] This is roughly akin to that which Crisp has described as 'local settlement' or 'temporary local integration'.[48] Although an important rhetorical tool, it is questionable whether the effect on the ground is in fact any different than if what was being done was described as 'local integration'.[49]

Further, there do remain, as before, significant political motivations for the Georgian government to continue to push for IDPs to return to South Ossetia when the time is right (or at least when security permits it) as part of reasserting Georgian authority over the area. As such, the approach taken to IDP settlement is not grounded solely in the humanitarian needs of IDPs but serves a purpose for the Georgian government in keeping IDPs grouped together. One Western observer recently wrote of driving past the 'sea of tiny houses' in the new settlements, which were 'aesthetically depressing in their uniformity'.[50] In pursuing local integration in this way the Georgian government may be able to continue to use IDPs as a vivid illustration of the plight of IDPs and the need for a political solution.[51]

To conclude here, while there continues to exist a strong undercurrent of desire for return on the part of IDPs themselves as well as government and international actors, there has clearly been a revolutionary shift in the approach to durable solutions for IDPs in Georgia. This shift is both evidence of a recent global movement towards use of the range of durable solutions, and an important precedent for displacements to come, in which non-return solutions might likewise be considered early on and provided significant financial and operational support. The last section explores the need for a strengthened international framework to support this normative shift.

A new 'Law of Durable Solutions'?

A legal or policy framework that accepts the range of durable solutions is less easily crafted than one that prioritises the right of return. Some challenges are highlighted by the Russia–Georgia example, and some will only arise when the lessons of Georgia and the larger shift in international refugee policy are applied to other displacement situations. If all durable solutions are to be considered acceptable depending on the circumstances – which this chapter argues is a positive development – then a more substantial framework is required for determining what durable solutions will be appropriate in a given displacement situation.

In considering the existence of an 'international rule of law', Chesterman questions whether 'the process of international rule-making can itself be said to be governed by laws…if the rule of law is understood in the core, formal sense …'[52] The international community's approach to durable solutions seems at present to mix law and policy in a way that makes a conclusion that the rule of law is present – or even relevant – problematic.[53]

It seems a fair conclusion that something short of the certainty and predictability[54] demanded by the rule of law currently exists as concerns the crafting of durable solutions to displacement. As discussed above, most of the contemplation of durable solutions happens at the level of policy rather than law, yet in recent years the right of return appears to have been elevated to the status of international law. The conclusion is then easily reached that the right of return, having legal force, deserves and receives a higher level of protection than local integration and resettlement, which remain policy-based alternatives. Yet this is a perversion of the origins of the durable solutions trilogy. Further, as experience has shown, an excessive focus on return often does no favours for refugees and IDPs themselves, regardless of the vehemence of their stated desires to return home. A singular focus on return leads more often than not to long warehousing rather than the desired prompt return to their pre-conflict lives and homes or opportunities to move on with their lives. When return does not take place, refugees and IDPs are left in an uncomfortable and often powerless situation, waiting for something to be done to improve their situations from a humanitarian perspective, with little recourse from a rights-based perspective.

If the concept of the 'rule of international law' is to be useful in this area, then a preferable approach would be the elevation of a refugee or IDP's *right to a durable solution* to the level of international law, with return, local integration and resettlement holding equal status as potential durable solutions. It should then be possible to craft a framework ensuring predictability and certainty in the determining of which durable solution(s) will be available in a given displacement situation. This might contribute to a more general and consistent application of durable solutions options, rather than a durable solution being either subject to political whims or tied to an inflexible prioritization on return. The Pinheiro Principles were a step towards certainty in the way in which the justice issues of forced migration are addressed. Yet in their rigidity they instead contribute to a renewed narrow focus on return, rather than the creation of a predictable but flexible framework through which to address the finding of solutions to displacement.

Exactly what such a framework would look like would require significant study and consultation (the Pinheiro Principles, e.g., were the product of almost a decade of consideration by the UN Sub-Commission on the Protection and Promotion of Human Rights). A few points may be made here, however. First, a set of criteria is necessary that could be applied consistently but flexibly to determine which durable solution(s) would be offered in a given displacement situation. The second requirement should be a duty of consultation with refugees and IDPs when decisions regarding the durable solutions to be available to them are being made. Lastly, when local integration or resettlement options are viewed as preferable, these must be implemented in such a way as to provide for real integration in new communities. Each of these is discussed briefly below.

Criteria for selection of durable solutions

The 2008 Russia–Georgia conflict created a set of circumstances in which it was virtually impossible to argue that return was, or would become, a viable durable solution, leading to a prompt determination that some form of local integration must be facilitated. However, most displacement situations will not provide such obvious solutions. It would be helpful for international legal instruments – even soft law such as the Pinheiro Principles – to elucidate the factors to be considered in determinations of what durable solutions will be pursued. These will undoubtedly include the types of factors already taken at least implicitly into consideration at a policy level in assessing any possible return programme, such as (particularly for pre-existing displacement situation) length of displacement, political stability of home and host communities, infrastructural damage, economic opportunities available in home and host communities, and ethnic relations.

A duty to consult

The 2008 conflict and the events following it once again illustrate the need for states and international actors to consult with refugees and IDPs themselves when durable solution plans are being considered. In many cases consultations do take place, but this is far from systematised. In general, IDPs in Georgia have complained of a lack of consultation on the possible approaches to durable solutions taken by the state and international actors.[55] Many Georgian IDPs have reported being much happier with the new settlements than with collective centres (and indeed some reportedly queued as long as two weeks to be granted a place in a new village),[56] yet some have also been quoted as saying that they feel their right of return has been completely sold off, that even more than the last time the Georgian government is now prepared to forget about them. A legal 'duty to consult' with refugee and IDP groups, before important decisions about their durable solutions are made, would add the type of predictability and certainty to the international refugee law regime which the rule of law demands.

Sustainability/location of integration programmes

The Georgian example points to the need for careful planning of local integration programmes, and in particular careful consideration of the location of integration settlements for refugees and IDPs, to ensure that true integration can be attained. The recent creation of IDP settlements in Georgia provided a solution which for most was preferable to collective centres. Yet, likely both for political reasons and simply through a lack of planning or resources, the Georgian government and international agencies may have stopped short of creating a viable full local integration option. The location of the new settlements – separate from established towns and cities and often in areas where there is little employment available or possibilities for farming – creates an enormous impediment to a sustainable local integration.[57] In his comprehensive 1993 report on shelter provision for refugees and IDPs, Zetter repeatedly emphasised the importance of location, in particular proximity to local settlements and livelihoods, in predicting the successful local integration of refugees and IDPs.[58] There is more work to be done on ensuring that local integration initiatives consistently provide real integration possibilities and not simply a more sustainable version of warehousing.

This latest displacement crisis in Georgia has been approached in a strikingly different way from previous ones, and is likely evidence of a shift taking place in international refugee law and policy towards a greater use of the range of durable solutions to displacement – return, local integration and resettlement. The development of a suitable and more substantial international legal framework to support such an approach promises to be a positive step for states, international actors and, most importantly, refugees and IDPs.

Notes

1. The title of this chapter is borrowed from a blog entry by a Western observer describing new settlements built for displaced persons in Georgia proper in 2008, quoted in full at *infra* note 50.
2. On this, and more generally on the protection of housing and property rights of after displacement, see A. Smit (forthcoming 2010) *The Property Rights of Refugees and IDPs: Beyond Restitution* (London: Routledge).
3. *Law of Georgia on Internally Displaced Persons* (2006, English translation published in 2002) IDPs Reference Book (Tbilisi: UNHCR, Ministry of Refugees and Accommodation of Georgia, and Association Migrant), p. 322.
4. 'Study on IDP Rights' UN Development Programme (December 2003), p. 10, online: www.undp.org.ge.
5. See, for example, Resolution #107 of Cabinet of Ministers on Privatization (Free of Charge Transfer) of Apartments in the Republic of Georgia (February 1, 1992, as amended).
6. 'Collective Center Privatisation Justification and Mechanisms' Working Paper of the IDP Collective Centers Privatization Working Group, UN Development Programme (14 December 2004) (copy on file with the author).

7. Of course, given that Georgian government authority is not recognised in South Ossetia, this Law could only have effect on the territory of Georgia proper – that is, it could only apply to Ossetians' right to restitution of their homes in Georgia proper and could not provide restitution for ethnic Georgians who had lost their homes in South Ossetia.
8. See, the Report of the Independent International Fact-Finding Mission on the Conflict in Georgia (IIFFMCG) (30 September 2009), Volume II, 113, online: http://www.ceiig.ch/Report.html.
9. Quoted in M. Corso, 'Georgia Promotes Property Payback for South Ossetia Peace', *Eurasia Insight*, EurasiaNet (17 April 2006), online: www.eurasianet.org.
10. G. Meladze, Liberty Institute NGO, quoted *ibid*.
11. M. Tsaboshvili, human rights activist, quoted in Corso, *supra* note 9.
12. P. Zakareishvili, quoted in V. Gujelashvili, 'Property Restitution Deal for South Ossetia', *Caucasus Reporting Service* No. 332 (24 March 2006), online: www.iwpr.net.
13. A. Remtulla, 'No Vacancy at the Iveria Hotel', *CBC News Viewpoint* (20 August 2004), online: www.cbc.ca.
14. IIFFMCG Report, *supra* note 8, Volume II, 381.
15. *Ibid.*, 397.
16. *Ibid.*, 224.
17. *Ibid.*, 279.
18. Convention Relating to the Status of Refugees, 14 December 1951, 189 U.N.T.S. 150 (entry into force 22 April 1954).
19. Indeed the term 'durable solutions' was not even mentioned in the Refugee Convention.
20. Memorandum by the Secretary-General to the Ad Hoc Committee on Statelessness and Related Problems, UN Doc. E/AC (3 January 1950), 6–7.
21. Note, however, that the Universal Declaration of Human Rights declared in 1948 at Article 13(2) that everyone has the right to leave his country and to return to it (Universal Declaration of Human Rights, UN General Assembly Resolution 217A (III), UN Doc. A/810 (10 December 1948), Article 13(2)).
22. See, for example, B.S. Chimni (1999) 'From Resettlement to Involuntary Repatriation: Towards a Critical History of Durable Solutions to Refugee Problems', *New Issues in Refugee Research* Working Paper No. 2, UNHCR, online: www.unhcr.org.
23. See E. Rosand (1997) 'The Right to Return Under International Law Following Mass Displacement: The Bosnia Precedent?', *Michigan Journal of International Law*, 19, 1121. See also discussions of the right of return in K. Lawand (1996) 'The Right to Return of Palestinians under International Law', *International Journal of Refugee Law*, 8, 532; and E. Rosand (2000) 'The Kosovo Crisis: Implications of the Right to Return', *Berkeley Journal of International Law*, 18, 229.
24. GA Res. 60/L.1.
25. The Pinheiro Principles: United Nations Principles on Housing and Property Restitution for Refugees and Displaced Persons, UN Doc. E/CN.4/Sub.2/2005 (11 August 2005). Although non-binding, the Principles have been taken up widely by governments and NGOs alike as a guiding document.
26. See, for example, L. von Carlowitz (2005) 'A Universal Human Right of Property for Refugees and Displaced Persons?: On the Development of Property-Related Customary International Law by the International

Administrations in Bosnia and Herzegovina and Kosovo', 7, online: http://www.irmgard-coninx-stiftung.de/en/download/118%20Carlowitz.pdf.
27. As Zetter and others have noted, refugees are far more likely to return home spontaneously than in organised programmes, see R. Zetter (1994) 'The Greek-Cypriot Refugees: Perceptions of Return under Conditions of Protracted Exile', *International Migration Review*, 28, 307.
28. Interview with the author, Tbilisi (16 September 2003).
29. A 2004 study suggested that of 12 million refugees in the world, seven million were warehoused, M. Smith, 'Warehousing Refugees: A Denial of Rights, A Waste of Humanity' *US Committee for World Refugee Survey* (2004).
30. See, for example, Smith, *ibid.*
31. See, for example, J. Milner (2005) 'Resettlement', 'Burden Sharing', 'Refugee Warriors' and 'The Comprehensive Plan of Action' in M.J. Gibney and R. Hansen (eds) *Immigration and Asylum: From 1900 to the Present* (Santa Barbara, CA: ABC-Clio).
32. 'State of the World's Refugees 2006' (Geneva: UNHCR) (2006), Chapter 6, online: www.unhcr.org.
33. 'UNHCR Policy on Refugee Protection and Solutions in Urban Areas: September 2009', *International Journal of Refugee Law* (2009) 21, 4, 846.
34. A. Slaughter and J. Crisp (2009) 'A Surrogate State? The Role of UNHCR in Protracted Refugee Situations', *New Issues in Refugee Research* EPAU Research Paper No. 168, 10, online: www.unhcr.org.
35. G. Paglione (2008) 'Individual Property Restitution: From Deng to Pinheiro – and the Challenges Ahead', *International Journal of Refugee Law*, 20, 3, 405.
36. Prior to the 2008 conflict there had been a period of relative peace between Ossetians and Georgians, with Georgians able to travel safely through South Ossetia and inter-ethnic co-operation on trade, for example.
37. Quoted in S. Elverland, 'Georgia: IDPs Cautiously Return Home' (27 August 2008), Norwegian Refugee Council, online: www.nrc.no.
38. Report of the Representative of the Secretary-General on the human rights of internally displaced persons, Walter Kälin, UN Doc. A/HRC/10/13 (9 February 2009), para. 41.
39. See, for example, press release 'Kakha Bendukidze Meets Representatives of International Organisations in Georgia' (4 September 2008), Government of Georgia, online: http://www.government.gov.ge/index.php?lang_id=ENG&sec_id=103&info_id=2177.
40. M. Corso, 'Georgia: IDPs have Found Homes, but Not Work', *Eurasia Insight*, EurasiaNet (16 August 2009), online: http://www.eurasianet.org/departments/insightb/articles/eav081809.shtml.
41. N. Naskidashvili, 'A Year in the Life of IDP Camp Residents', *Georgia Today* (7 August 2009), online: http://www.georgiatoday.ge/article_details.php?id=7127.
42. The significance of the attainment of ownership rights is much debated in international development circles, but one significant camp holds that ownership is key to development and self-sufficiency. See, for example, H. de Soto (2000) *The Mystery of Capital: Why Capitalism Triumphs in the West and Fails Everywhere Else* (London: Transworld).
43. 'Georgia Housing Voucher Purchase Programme', Urban Institute, online: http://www2.urban.org/centers/idg/pdsdev/pdescrip.cfm?ProjectID=328&allprojects=1.

44. See, for example, B. Zeynalova, 'New Homes for 52 IDP Families' (28 June 2007) Norwegian Refugee Council, online: http://www.nrc.no/?did=9183464. The heavily-criticised Rwandan experience of *imidigudu* in the 1990s should also be mentioned here as a much less successful example, although that programme stretched far beyond the creation of settlements for refugees into a full-blown recreation of the Rwandan rural landscape. See, for example, D. Hilhorst and M. van Leeuwen (2000) 'Emergency and Development: The Case of *Imidugudu*, Villagization in Rwanda', *Journal of Refugee Studies*, 13, 3, 264–280.

45. *Case Concerning Application of the International Convention on the Elimination of all Forms of Racial Discrimination (Georgia v Russian Federation) Request for the Indication of Provisional Measures*, Order of 15 October 2008, para. 149, International Court of Justice, online: http://www.icj-cij.org/docket/files/140/14801.pdf.

46. IIFFMCG Report, *supra* note 8, Volume II, 396.

47. G. Lomsadze, 'Post War, Georgia's Displaced Villagers Start New Life', *Eurasia Insight*, EurasiaNet (13 November 2008), online: http://www.eurasianet.org/departments/insightb/articles/eav111308d.shtml.

48. J. Crisp (2004) 'The Local Integration and Local Settlement of Refugees: A Conceptual and Historical Analysis', EPAU Working Papers, online: www.unhcr.org. See also K. Jacobson (2001) 'The Forgotten Solution: Local Integration for Refugees in Developing Countries', *New Issues in Refugee Research* Working Paper No. 45, online: www.unhcr.org.

49. Others have also made this rhetorical distinction: see, for example, Smith, *supra* note 29.

50. D. McBrayer, 'Reflections on Georgia and the Caucasus' (11 January 2009), online: http://reflectgeorgiacaucasus.blogspot.com/.

51. See also N. Kuprashvili and D. Gaimsonia, 'Georgian Conflict Exploitation Concerns', *Caucasus Reporting Service* No. 525, (24 December 2009), online: www.iwpr.net.

52. S. Chesterman (2008) 'An International Rule of Law', *American Journal of Comparative Law*, 56, 342.

53. In the case of refugee law, another hurdle must be addressed: traditionally states, rather than individuals (including refugees), have been considered the primary actors at international law. However, some – including Beaulac – recognise the need to consider further the position of non-state actors, including individuals, in assessing the existence of an international rule of law, S. Beaulac (2007) 'An Inquiry into the International Rule of Law', EUI Working Papers, MWP 2007/14, online: http://papers.ssrn.com/sol3/papers.cfm?abstract_id=1074562.

54. J. Waldron (2009) 'Are Sovereigns Entitled to the Benefit of the International Rule of Law?' *New York University Public Law and Legal Theory Working Papers*, 3, online: http://lsr.nellco.org/nyu_plltwp/115/.

55. United Nations Human Rights Council, Report of the Representative of the Secretary-General on the human rights of internally displaced persons, Walter Kälin, Addendum, Mission to Georgia, UN Doc. A/HRC/10/13/Add.2 (13 Feburary 2009).

56. See, for example, Lomsadze, *supra* note 47.

57. Corso, *supra* note 40.

58. R. Zetter (1993) 'Shelter Provision and Settlement Policies for Refugees', *Studies on Emergencies and Disaster Relief Report No.2* (Uppsala, Sweden: Nordiska Afrika Institutet), p.34, 46ff.

7
The Battles after the Battle: International Law and the Russia–Georgia Conflict

Christoph H. Stefes and Julie A. George

Introduction

During the violence and in the aftermath of the August 2008 conflict, the leaders of Georgia and the Russian Federation couched their public statements in the language of international law.[1] Georgian President Mikheil Saakashvili, citing the United Nations (UN) Charter, claimed that Russian actions were unlawful and violated Georgian state sovereignty. Using the rhetoric of humanitarian intervention, Russian President Dmitri Medvedev stated in a speech that Georgia's actions constituted 'the crudest violation of international law'.[2] Even as the ink dried on Nicholas Sarkozy's ceasefire text, both sides' attorneys prepared for a legal battle ahead. By January 2009, Russian and South Ossetian individuals – with official Russian assistance – had filed over 3,300 lawsuits in the European Court of Human Rights, most concerning alleged abuses conducted by Georgian troops against South Ossetian civilians and Russian peacekeepers. Georgia and individual Georgian citizens filed their own suits as well, charging abuses by South Ossetian militias and Russian soldiers against ethnic Georgian civilians living along the disputed border areas, as well as in undisputed Georgian territory. Georgia has also filed suit against Russia in the International Court of Justice, contending that Russia sought to change the ethnic demography of Abkhazia and South Ossetia through 'directing' the expulsion of ethnic Georgians from those territories.[3]

This volume is concerned about the development of international law and its application to the conflict. That international law mattered to the actors calling the shots is undisputed; but how did they understand the role of international law in either bringing about beneficial outcomes or in constraining their own behaviour? What do the ways in which the parties resorted to international law in their rhetoric tell us about the importance of international rules and norms in structuring international relations?

International relations scholars disagree about the extent to which states behave according to international legal precepts and accept the enforcement power of the bodies that adjudicate international law. Realists emphasise state power within a condition of international anarchy, noting that sovereign states can choose to forego enforcement if their power and interests permit them. Neoliberal institutionalists disagree with the realist position, contending that international institutions and law provide real benefits to state actors by diminishing the costs of diplomacy and negotiation while bringing a decline in arbitrary state coercive action. Constructivists argue further that, over time, international rules and norms are internalised by states insofar as these rules and norms shape the identity and interests of states. Once states become used to acting according to institutional precepts, they will accept the new environment of law as a natural component of their political environment.

Analysts have already begun dissecting how the August 2008 conflict falls within these theoretical paradigms. In Chapter 1 of this volume, Christopher Waters finds that international law constrained state behaviour, particularly Russia's, since it had the capacity to inflict far more damage on Georgia than it ultimately did during the conflict.[4] Other scholars have framed the conflict as interest-based, the result of Russian regional dominance and neo-imperialism.[5] We find, contrary to both perspectives, that while international law has not become institutionalised to fully govern state behaviour, even powerful states like Russia have come to frame their motivations and actions in terms of international law. In this way, both realism and constructivism bring insight into our understanding of the 2008 conflict; at the same time, adherence to any one school of thought will limit our ability to appreciate the conflict's complexity. In many regions of the world, the post-Soviet region significant among them, international rules and norms are contested, in flux, and unstable. International rules and norms are then tools of both communication and contest.

International law and common theories of realism and constructivism

Scholars of international relations are divided on the impact and power of international laws and international institutions, particularly those endowed with the power of legal adjudication. The realist paradigm of the twentieth century emphasised the power of states as the fundamental actors in the state system, having internal sovereignty – that is, governance authority and control over the legitimate use of force within their territorial boundaries. The international system of Westphalia established sovereignty as a mechanism of international politics. The state, being the highest level of governing authority, could act with liberty. States could not intervene in other states' domestic matters without permission.[6]

Realism developed from a perception that states in the international system functioned in a state of anarchy, where states existed in conditions of vulnerability. For some realists, anarchy combined with man's naturally selfish motivations permit power hungry states to seek hegemony, if not balanced with power by other states.[7] Other scholars of realism, led by Kenneth Waltz, argued that states in the international system do not naturally seek power for power's sake, but rather are forced to continue amassing power in order to guard against vulnerability in a world ungoverned by law and enforcement mechanisms.[8] At the heart of both schools of thought is the currency of power in the international system, borne of the indelible reality of anarchy. The importance of power in structuring international relations, argue many realists, limits the influence of international norms or law, particularly in matters of high-stakes such as national security. Some realists go so far as to say that international organizations and law are entirely subject to power political interests, others merely argue that keeping international rules and norms will be a priority based on state interests and will be abandoned for more important goals.[9]

Neoliberal institutionalist scholars, such as Robert Axelrod and Robert Keohane, find that international institutions might help mitigate the dangers of the anarchic world system by providing alternative incentive structures for states to co-operate in the international system. The establishment of international legal structures and the institutions to enforce these structures decreases state vulnerability to the arbitrary whims of other state actors. These states, upon joining these institutions, increasingly have a stake in the international system of law.[10] As such, although states in conditions of Westphalian sovereignty enjoy independence from external meddling, they might nonetheless take actions that may conflict with their short-term, but aid their long-term, interests.

The most far-reaching critique, however, comes from social constructivism. If realists were right and international law matters little and merely serves the interests of powerful states, we would frequently observe powerful states violating international law with impunity. Yet states usually comply with international law. Moreover, when they act outside international rules and norms, 'they seek to justify their actions as consistent with prevailing law, and if they fail to do this persuasively they often pay high costs to their reputation and perceived legitimacy'.[11]

Constructivists acknowledge that material resources are part of the social structure of international relations. Yet they argue that 'material resources only acquire meaning for human action through the structure of shared knowledge in which they are embedded'.[12] Norms and ideas form the core of this social structure, and they emerge out of and are maintained by states' interactions. 'Norms are [therefore] intersubjective in that they are beliefs rooted in and reproduced through social practice.'[13] Once internalised, intersubjective beliefs in turn form the identities of states and thereby shape their interests. Such beliefs inform state actors about the appropriateness of action in a given situation.

The assumption of 'rule-guided behaviour' starkly contrasts with the interest-based behaviour that realists and liberal institutionalists argue is prevalent in international relations, as Thomas Risse points out: 'Rule-guided behaviour differs from instrumentally rational behaviour in that actors try to "do the right thing" rather than maximizing or optimizing their given preferences.'[14] As norms assume a prominent position in social constructivism, the role of international law in shaping state behaviour gains prominence. For realists, international law is not really law, because it lacks an external enforcement mechanism. Without external enforcement, powerful states can violate international norms and obligations with impunity. And both realists and liberal institutionalists assume that international law is primarily of instrumental value to states. States follow international law only to the extent that it serves their interests.[15]

Social constructivists conceptualise the role of law in international politics in a radically different way than the realists. Instead of an 'artefact', something purposefully created to serve the exogenously given interests of states, social constructivists emphasise law as a process: 'Much of what legitimates law and distinguishes it from other forms of normativity are the processes by which it is created and applied.'[16] These processes in turn 'play a *constitutive* role in the formation of actors' identities and interests and in the structure of the international system itself...[Social constructivism thereby] rejects a simple law/ power dichotomy, arguing instead that legal rules and norms operate by changing interests and thus reshaping the purposes for which power is exercised.'[17] In short, creating and applying international law is a mutually constitutive process that shapes the identities and interests of states. Once international rules and norms are internalised, states follow international law not *only* because it serves their interests but because it is the proper thing to do.

If international rules and norms indeed shape the identities and interests of states, the puzzle as to why most states comply with international law most of the time is resolved. The problem is that sometimes some states violate international law. How do constructivists explain illicit or non-conforming state behaviour? Alexander Wendt emphasises that states' intersubjective understanding of the international system and their role in it can be either conflictual or co-operative, arguing that 'anarchy is what states make of it'.[18]

Going beyond the conflict/co-operation dichotomy, Vaughn Shannon argues that states violate international rules and norms *if* they conflict with national interests *and if* the situation and/or the norms are indeterminate enough to allow states to claim that they still 'do the right thing'. Paraphrasing Wendt's famous dictum, Shannon argues that 'norms are what states make of them',[19] This would allow social constructivists to concede less space (literally) to realists than Wendt does. Yet Shannon's theory also means that 'norms are not as powerful as the sociological [i.e. constructivist] school think, nor as weak as rationalists think'.[20]

Finally, building on Habermas' theory of communicative action, Risse argues that beyond norm-conforming and self-interested behaviour, 'actors have a third mode of social action at their disposal: arguing and deliberating about the validity claims inherent in any communicative statement about identities, interests, and the state of the world'.[21] In other words, if states are confronted with an uncertain situation and imprecise norms, they might not simply violate or obey norms, but argue with other states about the meaning of the situation and the norms. In this process, states reveal self-interested behaviour insofar as they try to convince others to adapt their interpretation of the situation and/or norms. At the same time, the logic of appropriateness limits the range of interpretations insofar as outlandish claims will be considered illegitimate by other states. 'Finally, the logic of argumentative rationality and truth-seeking behaviour is likely to take over if actors are uncertain about their own identities, interests, and views of the world and/or if rhetorical arguments are subject to scrutiny and counterchallenges leading to a process of "argumentative self-entrapment".'[22] Following social constructivist logic, the process of arguing and deliberating should ultimately strengthen international rules and norms, as it is precisely through this type of state interaction that rules and norms are clarified and internalised by states. Arguing is then a first step towards a more co-operative social structure in international relations.

In sum, social constructivists contend that international rules and norms have a powerful influence on state behaviour, as states would rather do what is right than what is in their immediate self-interest. If self-interest conflicts with fuzzy situations and norms, states might decide to engage in norm-violating behaviour (still claiming, though, that they act in accordance with the norm). Yet it is also possible that states will decide to argue about the meaning of norms. Such actions might ultimately strengthen the norms themselves, insofar as the conflict between self-interested and norm-conforming behaviour increasingly becomes resolved more often in favour of norm-conforming behaviour.

Approach

This chapter examines the cross section of interest-based and norm-based claims and actions in the 2008 Russia–Georgia conflict. We trace the rhetoric surrounding the conflict as emblematic of both realist and constructivist schools. In doing so, we assess not only how the language used by both sides underscores this continuing debate in international relations theory, but we also note that the parties to the conflict themselves are deliberately using the language of both programs in different contexts, both international and domestic. In particular, we examine the domestic news outlets, the statements made to international news media, and the arguments made toward international institutions. This latter group includes arguments made in the UN Security Council and the official claims offered by each side to the European Union (EU)'s Independent International Fact-Finding Mission on the Conflict in Georgia (IIFFMCG), led by Heidi Tagliavini, formerly the Head of the UN Mission in Georgia (UNOMIG) and the Special Representative of the UN Secretary-General in Georgia. The IIFFMCG Report was published in September 2009, over a year after the conflict's beginning and ceasefire.

We are not invested in determining whether the conflict acts as a repudiation of realism or constructivism. Notably, international scholars themselves differ on the standards of evidence for concluding the relative strength of each argument. Realists look for evidence that states behave in ways outside their immediate interests. Liberal institutionalists cite circumstances where states benefit from co-operating in international institutions. Constructivists aim at discovering norm-guided behaviour that cannot be explained by states' national interests. Our findings here illustrate the complexity of assessing state behaviour as interest-based or norm-contingent. Although we find evidence of both realism and constructivism based argumentation by both states, we find that Russia and Georgia often couched their language in a legal frame, particularly for international audiences. Yet, according to the IIFFMCG investigation, both states violated international law.[23]

With our focus on the arguments and claims that Russia and Georgia used to defend their decisions to use military force, we are neglecting several important aspects of the conflict, which we should mention and explain. We omit a full discussion of the South Ossetian and Abkhaz claims. We likewise neglect discussion of the allegations of violations of international humanitarian and human rights law. Civilians suffered enormously in this conflict and the involved parties have used accusations of genocide and ethnic cleansing. The IIFFMCG Report has offered some conclusions about crimes against civilians that we do not recount here.[24] We do not explore these two frames due to space constraints and the focus of this book on the Russia–Georgia component. Additionally, from a theoretical standpoint, social constructivism and realism explicitly focus on sovereign state actors. As such, they are ill-equipped to contend with the complex status of Abkhazia and South Ossetia. Our analysis therefore is limited to the Russian and Georgian arenas. However, we wish to remark that we appreciate the complexity of this conflict and its impact on the Abkhaz and South Ossetian populations, in addition to the Russian and Georgian experiences.

Legal rhetoric, actions and the Russia–Georgia conflict

Georgian rhetoric and action

For the Georgian side, the conflict was the culmination of a campaign by Russia 'to subvert the Georgian state and control Georgian territories'.[25] In fact, Georgia emphasised that the Russian denial of Georgia's independence dated back to Georgia's forceful incorporation into the Soviet Union in 1921, through Russia's support of the South Ossetian and Abkhaz secessionism in the early 1990s, and eventually the Russian invasion of Georgia in 2008. Russia thereby used Abkhazia and South Ossetia 'to divide and rule its southern neighbour'.[26] Especially after the Rose Revolution, Russian hostilities towards Georgia intensified, presumably because the newly elected government under President Saakashvili advanced a pro-Western foreign policy agenda with the declared goal of eventually joining the EU and NATO. 'Moscow activated a premeditated series of legal, military, paramilitary, and diplomatic manoeuvres intended to create a pretext for invasion.'[27] Among these 'manoeuvres' were the handing out of Russian passports to South Ossetian and Abkhazian citizens, the establishment of formal contacts between Moscow and the separatist governments, the staffing of South Ossetian government positions with Russian citizens, a military build-up in the conflict zones, armed provocations against and killings of Georgian security and peacekeeping forces.

According to the Georgian claims, on 7 August 2008 'Russian armed forces, already pre-positioned on Georgia's northern border with the Russian Federation, launched a massive, coordinated, and – given the scale of the enterprise – premeditated assault on Georgia.'[28] The Georgian government cast its military action as solely defensive, justified by Georgia's right to protect its citizens, sovereignty, and territorial integrity. Furthermore, Georgia pointed towards the strategic location of South Ossetia that could be used by enemy forces as a springboard to take the Georgian capital and split the country into two halves.[29] Nevertheless, the Georgian government emphasised that it had made numerous diplomatic efforts up to 7 August to de-escalate the situation. The government offered regrets that its efforts and warnings were only taken seriously by the international community when it was too late.[30]

For the Georgian government, the main thrust of its legal campaign was Russia's violation of a critical norm of international relations, the prohibition of the use of force 'against the territorial integrity or political independence of any state' as codified in Article 2(4) of the UN Charter. Tacitly acknowledging that under certain circumstances a violation of this norm is justified, Georgia emphasised that Russia lacked a convincing reason for the invasion of South Ossetia, Abkhazia, and other parts of Georgia. The UN Security Council had not authorised the invasion. An attack on Russia was not imminent, which could have justified a pre-emptive strike. Furthermore, Russia could not defend the invasion for humanitarian reasons, as accusations of genocide were unfounded. Nor could Russia demonstrate that the protection of Russian nationals and peacekeepers justified a military intervention. Peacekeepers were not attacked prior to Russia's invasion, while the issuing of Russian passports to South Ossetian and Abkhazian residents constituted a violation of Georgia's sovereignty and mainly served as a pretext for the invasion.[31] In fact, so claimed the Georgian government, Russia's military assault on Georgia 'was part of a broader, premeditated plan to redraw the map of Europe'.[32] Georgia thereby characterised Russia as a pariah state that constituted a threat to international security. Said President Saakashvili, '[m]y appeal to the free world is to condemn and reject Russia's dangerous and irrational decision – NOT only for Georgia's sake – but for the sake of preserving the fundamental basis of international law and order'.[33]

The Georgian government repeatedly argued that in contrast to Russia's premeditated and unlawful invasion, it tried everything to avoid a military confrontation, favouring instead a diplomatic solution to the conflict. When diplomacy failed, according to this perspective, 'the Georgian response to the Russian armed attack was confined entirely to its own sovereign territory, was reluctantly undertaken, and was proportionate, necessary and wholly justified exercise of its customary and [UN] Charter right to use force in self-defence'.[34] The Georgian government invested a great deal of effort in its attempt to persuade the world that Georgia not only was acting in self-defence, but that it was acting in accordance with international law as it did so. In contrast, Georgia argued, Russia and its 'proxies' violated international law during and after the conflict on a massive scale, notably with the forceful expulsion – or rather, ethnic cleansing – of ethnic Georgians from South Ossetia and Abkhazia.[35]

While the Georgian government portrayed its actions as law-abiding, the IIFFMCG Report noted several violations of international norms. Notably, the Report supported Russia's accusation that Georgia did not act in self-defence, but initiated hostilities with an indiscriminate rocket and artillery barrage in violation of international humanitarian law. However, the Report also stated that Russia politically and militarily provoked Georgia for years before the assault and then responded with disproportionate force, advancing its military assault deep into undisputed Georgian territory. Moreover, it found that Russia's offering passports to South Ossetians and Abkhazians was unlawful and thus they did meet international legal standards for consideration as Russian nationals.

In Georgia's attempt to justify its own actions and discredit Russia, two details are especially noteworthy. First, Georgia has portrayed the conflict exclusively as an inter-state armed conflict between Russia and Georgia – an interpretation that Russia (not to mention South Ossetia and Abkhazia) sharply rejects.[36] According to the Georgian government, the South Ossetian and Abkhaz leaderships merely acted as 'proxies' of Russian interests: 'Throughout the armed conflict, the Russian

Federation, in conjunction with proxy militants *under their control*, conducted indiscriminate and disproportionate attacks.'[37]

The obvious reason for Georgia's insistence on this characterization of the conflict is that the international community never recognised the sovereignty of these two breakaway regions. By law, Abkhazia and South Ossetia continued to belong to Georgia even though Georgia had lost the *de facto* control over them. Any acknowledgment of Abkhazia and South Ossetia as autonomous actors in this conflict would have elevated their status. Portraying this conflict as an inter-state war has helped Georgia in two other ways. For one, international norms pertaining to inter-state conflicts are more determinate than those that relate to intra-state conflicts. In the latter cases, the norms of territorial integrity conflict with the right of self-determination. Yet for the Georgian government, the territorial integrity of Georgia in its 1991 borders has been inviolable. Shortly after the 2008 conflict, for instance, 91% of Georgians polled declared that they would never accept the independence of these two regions.[38] Furthermore, to portray the conflict as an act of aggression by a far more powerful hegemonic state against a much smaller neighbouring state would inevitably generate international sympathy for Georgia.

A second detail that deserves mentioning is Georgia's legal and public relations campaign following the conflict, which was impressive given its breadth and intensity. The Georgian government and Georgian individuals instituted proceedings before the European Court of Human Rights and the International Court of Justice, alleging that Russia had violated the European Convention on Human Rights and the International Convention on the Elimination of All Forms of Racial Discrimination, respectively. Furthermore, government officials – foremost, President Saakashvili – have frequently defended Georgia's position in the international media and when the media began to question Georgia's version of events, the government launched a new information campaign intended 'to debunk the inaccurate and incomplete accounts in several respected media outlets'.[39] Finally, the Georgian government liberally provided international governmental and non-governmental organizations (e.g. the Tagliavini Commission and Human Rights Watch) as well as foreign governments, with detailed reports aimed at documenting Georgia's full compliance with international rules and norms.

To understand Georgia's frequent invocation of international norms, realist and social constructivist interpretations are possible. From a realist point of view, one could argue that Georgia has tried to situate itself in the community of European states. Proving to be a law-abiding state is therefore politically and economically expedient, as Georgia has frequently expressed its desire to join the two most powerful Western organizations, NATO and the EU. Doubts about Georgia's willingness to play by the rules would constitute a major setback for President Saakashvili's foreign policy. A social constructivist interpretation would be norm-based rather than interest-based. Georgia's actions towards the international community, then, demonstrate an acceptance of rule-based authority as a mechanism to pattern behaviour. We might also recall Risse, who takes the view that legal arguments 'increase the influence of the materially less powerful [actors such as] small states'.[40]

To determine which theoretical approach offers more explanatory traction is difficult, as it is clear that the Georgian government promoted two sets of narratives to justify its military actions in South Ossetia. The first one, summarised above, was common in international media outlets and official government statements intended for distribution among international organizations and foreign governments. The other narrative has had the Georgian population in mind. In this narrative, the Georgian government emphasised that the military intervention was necessary to 'restore the constitutional order in South Ossetia'.[41] As South Ossetia was formally part of Georgia, restoring the constitutional order could only mean driving the separatists from power. President Saakashvili went even so far as to characterise the Georgian military action as a 'liberation' of South Ossetia.[42] While the international community recognised the inviolability of Georgia's territory, Georgia had signed the 1992 Sochi Agreement in which it committed itself to abstain from using force to change the status quo. If the Georgian attack on South Ossetia occurred before the Russian army entered Georgia, as the IIFFMCG Report implies, and was therefore not motivated purely by self-defence, as the Georgian government claims, Georgia clearly violated this international agreement and thus international law.

Russian rhetoric and actions

Russia's rhetoric and actions in the early days of its military efforts in South Ossetia showed a clear attention to international law in its framing of its state policy. Russia offered its version of events in statements before the UN Security Council and invoked Article 51 of the UN Charter, which permits states to use force in self-defence, in a written notification to the Security Council on 11 August 2008.[43] Yet, as in the case of Georgia, not all of the Russian rhetoric and actions conformed with international legal standards.

The Russian leadership offered six explanations and goals for its actions during the August conflict. These explanations surfaced in the Russian media as well as in American news outlets (notably Vladimir Putin's interview on CNN), and culminated in the IIFFMCG investigation. The six explanations centred on self-defence for Russian peacekeepers and citizens, humanitarian concerns for South Ossetians, a suspicion that the United States was using Georgia to expand its empire into the Russian sphere of influence by controlling Georgian action, a collective security argument that centred around South Ossetia's request for Russian military support, a need to punish Mikhail Saakashvili for his 'criminal' behaviour, and Russia's position as a regional power and status as a guarantor of stability in the Caucasus. Some of these contentions were not reflected in the official statements offered to the compilers of the IIFFMCG Report, implying complexity as to how the conflict is contextualised in Russia by elites, scholarly observers, and in basic public opinion. They also give us insight into how Russian actors sometimes legitimised international law and sometimes expressed motivations outside the realm of the international legal sphere.

Self-defence

The bulk of the Russian argument for its military effort during the 2008 conflict centred on self-defence.[44] Upon the outbreak of violence in South Ossetia, Russia took its position to the UN Security Council claiming its right to defend the lives of its peacekeepers stationed in South Ossetia and the South Ossetians who held Russian passports. Russian peacekeepers had been stationed in garrisons primarily in Tskhinvali since the signing the Sochi ceasefire in 1992. Citing the deaths of two of its peacekeepers and the wounding of others in the 2008 hostilities, the Russian Ambassador to the UN wrote that Russia 'pursues no other goal but to protect the Russian peacekeeping contingent and citizens of the Russian Federation...and to prevent future armed attacks against them'.[45]

The Russian passportisation of Abkhazians and South Ossetians has been a point of controversy between the Russian and Georgian regimes.[46] It occurred without the consent of the Georgian government, which had conferred Georgian citizenship broadly over the population of its territory, no matter their ethnic make-up or level of desire for Georgian citizenship, in 1993.[47] Many Ossetians and Abkhazians in the secessionist territories rejected Georgian citizenship for reasons linked to their desire to obtain independence. They were loath to accept Georgian passports to travel overseas or receive government paid pensions and the like. Georgian documentation meant that legal travel into Russia in particular was difficult to impossible, given that state's visa requirements for Georgian citizens. Russian passports enabled the South Ossetians and Abkhazians to travel across the border to conduct border trade and obtain social welfare benefits.

There were also political implications. In the 1990s, the Russian Duma passed a law enabling the state to act in support of its citizens anywhere in the world where they were endangered. Just prior to the outbreak of conflict in August 2008, Yury Popov, a special envoy from the Russian Foreign ministry, warned of the likelihood of a Russian intervention: 'if the events develop according to the gloomiest violent scenario, Russia will not be able to let itself remain indifferent, given that South Ossetia, including the conflict zone, is home to some Russian citizens'.[48]

Humanitarian concerns

In an address offered on 8 August 2008, the first full day after Georgia's late evening/early morning incursion into South Ossetia, Russian president Dmitri Medvedev accused the Georgian forces of committing 'the crudest violation of international law' and stated that '[c]ivilians – women, children, and elderly people – are being killed in South Ossetia.'[49] Ivan Melnikov, the Vice-Speaker of the Russian State Duma, categorised the Georgian strike as a 'genocide of the Ossetian people'.[50]

Putin furthermore contended that intervention was obligatory: 'In compliance with the existing international agreements ... Russia [was] obliged to defend another party if one of the sides violates the agreement on ceasefire. We did this towards South Ossetia.'[51] Russian news of the time stressed the humanitarian element of the mission, particularly with regard to protecting Russian citizens and Russian peacekeepers within South Ossetia. In a press conference on 12 August, Medvedev praised the success of the Russian military effort in averting casualties: 'We did not have any other options to respond [to the conflict] ... If we had not done so, the number of deaths would have been much larger.'[52]

Upon its recognition of South Ossetian and Abkhaz independence, Russia faced criticism from observers who noted its resistance to the Western recognition of independence for Kosovo. Noted Medvedev, 'I would like to emphasize once again that each state decides on its own whether it should recognize some nation as an entity under international law or not.'[53] Further citing international law, Medvedev commented that 'considering that ethnic cleansing and instances of genocide have occurred (in South Ossetia) for seventeen years', there were 'grounds to apply the UN Charter, the conventions of the 1970s and the Helsinki Act of 1975 as grounds to recognize independence of these two entities'.[54] The humanitarian rhetoric seemed to have resonance in the Russian population. When asked in a public opinion poll about the Western outcry against Russia's military action in Georgia, the Russian population responded in confusion – presumably because the humanitarian mission was self-evident. Of those asked 'how do you feel about negative reaction by the Western countries on Russia's action in the relations of Georgia?', only 5% said that they agreed or understood, 20% said 'puzzled,' 22% said 'uneasy,' and 39% (the plurality) said 'disturbed'.[55]

Russia's recognition of Abkhaz and South Ossetian independence, likewise, was cast as an obligation and requirement in order to ensure their safety. Sergei Mironov, Speaker of the Federation Council, referred to the recognition as a duty and noted: 'The recognition by Russia of Abkhazia and South Ossetia's independence is the necessary condition for ensuring the security of these peoples.'[56] The Russian recognition of Abkhazia and South Ossetia was explicitly linked to international law and to the Western decision-making regarding Kosovo (although not all Western states have recognised Kosovo). Russian Deputy Foreign Minister Grigory Karasin noted that: 'We warned long and patiently of the consequences if international law was trampled upon in Kosovo. In reply we heard every time that Kosovo was only a special case. Now we see that it was not so.'[57]

United States' Plans/Manipulation

The Russian perspective on the conflict corresponds to a wariness regarding the expansion of Western – particularly the United States' – influence in former communist and former Soviet space. The Russian leadership has long considered the discussion of NATO expansion into Ukraine and Georgia as a violation of its long-standing interests in those regions.[58] The Bush administration's support of Saakashvili concerned many in Russia, especially with the United States' declaration in April 2008 that Georgia would someday become a member of NATO. Although that statement was diminished somewhat by the reality that Georgia had been refused Membership Action Plan status, the promise boded ill for Russian interests in the region.[59] With the considerable financial and military support the West had offered Georgia after the Rose Revolution, Russia's focus on Georgia included some concern for Western expansion against its own interests.

In their book entitled *Recognizing the Independence of South Ossetia and Abkhazia: History, Politics, Law*, Vladimir Akeksandrovich Zakharov and

Andrei Grigorevich Areshev opened their introduction by linking Georgian actions in August 2008 with American interests: 'The events in South Ossetia and Abkhazia were intensified not only by relationships between Georgia and Russia, but by all the western world with our country. In the beginning, the United States of America, and then the European Union, presented Russia with one ultimatum after another.'[60] Although a great deal of their book contends with broad historical precursors to the secessionist conflicts that erupted in the early 1990s, the authors also argue that Western actions were critical to Georgia's decision to enter Tskhinvali militarily. According to the authors, joint United States–Georgian exercises held in July 2008 were the sort 'which mastered many of the elements of the future operation of the seizure of Tskhinvali'.[61]

Although Zakharov and Areshev are both academics, their emphasis nonetheless reflects a conversation about perceived Western imperialism within the actions of Mikhail Saakashvili. Vladimir Putin most famously espoused this perspective in his interview with CNN just following the conflict. In it, he asserted not only that United States personnel were on the ground fighting on the Georgian side during the conflict, but that 'there are grounds to suspect that some people in the United States created this conflict deliberately in order to aggravate the situation and create a competitive advantage for one of the candidates for the US presidency'.[62] While Putin's comments were perceived in the West as shrill and unfounded,[63] the linkage of possible American aggression against Russia during the 2008 presidential election was not unprecedented. In 2006, a document surfaced in the Russia Duma entitled 'On a Likely Scenario of Action of the United States Toward Russia in 2006–2008'. This document, termed by Georgy Bovt of the *Moscow Times* as 'undoubtedly the largest-scale and most comprehensive anti-US program that post-Soviet Russia has seen', anticipated an attempt to displace Putin's leadership during the 2008 United States elections in an effort to dismantle Russia's 'sovereign democracy'. The document further predicted 'the United States will also work to undermine "Russia's energy sovereignty", and simultaneously push for Georgia to be accepted into NATO'.[64]

The Russians also invoked collective self-defence, arguing their right to intervene at the behest of the South Ossetian government. According to the Russian statement given to the EU diplomats compiling the Report, the South Ossetian Security Council 'appealed to Russia for help'. This request, and the deaths of two Russian peacekeepers on 8 August, 'entitled the Russian Federation leadership to take the decision to send additional troops to South Ossetia'.[65]

Two final explanations offered, albeit more rarely than others, were Russia's traditional sphere of influence in the Caucasus and the need to punish the Georgian government for its actions. In his rhetoric concerning the Georgian strike, Medvedev noted: 'We have invariably seen our task in the preservation of peace. Historically, Russia has been the guarantor of security of Caucasus peoples, and it will remain so in the future.'[66]

On the punitive front, Medvedev announced at a meeting of the Russian Security Council that 'we will not let allow the deaths of our compatriots to go unpunished. Those guilty will receive due punishment.'[67] The Russian claim offered in the IIFFMCG Report stressed its actions as a response to Saakashvili specifically. In explaining the Georgian actions leading up to the conflict, the Russians cast the Georgian 'aggression' as 'a logical progression of policies conducted by the Saakashvili regime'. In its conclusion, the Russian claim added, '[i]t might be worth noting that ever since Mr. Saakashvili came to power in 2004 he was known to frequently take rash actions both in his domestic and foreign policies clearly demonstrating such character traits as adventurism and propensity for taking risks.'[68] Later, Medvedev would refer to Saakashvili as 'a political corpse'.[69] Putin famously offered description of how he would treat Saakashvili's genitals if he were to be able to bring him to Moscow.[70]

Several of these explanations of Russian military action dovetail with international norms, namely the claim to self-defence for Russian peacekeepers and citizens, the reference to South Ossetia's invitation for Russian protection (collective self-defence), and humanitarian claims. Others do not: the allegations of American involvement, the invocation of Russia's sphere of influence in the Caucasus, and the punishment targeted towards Saakashvili. Of these six claims, two were officially part of the explanation for Russian military action in the IIFFMCG Report: the rights of individual self-defence and of collective self-defence. Notably, although Russia included humanitarian concerns for South Ossetian civilians in its claims of human rights violations by Georgia, it did not use humanitarian intentions as a legal explanation for its military action in Georgia.[71]

Complicating the humanitarian argument for the Russians has been its rejection of humanitarian motivations in Western military intervention in Kosovo, which the Russians vociferously opposed. Indeed, a great deal of the rhetoric offered by Russian policymakers after the conflict included references to Kosovo as though to draw parallels between the Western action there and Russian actions in South

Ossetia. For example, the military claims to the IIFFMCG (while careful not to invoke humanitarian reasons for intervention) noted that from the 1992 ceasefire up until the Georgian military action, 'Russia complied with its peacekeeping and intermediary obligations in good faith, while trying to help in reaching peace agreements, and demonstrated self-restraint and patience in the face of provocations, unflinchingly maintaining its position even after Kosovo's unilateral declaration of independence.'[72] The out of context reference to Kosovo in reference to a 'provocation' that Russia withstood that could have led to an action in Georgia – clearly an entity outside of the Balkans – hints at other motivations than Georgian and South Ossetian politics behind Russian action. In an article in *Russia in Global Affairs*, Vladimir Ovchinsky, retired Major-General of the Russian Police and holder of a doctorate in law, reflected upon the ambiguity of international law and the ability of Russian foreign policymakers to turn Western humanitarian rhetoric on itself. He argued that Russia showed in the August 2008 conflict that it, like the United States after 11 September 2001 or NATO in Kosovo, could now use humanitarian rhetoric as a means to rationalise missions whose actions were not really humanitarian:

> The reality that developed after September 11, 2001 and August 8, 2008 is such that the 'catches' of self-defence, self-determination and peacekeeping in ambiguous UN documents can be used to justify war against sovereign states. This requires military might and political will. The United States demonstrated this capability after September 11, and Russia – after August 8.[73]

For its part, the IIFFMCG Report rejected the humanitarian argument the Russians made in the informal arena for the military action in South Ossetia.[74] The Report also found that Russia's claim to self-defence did not extend to the South Ossetian citizens of Russia, since that citizenship was unlawful and unaccepted by the Georgian government.[75] It also rejected the claim of collective self-defence, finding that states do not have the right to intervene in other sovereign states at the request of separatist groups.[76] Although the Russians did not offer claims of a sphere of influence to the EU body, the Report rejected the concept of such influence, stating that a claim to a sphere of influence outside a state's borders would violate other states' sovereign interests and therefore international law.[77]

The only Russian action the IIFFMCG Report found to be lawful was its defence of peacekeepers if fired upon first by Georgian military units, although IIFFMCG did not find independent evidence that the Georgians fired first (the Russians said they did; the Georgians claimed the Russian peacekeepers were the first to fire).[78] The Report further noted, however, that the Russian response to the attack of its peacekeepers (if such existed) was disproportional and thus unlawful.[79]

Conclusion

The conflict of August 2008 took about 750 lives and wounded thousands others. It led to the migration of tens of thousands and many have not returned to their homes and perhaps never will. The conflict reopened and heightened tensions between neighbours, few of whom acted particularly neighbourly before, during and after the wartime events. The conflict has deepened some long-standing rifts and constructed many anew. Moreover, any hopeful conclusions one might have about the increasing influence of international legal norms in governing or mitigating state behaviour risks diminishing these losses. Yet with these caveats, the Russia–Georgia conflict might offer an intriguing case for scholars to draw a clear line between realist, interest-based behaviour, on one hand, and rhetoric, actions and speech that shows an adherence to and internalization of international legal norms, on the other (social constructivism). We find that we cannot draw this line. We argue instead that these approaches taken together (rather than taken individually) help us to understand better the complexity of how international law is used in international relations and conflict.

It is tempting to conclude that the realist approach is the most salient for our understanding of the Russia–Georgia conflict. All sides have repeatedly violated international rules and norms in the course of this military conflict. According to the IIFFMCG Report, the build-up to the conflict included all sides increasing tensions rather than decreasing them. Georgia's claims to self-defence against Russia were not substantiated by the Report, and its early August rhetoric about 'liberation' and 'restoring constitutional order' hints at motivations beyond self-protection from Russian aggression. Likewise, the Russian rhetoric about humanitarian intervention seemed to be about punishing the West for its actions in Kosovo in addition to protecting South Ossetians from Georgian actions. The Russian passportisation of South Ossetians and Abkhazians, while offering real benefits to those vulnerable populations, was found by the IIFFMCG Report to be unlawful and by others to be suspiciously akin to territorial annexation of strategic parts of Georgian territory.

With this rendering, social constructivists could at best point out that the intersubjective understanding of Russia and Georgia was shaped by conflict and not co-operation. Yet to say that the social structures of the Caucasus region are conflictual merely concedes to realists that the subsystem of international relations in the Caucasus resembles a self-help system. If that were indeed correct, realists could rightly argue that Georgian and Russian references to international rules and norms were at best poor excuses for barely veiled wrongdoings and at worst cynical gestures meant to demonstrate the ambiguity and the insignificance of international law. Russia's repeated references to Kosovo might serve as a case in point.

Yet realism's interpretation of the invocation of international law during and after the conflict is flawed as well. The conflict did not take place in a lawless area. Georgia and Russia are members of numerous international and regional organisations and parties to the main universal and European human rights treaties. Both sides have repeatedly referred to these underlying rules and norms to justify their own actions and expose the wrongdoings of the other party. If international rules and norms were so inconsequential, why did both sides go to such a great length invoking them? It has been an obvious concern for both Russia and Georgia to demonstrate to the rest of the world that their actions were 'appropriate' – that is, in accordance with international law. At the same time, they have also invested significant time and effort in portraying the adversary as behaving 'inappropriately'. Russian and Georgian governments have thus tried to communicate with each other, their citizens, and the governments in the United States and in Europe. While the recurring invocation of international rules and norms were thereby meant to support specific storylines that legitimise the actions that each party took during the conflict, it has also been about constructing particular narratives that outline specific understandings of the international system, the role of the adversaries in this system, and one's own role in this system. As Theo Farrell rightly argues, 'international law not only defines legitimate state practice, it also legitimates states and allows them to behave in ways that have meaning for other international actors'.[80]

The problem for social constructivism in interpreting this conflict is the conflict itself, constituting massive violations of international rules and norms. Risse's theory does not help much in this regard, as the deliberation over the validity of the various claims and counter-claims took place *after* the violations had occurred. At least in the future, the process of arguing and deliberating might ultimately strengthen international law and thereby lead to amicable relations between Georgia and Russia. Yet the persistent violations of international agreements long after the signing of the EU-brokered ceasefire (e.g., Russia's breach of the EU-sponsored ceasefire agreement and recognition of Abkhazia and South Ossetia as sovereign states), do not bode well for more peaceful relations between the two states.

Following Shannon, one might argue that both sides violated international law because it conflicted with their national interests *and* because the situation and/or the norms were indeterminate enough to allow them to claim that they still did the right thing. The fundamental norms that were violated in this conflict were determinate, being part of international law. The situation in the weeks and months before the conflict was arguably indeterminate. Yet both sides had purposefully contributed to this situation in preparation for this conflict (e.g., the Russian government by distributing passports to South Ossetians, which later allowed Russia to justify its military intervention claiming that it needed to protect its citizens).

In short, international rules and norms barely constrained the behaviour of Russia, Georgia and the leaders of the two separatist regions. Nevertheless, the aftermath of the conflict has shown that international rules and norms have played important roles in giving meaning to what happened and determining the ways governments talked to each other, to the outside world and with their citizens. It is clear that states find it inconceivable to engage in actions that other states might consider unlawful without trying to justify their behaviour by invoking international law.

Notes

The authors wish to thank James Green and Christopher Waters, the Centre for Transnational Law and Justice, University of Windsor, and the School of Law, University of Reading, Rachel Epstein, Jack Donnelly, Peter Liberman, and Quinn Patterson.

1. As discussed below, two other parties to the larger conflict were Abkhazia and South Ossetia, both of which also have offered rhetoric couched in international law. This chapter reflects the book's focus on the Russia–Georgia component of the conflict and so does not emphasise these two very important players in the August 2008 events.
2. 'Georgian Aggression Is Crude Violation of International Law – Medvedev', *TASS* (8 August 2008).
3. Human Rights Watch, 'Up in Flames: Humanitarian Law Violations and Human Victims in the Conflict Over South Ossetia' (2009), 74, online: http://www.hrw.org/en/reports/2009/01/22/flames-0. See *Case Concerning Application of the International Convention on the Elimination of All Forms of Racial Discrimination (Georgia v Russian Federation), Request for the Indication*

of Provisional Measures, Order of 15 October 2008, International Court of Justice, online: http://www.icj-cij.org/docket/files/140/14801.pdf.
4. See Chapter 1 of this volume. Charles King has also argued that the Russian behaviour exhibited constraint, although his emphasis was not international law, see C. King, 'Russo-Georgian Conflict Is Not All Russia's Fault', *The Christian Science Monitor* (11 August 2008).
5. See S.E. Cornell, J. Popjanevski and N. Nilsson (2008) 'Russia's War in Georgia: Causes and Implications for Georgia and the World', Central-Asia Caucasus Institute/Silk Road Studies Program; and S.E. Cornell and S.F. Starr (2009) *The Guns of August 2008: Russia's War in Georgia* (New York: M.E. Sharpe).
6. E. de Vattel (1884) *The Law of Nations or Principles of the Law of Nature, Applied to the Conduct and Affairs of Nations and Sovereigns*, trans. by Joseph Chitty, 6th American edn (T. & J.W. Johnson).
7. E.H. Carr (1946) *The Twenty Years' Crisis: An Introduction to the Study of International Relations* (London: Macmillan); H. Morgenthau (1978) *Politics Among Nations: The Struggle for Power and Peace* (New York: Knopf); and R. Niebuhr (1936) *Moral Man and Immoral Society: A Study in Ethics and Politics* (New York: C. Scirbner's).
8. K. Waltz (1979) *Theory of International Politics* (Boston: McGraw-Hill).
9. J.J. Mearsheimer (1994–1995) 'The False Promise of International Institutions' *International Security*, 19, 3; and R.L. Schweller and D. Priess (1997) 'A Tale of Two Realisms: Expanding the Institutions Debate', *Mershon International Studies Review*, 41.
10. R. Axelrod (1990) *The Evolution of Co-operation* (London: Penguin); and R.O. Keohane (1984) *After Hegemony: Co-operation and Discord in the World Political Economy* (Princeton: Princeton University Press).
11. C. Reus-Smit (2008) 'International Law' in J. Baylis, S. Smith and P. Owens (eds) *The Globalization of World Politics. An Introduction to International Relations* (New York: Oxford University Press), p. 290.
12. *Ibid.*, 73.
13. T. Farrell (2004) 'Constructivist Security Studies: Portrait of a Research Program', *International Studies Review*, 4, 1, 49.
14. T. Risse (2000) '"Let's Argue!" Communicative Action in World Politics', *International Organization*, 54, 1, 4.
15. H.H. Koh (1997) 'Why Do Nations Obey International Law', *The Yale Law Journal*, 106, 8, 2602.
16. M. Finnemore and S.J. Toope (2001) 'Alternatives to "Legalization": Richer View of Law and Politics', *International Organization*, 55, 3, 750.
17. A.-M. Slaughter, A.S. Tulumello and S. Wood (1998) 'International Law and International Relations Theory: A New Generation of Interdisciplinary Scholarship', *The American Journal of International Law*, 92, 3, 367–397.
18. A. Wendt (1992) 'Anarchy Is What States Make of It: The Social Construction of Power Politics', *International Organization*, 46, 2.
19. V.P. Shannon (2000) 'Norms Are What States Make of Them: The Political Psychology of Norm Violation', *International Studies Quarterly*, 44.
20. *Ibid.*, 294.
21. Risse, *supra* note 14, 33.
22. *Ibid.*, 23.

23. The Report of the Independent International Fact-Finding Mission on the Conflict in Georgia (IIFFMCG) (30 September 2009), Volume II, online: http://www.ceiig.ch/Report.html.
24. *Ibid.*
25. *Ibid.*, Volume III, 7.
26. *Ibid.*
27. *Ibid.*, 7f.
28. *Ibid.*, 7.
29. *Ibid.*, 11.
30. *Ibid.*, 9.
31. *Ibid.*, Volume II, 186f. See also the discussion by James Green in Chapter 3 of this volume.
32. M. Saakashvili, 'Statement by the President of Georgia', *New York Times* (26 August 2008).
33. *Ibid.*
34. IIFFMCG Report, *supra* note 23, Volume II, 187.
35. *Ibid.*, Volume III, 274, 77–78.
36. *Ibid.*, Volume II, 188.
37. *Ibid.*, 337.
38. *Georgian National Survey, September 23-October 1, 2008*, International Republican Institute, online: http://www.iri.org/eurasia/georgia/pdfs/2008%20November%2021,%20Survey%20of%20Georgian%20Public%20Opinion,%20September-October,%202008.pdf.
39. Government of Georgia, *Factual Evidence Contradicts War Claims in Recent Media Stories* (2005), online: http://www.usa.mfa.gov.ge/index.php?lang_id=ENG&sec_id=594&info_id=94. See also Risse, *supra* note 14.
40. Risse, *ibid.*, 33.
41. '"Georgia Decided to Restore Constitutional Order in S. Ossetia" – MoD', *Civil Georgia* (8 August 2008), online: http://www.civil.ge/eng/article.php?id=18941&search.
42. '"Most of S. Ossetia under Tbilisi's Control" – Saakashvili', *Civil Georgia* (8 August 2008), online: http://www.civil.ge/eng/article.php?id=18955&search=most%20of%20S.%20Ossetia.
43. UN Doc. S/2008/545.
44. For a detailed examination of the legal merits of the Russian self-defence claim, see James Green's analysis in Chapter 3.
45. Cited in IIFFMCG Report, *supra* note 24, Volume II, 269. The Report notes that the Russian representative at the Security Council on 10 August 2008 noted 12 peacekeeper deaths, although those numbers were later corrected to two.
46. The Russian passportisation policy has been considered previously in this volume: see, in particular, Chapter 3.
47. IIFFMCG Report, *supra* note 24, Volume II, 150–152.
48. 'Russia Cannot Remain Indifferent in Case of Extreme Escalation in South Ossetia', *Interfax* (5 August 2008).
49. 'Georgian Aggression Is Crude Violation of International Law – Medvedev', *supra* note 2.
50. 'Georgian Hostilities Are Genocide of Ossetian People – State Duma Vice-Speaker', *TASS* (8 August 2008). Accusations of Georgian genocide against

South Ossetians are not unprecedented. Both the South Ossetian and Russian allegations to the IIFFMCG included claims of genocide. The view has also obtained resonance within the Russian academic community, for example in Vladimir A. Zakharov and Andrei G. Areshev (2008) *Priznanie Nezavisimosti Iuzhnoi Osetii i Abkhazii: Istoria, Politika, Pravo (the Recognition of South Ossetian and Abkhazian Independence: History, Politics, Law)* (Moscow: MGYMO).

51. 'Putin Urges Georgia to Immediately Stop Aggression against S Ossetia', *TASS* (9 August 2008).
52. '"Russia's Actions Prevented Larger Number of Deaths in S. Ossetia" – Medvedev', *Russia & CIS Military Newswire* (13 August 2008).
53. 'Abkhazia, S. Ossetia Have Reasons to Claim Self-Determination – Medvedev', *Russia & CIS General Newswire* (26 August 2008).
54. *Ibid.*
55. 'Rossiyanye o Situatsii Vokrug Abkhazii i Iuzhnoi Osetii (Russian Citizens on the Situation Concerning Abkhazia and South Ossetia)', *Levada-Tsentr* (10 September 2008), online: available from http://www.levada.ru/press/2008091001.html.
56. 'It is Russia's Duty to Recognize Abkhazia, S. Ossetia's Independence – Mironov', *Russia & CIS Military Newswire* (25 August 2008).
57. 'Russia Has No Plans to Annex S. Ossetia, Abkhazia but Will Support Them – FM', *TASS* (25 August 2008).
58. J. Smith (2008) *The NATO-Russia Relationship: Defining Moment or Deja Vu?* (Center for Strategic and International Studies). On the Russian consideration of its sphere of influence, see P. Kubicek (1999–2000) 'Russian Foreign Policy and the West', *Political Science Quarterly*, 114, 4.
59. C. Bigg, 'NATO: On Georgia and Ukraine, a Meeting of "Old" And "New" Minds', *Radio Free Europe/Radio Liberty* (4 April 2008).
60. Zakharov and Areshev, *supra* note 50, 5.
61. *Ibid.*, 162. The South Ossetians made a similar claim in their responses to the questions of the IIFFMCG, see IIFFMCG Report, *supra* note 23, Volume III, 505–506.
62. 'Transcript: CNN Interview with Vladimir Putin', *CNN Online* (2008), online: http://www.cnn.com/2008/WORLD/europe/08/29/putin.transcript/index.html.
63. M. Chance, 'Putin Accuses US Of Orchestrating Georgian War', *CNN Online* (28 August 2008), online: http://www.cnn.com/2008/WORLD/europe/08/28/russia.georgia.cold.war/index.html.
64. G. Bovt, 'Handy Anti-Americanism', *The Moscow Times* (28 September 2006), online: *Russia in Global Affairs*, http://eng.globalaffairs.ru/engsmi/1058.html.
65. IIFFMCG Report, *supra* note 23, Volume III, 371.
66. 'Georgian Aggression Is Crude Violation of International Law – Medvedev', *supra* note 2.
67. 'Georgian Actions in South Ossetia Cannot Go Unpunished – Russian President', *Russia & CIS Military Weekly* (22 August 22 2008).
68. IIFFMCG Report, *supra* note 23, Volume III, 369.
69. 'Saakashvili A "Political Corpse"', *BBC News* (2 September 2008), online: http://news.bbc.co.uk/2/hi/7594860.stm.

70. C. Bremmer, 'Vladimir Putin "Wanted to Hang Georgian President Saakashvili by the Balls"', *The Times* (14 November 2008), online: http://www.timesonline.co.uk/tol/news/world/europe/article5147422.ece.
71. For more on this, see Chapter 3 of this volume.
72. IIFFMCG Report, *supra* note 23, Volume III, 336–37.
73. V. Ovchinsky (2008) 'The Flipside of September 11, 2001', *Russia in Global Affairs*, 4, online: http://eng.globalaffairs.ru/numbers/25/1236.html.
74. IIFFMCG Report, *supra* note 23, Volume II, 283–84.
75. *Ibid.*, 285–289.
76. *Ibid.*, 280–283.
77. *Ibid.*, Volume I, 36.
78. *Ibid.*, Volume II, 252–253 and 264–270.
79. *Ibid.*, 271–274.
80. Farrell, *supra* note 13, 50.

Index